Models of
EVANGELISM

Priscilla Pope-Levison

Baker Academic
a division of Baker Publishing Group
Grand Rapids, Michigan

Published by Baker Academic
a division of Baker Publishing Group
PO Box 6287, Grand Rapids, MI 49516-6287
www.bakeracademic.com

Printed in the United States of America

Library of Congress Cataloging-in-Publication Data
Names: Pope-Levison, Priscilla, 1958– author.
Title: Models of evangelism / Priscilla Pope-Levison.
Description: Grand Rapids : Baker Academic, a division of Baker Publishing Group, 2020. |
    Includes bibliographical references and index.
Identifiers: LCCN 2020011429 | ISBN 9780801099496 (paperback)
Subjects: LCSH: Evangelistic work.
Classification: LCC BV3790 .P638 2020 | DDC 269/.2—dc23
LC record available at https://lccn.loc.gov/2020011429

ISBN: 978-1-54096-349-9 (casebound)

20 21 22 23 24 25 26   7 6 5 4 3 2 1

In keeping with biblical principles of creation stewardship, Baker Publishing Group advocates the responsible use of our natural resources. As a member of the Green Press Initiative, our company uses recycled paper when possible. The text paper of this book is composed in part of post-consumer waste.

To Jack

We are one,
One flesh; to lose thee were to lose myself
(JOHN MILTON, *PARADISE LOST*)

CONTENTS

Acknowledgments   vii

Introduction   1

1. Personal   11

2. Small Group   31

3. Visitation   49

4. Liturgical   69

5. Church Growth   91

6. Prophetic   113

7. Revival   135

8. Media   157

Conclusion   181

Scripture Index   191

Subject and Name
    Index   193

ACKNOWLEDGMENTS

The genesis of this book is the classroom—more than twenty years of teaching Introduction to Evangelism at Duke Divinity School, Seattle Pacific University, and now Perkins School of Theology at Southern Methodist University. Typically, the first half of the course covers biblical, historical, and theological foundations of evangelism; the second half focuses on models of evangelism. The final project requires students to gather all this together into a yearlong evangelistic strategy for a concrete ministry setting; they must thoroughly implement at least one model in the assignment. Over the years, students' enthusiasm about these models—which challenge their preconceptions about the worth of evangelism and spark their imaginations about how to practice it intelligently and winsomely—inspired me to write this book. Perhaps, then, it is not so much the classroom that is the genesis of the book but the many eager and earnest students who, for more than two decades, have filled its pages with a spirit of learning.

Five years ago, I began a full-time administrative position as associate dean of external programs at Perkins School of Theology. This vocational shift came with less time for research and writing, which made my five-month leave of absence granted by Dean Craig Hill all the more precious. During those months, my husband, Jack, and I sequestered ourselves in an apartment under the eaves in the Internationales Begegnungszentrum in Munich, and I completed a full draft of the book. Our stellar graduate assistant, Andrew Klumpp, scanned and e-mailed me scads of articles and book chapters so I could keep up a feverish writing pace. Bridwell Library staff were immensely helpful as well. Sally Hoover requested countless interlibrary loan materials, Ellen Frost bought books to add to the Bridwell collection, and reference librarians David Schmersal (now at Austin Presbyterian Seminary) and Jane Elder searched for obscure and otherwise unattainable bibliographic references and citations. While I was away from campus, my dear colleagues in the Office of External Programs, Bart Patton and Mary Roberts, ran our events with aplomb and excellence. They are an absolute joy to work alongside, and I look forward each and every day to interacting with them as I climb the steps to the third floor of Selecman Hall, an old, brick building on the campus of Southern Methodist University.

A remarkable coterie of people, some of whom I have yet to meet in person, graciously took time from their own work to comment on parts of the manuscript or to contribute to it through meaningful conversations: Billy Abraham, Chris Alford, Jonathan Bedford-Strom, Angela Gorrell, Natasha Govekar, Robert Hunt, Dick Peace, Mark Teasdale, Patricia Walker, and Mark Wingfield. I am also grateful to the team at Baker Academic, who designed the book's fabulous cover and provided expert and careful copyediting, and especially to Bob Hosack, acquisitions editor, who helped shape this book over meals at the American Academy of Religion and the Wesleyan Theological Society—and who, not incidentally, championed it from the start.

Chloe and Jeremy, our daughter and son, surprised and delighted us by moving to Dallas—both of them—not long after Jack and I picked up stakes in Seattle and headed to Texas in 2015. They have kept me grounded in the midst of a major transition in geography and vocation. During the past half decade, we have discovered favorite places to walk, order great takeout pizza, and enjoy happy hour. What a joy it has been to be in their presence on nearly a daily basis.

Jack, my spouse of thirty-eight years, vociferously edited this entire book. He knew my time for a thorough edit was limited once my leave was over, so he offered to be my editor, and I readily accepted. The book improved immensely under his wise and expert pen. For his birthday last year, I gave him a card with the message "I love how we do life!" These words speak to our love-filled enjoyment of daily life together, fully and happily bound up in the other. I dedicate this book to Jack with love and gratitude for how we do life together.

INTRODUCTION

Bathsheba Kingsley was charged in 1741 with stealing a horse and riding away on the Sabbath without her husband's consent, which she did in order to preach the gospel in neighboring towns. She justified herself to the church council, which included Jonathan Edwards, by claiming that she had received a revelation from heaven and was merely obeying God's will. Bathsheba Kingsley was an evangelist.

Sarah Osborn hosted a women's prayer group for over twenty years. By 1766, the group grew to as many as 350 people, including men, women, children, and enslaved people, who flocked to her house for nightly prayer meetings and religious conversation. Sarah Osborn was an evangelist.

Harriet Livermore sang and preached to a standing-room-only crowd in Congress on January 8, 1827, with President John Quincy Adams in attendance. She preached to Congress three more times between 1831 and 1843. Harriet Livermore was an evangelist.

Jarena Lee traveled by foot, stagecoach, and boat from her home in Philadelphia throughout New England, north into Canada, and west into Ohio. She preached wherever a location presented itself—in churches, schools, camp meetings, barns, and homes. Her 1836 autobiography was the first published by an African-American woman. Jarena Lee was an evangelist.

Isaac Hecker converted to Catholicism in 1844. He and five other American-born priests formed the Congregation of St. Paul (or the Paulists) in 1858, as an apostolate to non-Catholics. They held evangelistic missions throughout the country. Isaac Hecker was an evangelist.

Jennie Fowler Willing never birthed her own child, but she encouraged women, especially mothers, to utilize their influence and authority in the service of evangelism. In an article published in 1896, Fowler Willing extolled the mother's power in evangelism. "Among the mightiest of undiscovered forces," she advised, "the mother's power for good ranks all."[1] Jennie Fowler Willing was an evangelist.

Mattie Perry founded Elhanan Training Institute in Marion, North Carolina, for penniless students called into evangelistic work. Her curriculum provided them with Bible classes and practical training. Working with her father and brother, she refurbished, furnished, and readied twenty-five rooms of the derelict Catawba Hotel in time for the watch-night dedication service on December 31, 1898. Mattie Perry was an evangelist.

Emma Ray and Mother Ryther were an interracial pair who visited brothels in Seattle's wharf district on the cusp of the twentieth century. Brothel owners gave them permission to visit and quieted the dancing and music so that Ray and Ryther could hold evangelistic meetings in the parlor. Emma Ray and Mother Ryther were evangelists.

Anna Prosser was healed after living with a disability for ten years. Armed with renewed health, she began to volunteer in a Woman's Christian Temperance Union rescue mission in Buffalo, New York, and she convened a Saturday evening Bible study for laboring men. Each Christmas she provided as lavish a feast for them as she could afford. When she felt called to open a new mission, the men elected to go and assist her. From then on, when talking about the mission, Prosser used the pronoun *we* to signify their partnership. Anna Prosser was an evangelist.

David Goldstein, a convert to Catholicism from Judaism, co-founded the Catholic Truth Guild in 1917 as a traveling evangelistic organization run and staffed by Catholic laypeople. With support from Boston's archbishop, William O'Connell, Goldstein traveled in a customized Model-T throughout New England in the summer and across the continent to California in the winter, holding outdoor evangelistic meetings along the way. David Goldstein was an evangelist.

Raymond Leong emigrated from southern China to Detroit and worked in a hand-laundry business. After becoming a Christian in 1953, thanks to the

---

1. Jennie Fowler Willing, "The Mother's Power in Evangelism," *Guide to Holiness* (December 1896): 220.

outreach efforts of local churches, he recruited other Chinese laundry work-ers to join group Bible studies. These evangelistic efforts led to the founding of the Detroit Chinese Bible Church. Raymond Leong was an evangelist.

Iva Dardanet spoke to her neighbor at the nondescript backyard clothesline of a post–World War II tract home built on the potato fields of Long Island, New York. In her strong Southern accent she asked, "How about a nice cold Coca-Cola?" Her neighbor, Norma Levison, accepted the neighborly gesture and within a matter of months made a commitment to Christ. Iva Dardanet was an evangelist.

Members of Oak Lane Presbyterian Church rang doorbells in their down-town Philadelphia neighborhood in the late 1960s for their visitation evange-lism program. This led to neighborly compassion—for example, purchasing hospital beds for the suffering—as the church demonstrated love to its Phila-delphia neighbors in practical ways. Oak Lane was changed in the process: they became a more ethnically diverse church that reflected the changing demographics of their neighborhood. The members of Oak Lane and their pastor, Richard Armstrong, were evangelists.

Rodney Woo—while serving as senior pastor of Wilcrest Baptist Church in Houston, Texas, from 1992 to 2010—led its transformation from an all-white church to one that is thirty-five times more racially diverse than the average congregation in the United States. "Wilcrest Baptist Church is God's multi-ethnic bridge that draws all people to Jesus Christ who trans-forms them from unbelievers to missionaries," announces the church's vi-sion statement.[2] Rodney Woo and the members of Wilcrest Baptist Church are evangelists.

Samira Izadi Page, born a Shia Muslim, fled Iran in 1989. Eventually, she crossed into the United States at the Texas border by walking through the Rio Grande and turned herself in at the border checkpoint. In Dallas, she became a Christian, earned two seminary degrees, and founded Gateway of Grace, an organization that mobilizes congregations to connect with refugees. Samira Izadi Page is an evangelist.

According to a recent Barna Group study, "A startling six in 10 Ameri-cans believe that any 'attempt to convert others' to one's own faith is 'ex-treme.' More than eight out of 10 'nones' say so! To be clear: A majority of US adults, and the vast majority of non-religious adults (83%), believe that

---

2. "Nations Reaching Nations," Wilcrest Baptist Church, 2020, http://wilcrestbaptist.org.

evangelism is religiously extreme."[3] That majority may just be right. After all, Bathsheba Kingsley stole a horse—committing a crime to be an evangelist. Harriet Livermore, after preaching to Congress for the last time, spent all her money traveling four times to Jerusalem to evangelize there and to witness to the impending, literal return of Jesus; she died alone in a Philadelphia almshouse and was buried, as she had requested, in an unmarked grave. Richard Armstrong, the pastor at Oak Lane Presbyterian Church and convener of its visitation evangelism program in downtown Philadelphia, made no bones about the fact that evangelism can be extreme. "The first effect of our Christian witness," cautions Armstrong, "may not be reconciliation but alienation, not peace but a sword, not confession but conflict. That is the risk we must take, for our calling is to be God's agents of reconciliation in such a world."[4]

Yes, the majority of American adults may be right when they claim that evangelism is religiously extreme. Yet they may be off the mark as well. Evangelism is not inevitably extreme. Sarah Osborn did not set out to orchestrate a multiracial meeting for hundreds of people. What she did was open her home for the women in town to gather in prayer. Iva Dardanet asked a neighbor if she wanted a Coke. That conventional invitation led to invitations to church and eventually to my mother-in-law's lifelong, durable, vibrant faith. Rodney Woo's vision for a multicultural church circulated in his veins even before he was born. His half-Chinese father served as a missionary to Hispanic people, African-American people, and Vietnamese immigrants in the border town of Port Arthur, Texas. Woo's multicultural experience intensified as he attended an all African-American elementary and middle school. Woo would claim that it is only natural—not religiously extreme at all—to expect churches to cross racial and ethnic lines in their communities.

The majority of Americans, then, are both right and wrong. Evangelism can be both—sometimes extreme, sometimes not. Either way, there remains something invigorating about it. Being actively engaged in evangelism encourages the evangelist to keep her own faith alive and resilient because she is motivated by a sense of optimism, of leaning into the possibilities that materialize when she engages others with the Christian gospel. Consider Mattie Perry, who recognized that evangelists and missionaries need training before heading out into full-time ministry. When no one else stepped up, Perry, despite a lack

---

3. Barna Group, *Spiritual Conversations in the Digital Age: How Christians' Approach to Sharing Their Faith Has Changed in 25 Years* (Ventura, CA: Barna Group, 2018), 23.
4. Richard Stoll Armstrong, *Service Evangelism* (Philadelphia: Westminster, 1979), 72.

of education and financial backing, founded a religious training school for students who could not afford a college or university education. Consider, too, Anna Prosser, how she wanted to give to others in gratitude for her healing after living ten years with a disability, so she spent her time and resources at her local rescue mission with those who were utterly destitute. Also consider Samira Izadi Page, who took her experience as a refugee and transformed it into an organization that serves—in the name of Jesus Christ—refugees of all faiths who have settled in Dallas, Texas.

The history of evangelism is a diverse litany. Male and female, rich and poor, itinerant and local, Catholic and Protestant, extreme and natural, public and private. Evangelists come in all shapes and sizes.

The English word *evangelism* is not so much a translation as a modified transliteration of the Greek word *euangelion*, which is composed of two parts: the preposition *eu*, meaning "good" (as in *euphoria* or *euphemism*); and the root *angelos*, meaning "angel" or "messenger." The content of evangelism is the gospel, the *euangelion*, the good news. The one who brings good news, the messenger, is an evangelist, a *euangelistēs*.

Jesus brought a message of good news, the *euangelion*. The first mention of Jesus's message, depicted in the earliest Gospel, uses precisely this word: "Now after John was arrested, Jesus came to Galilee, proclaiming the good news [*euangelion*] of God, and saying, 'The time is fulfilled, and the kingdom of God has come near; repent, and believe in the good news'" (Mark 1:14–15). The word *euangelion* occurs twice in this encapsulation of Jesus's vocation: Jesus proclaimed the good news of God (*to euangelion tou theou*) and told people to "repent, and believe in the good news" (*metanoeite kai pisteuete en tō euangeliō*).

Although we can trace the history and practice of evangelism to Jesus, definitions of evangelism vary widely. D. T. Niles, a Sri Lankan leader in the mid-twentieth-century ecumenical movement, set out one of the simplest definitions of evangelism: evangelism is "one beggar telling another beggar where to get food."[5] Southern Baptist evangelism professor Delos Miles offered a broad

5. Here is a fuller context for this famous line, in a chapter titled "The Non-Christian": "Evangelism is witness. It is one beggar telling another beggar where to get food. The Christian does not. offer out of his bounty. He has no bounty. He is simply guest at his Master's table and, as evangelist, he calls others too. The evangelistic relation is to be 'alongside of' not 'over-against.' The Christian

definition, based in part on Mark 1:14–15: "Evangelism is being, doing, and telling the gospel of the kingdom of God, in order that by the power of the Holy Spirit persons and structures may be converted to the lordship of Jesus Christ."[6] Central to Miles's definition is the directive that evangelism can be transformative for both individuals and structures. Essential, too, is the presence of the Holy Spirit, which signals that evangelism is not a mechanical process.

Contemporary author and speaker Martha Grace Reese derived a definition based on interviews with over one thousand individuals from hundreds of churches: "At its core, evangelism is people sharing with others their personal understandings that life is better, richer, truer if one has faith in Christ and lives in a faith community."[7]

Pope Francis offers yet another definition, highlighting the centrality of hospitality in the task of evangelism. "Christians have the duty to proclaim the Gospel without excluding anyone," he advises. "Instead of seeming to impose new obligations, they should appear as people who wish to share their joy, who point to a horizon of beauty and who invite others to a delicious banquet."[8]

No one definition of evangelism is universally accepted, yet common to those presented here is the promise of evangelism that issues invitations, forges relationships, relieves hunger, quenches thirst, restores fruitfulness, and reconciles estranged parties. If a single biblical text can encapsulate this vision, it is Isaiah 52:7:

> How beautiful upon the mountains
>> are the feet of the messenger who announces peace,
> who brings good news,
>> who announces salvation,
>> who says to Zion, "Your God reigns."

In this lovely encomium, the verb *euangelizō* ("to bring good news") appears twice in the Greek translation of the Old Testament (the Septuagint). The

---

stands alongside the non-Christian and points to the Gospel, the holy action of God." D. T. Niles, *That They May Have Life* (New York: Harper & Brothers, 1951), 96.

6. Delos Miles, *Introduction to Evangelism* (Nashville: Broadman, 1983), 47.

7. Martha Grace Reese, *Unbinding the Gospel: Real Life Evangelism* (St. Louis: Chalice, 2006), 6.

8. Pope Francis, *Evangelii Gaudium*, Vatican Publishing House, November 24, 2013, http://www.vatican.va/content/francesco/en/apost_exhortations/documents/papa-francesco_esortazione-ap_20131124_evangelii-gaudium.html, III.15.

messenger brings good news of peace and salvation—which, in the context of Isaiah 40–55, is restoration to wholeness and return from the harsh realities of Babylonian exile. In essence, the promise is of a return to a place of safety and prosperity, which, when we think about it, is a splendid description of the purpose of evangelism.

The eight models of evangelism selected for this book exemplify the broad expanse that makes up evangelism.[9] In short, the models vary dramatically. Think here about the difference between personal evangelism (a one-on-one experience, often among friends) and a revival (a highly orchestrated, typically large rally focused on a message proclaimed to everyone simultaneously). Or ponder the difference between media evangelism, which employs the latest in technological advances, and liturgical evangelism, which is grounded in millennia of worship and catechetical traditions. Given this wide spectrum—this alone is one of the contributions of this book—each reader will no doubt gravitate to some models, resist others, and perhaps (and I encourage this) combine elements of several models, in concert with one another, to develop a distinctive model of evangelism uniquely suited to a particular context.

These eight models are organized from the most intimate to those with the widest possible reach:

- Personal: developing a one-on-one relationship that provides a comfortable context for evangelism
- Small group: convening eight to twelve people for a short-term, focused study on the gospel
- Visitation: knocking on doors, getting to know neighbors' needs and religious inclinations, and initiating conversations about the gospel
- Liturgical: integrating evangelism into the church's worship as it follows the Christian calendar

9. I chose evangelism models that met three criteria: (1) demonstrated longevity, having been practiced for at least a generation and in most cases much longer; (2) provided a substantial body of literature that discussed four foundations, biblical, theological, historical, and practical; and (3) represented a significant number of proponents. In some cases, when several models closely overlapped, I merged them into one model. For instance, in personal evangelism, I integrated lifestyle evangelism as step 1 in the model and discipleship evangelism as step 4. The eight models discussed here do not exhaust the potential models; nevertheless, they represent a wide, diverse, and timeless swath of the ways evangelists have engaged—and continue to engage—in evangelism.

- Church growth: establishing new ports of entry that receptive people can easily join in order to be introduced to the gospel
- Prophetic: challenging individuals and structures to pursue the gospel in word and deed and in its social, political, and economic fullness
- Revival: an organized, crowd-based gathering that typically includes music, an evangelistic message, an invitation, and follow-up
- Media: appropriating media ranging from the printed word to the internet for an evangelistic purpose

The organization of this book is straightforward with a chapter devoted to each model. Each chapter follows the same format:

- opening with an anecdote or observation to set the stage for a discussion of that model
- analyzing the primary *biblical* bases of that model
- exploring at least two *theological* themes that anchor each model
- conveying a brief *historical* discussion of several notable, principally North American, practitioners of that model
- providing a step-by-step *practical* breakdown to facilitate implementation of that model
- offering an appraisal of each model

This book, then, provides a study of eight influential models of evangelism under these same rubrics: biblical, theological, historical, and practical.

The analysis in each chapter is eclectic, by which I mean that the presentation of each model is drawn from a wide, representative range of proponents and approaches rather than from only one approach or proponent as *the* representation of the model. For instance, in my analysis of visitation evangelism, I draw from James Kennedy's highly orchestrated, salvation-centered Evangelism Explosion alongside Richard Armstrong's service-oriented model. Both represent visitation evangelism, but they represent it in noticeably different ways. This approach allows the reader to view a model from a multiplicity of perspectives.

When proponents of these models did not provide adequate biblical, theological, historical, or practical underpinnings, I supplemented and strengthened their approaches by filling in gaps and underscoring emphases. You will see traces of my hand in the "Biblical Foundations" sections, where I include significant supplementary study of texts that have often been cited without enough comment on original languages, historical context, and literary artistry.

You will see more traces in the "Theological Foundations" sections because I frequently found the theological articulation of these models to be somewhat superficial. Evangelism falls under the rubric of practical theology, but these models, on the whole, tend to lean toward the practical at the expense of the theological. To provide consistency of theological reflection, I often incorporated insights from Avery Dulles's *Models of the Church* to draw out theological implications related to ecclesiology (the doctrine of the church). Dulles's book also served as the inspiration for this book's title, *Models of Evangelism*.

You will see traces of my hand in the "Historical Foundations" sections too, since I am first and foremost a historian. I have analyzed these models with what I hope will be seen as historical perspicacity and insight.

In the "Practical Foundations" section of each chapter, you will see my hand largely in selection and organization. These models, on the whole, do not lack practical strategies, but no one, to my knowledge, has provided a comprehensive, organized, and accessible analysis of how to implement each of them. *Models of Evangelism* does.

My hand is heaviest toward the conclusion of each chapter, in the "Appraisal" section, in which I raise several questions about each model. These questions are intended to provide an evenhanded evaluation of each model. Then, to facilitate interaction by the reader, each chapter closes with five reflection questions. The last question is always the same: *Which other model of evangelism best complements this model?* This question is essential to the book—and the ongoing work of evangelism—because the impression this book may give is that evangelism requires the mastery of a single model (personal, small group, visitation, liturgical, church growth, prophetic, revival, media). On the contrary, a vital, promising future for evangelism will happen only as individual models combust to create a model uniquely suited to each particular context. Such a combustion is the promise and potential of *Models of Evangelism*.

ONE

PERSONAL

To envision how effective a model of evangelism can be, in which one person shares her faith one-on-one with another, simply recall a time when you got caught up in a friend's enthusiasm for the amazing food she ate last night at a trendy downtown restaurant, or the movie he saw over the weekend that you just *have* to see, or—yes, this is true—a revolutionary new hair product, as Kevin Harney experienced: "I once saw a woman come up to her friend and say, 'Smell my hair.' It seemed like a strange request. But to my surprise, the other woman leaned over and took a big whiff. This led to an extensive conversation about a particular hair-care product. They chatted for a good ten minutes about it. The first woman touted the benefits of her new shampoo with great enthusiasm and passion. The second listened, asked questions, and seemed quite intrigued." Harney, an advocate of personal evangelism, goes on to make the point that "we evangelize all the time. . . . The truth is, when we are zealous about something, when we really love it, we talk about it. We invite others to experience it. We want to share the joy."[1]

It sounds so easy, but talking about a hair-care product or a restaurant is much easier—and typically far less liable to resistance on the part of the hearer—than conversing about religion. Who doesn't want to eat a delicious

1. Kevin Harney, *Organic Outreach for Ordinary People* (Grand Rapids: Zondervan, 2009), 13–14.

meal, watch a good movie, or have hair with, oh, that perfect luster and bounce? But religion? Faith? Christianity? A recent study by the Barna Group documented two reasons in particular why people do not talk often about faith: avoidance and ambivalence.

- Religious conversations always seem to create tension or arguments: 28%
- I'm put off by how religion has been politicized: 17%
- I don't feel like I know enough to talk about religious or spiritual topics: 17%[2]

The conundrum that avoidance and ambivalence presents is that fewer and fewer Christians in the United States are willing to engage in what is the most effective model of evangelism. As Tom Stebbins writes, "The gospel spreads most effectively across an existing network of trust relationships."[3] What then to do? If you are someone who resists the very thought of personal evangelism, I would ask you to suspend your hesitation, put down your crossed arms, and quiet your criticisms just long enough to read carefully the rest of the chapter, in which you may find some surprising, even admirable, qualities of personal evangelism that you have yet to encounter or consider.

Biblical Foundations

Though it is possible to find countless examples in Scripture of individuals sharing good news one-on-one, there are enough illustrations in John's Gospel to prompt us to begin there. In John 1:39, Jesus responds to a question from Andrew, one of John the Baptist's disciples, by inviting him to "come and see" where he is staying. Andrew then finds (*heuriskei*) and brings (*ēgagen*)—the Greek verb *agō*, perhaps better translated as "led"—his brother, Simon Peter, and the two brothers end up becoming two of the twelve disciples (1:40–42). In the next verse—the next day chronologically—Jesus finds (*heuriskei*) Philip and calls him to follow (v. 43). Philip responds affirmatively and then invites a more skeptical Nathanael—who cannot believe that anything good could

2. "Why People Are Reluctant to Discuss Faith," Barna.com, August 14, 2018, https://www .barna.com/research/reasons-for-reluctance. These are three of the top four responses given.

3. Tom Stebbins, *Friendship Evangelism by the Book: Applying First-Century Principles to Twenty-First-Century Relationships* (Camp Hill, PA: Christian Publications, 1995), 72.

come from Nazareth—with the simple words, "Come and see" (v. 46), which Jesus had spoken earlier.

So many simple words in this first chapter of John's Gospel, words that encapsulate the essence of personal evangelism. *Come and see. Found. Led. Found. Come and see.* In the first chapter of John's Gospel, the good news spreads one by one via personal invitation among friends and family, underscoring a central thrust of personal evangelism: the gospel spreads most effectively and efficiently across an existing network of relationships.

Two chapters later, Jesus interacts with another person, Nicodemus, "a leader of the Jews" (John 3:1). This time, Nicodemus is the one who initiates the encounter, with questions he wants to discuss (vv. 1–21). After Jesus's crucifixion, Nicodemus shows up with a large amount of spices and helps Joseph of Arimathea place Jesus's body in the tomb (19:38–42). Whether Nicodemus ever comes to believe in Jesus as the Messiah is a question left unanswered; his response in this respect is not at all like Andrew's and Philip's. The ambiguity that marks Nicodemus's final appearance in John's Gospel is something for which we can be grateful, since it is true to life: spiritual conversations can be tricky and tentative, and they often end without a clear decision, a certain conversion.

In the fourth chapter of John's Gospel, one of the most successful examples of Jesus as an evangelist occurs in a most unlikely, even unseemly, encounter with a woman whose sexual promiscuity is legendary. In Jesus's longest conversation, he talks alone with the Samaritan woman at the Sychar well in the heat of the noon sun (4:1–42). Jesus prompts the conversation with a simple request. "Give me a drink," he says (v. 7). The woman proceeds to ask several questions, which Jesus answers, and the conversation continues, touching on topics from her personal life to divisive religious issues. When the disciples return, the woman leaves her water jar at the well and rushes back to town with these words on her lips: "[He] told me everything I have ever done" (v. 29). As a result of her testimony, the townspeople come to Jesus to hear more for themselves. Jesus stays for two days, and many, whose curiosity was piqued initially because of the woman's words, come to believe that Jesus is the Messiah.

The Gospel of John is not the only New Testament book to offer clear models of personal evangelism.[4] The book of Acts, which narrates the story

---

4. More examples abound throughout the Gospels, such as Jesus calling up to Zacchaeus as he crouches in the tree for a better view (Luke 19:1–10) and the many people Jesus heals, like the Gerasene demoniac (Mark 5:1–20). In these stories, Jesus meets people where they are

of the early church, contains a breathtaking account of personal evangelism involving Philip and an Ethiopian eunuch (8:26–40). Note Philip's responsiveness to God's messenger. Immediately and obediently, he gets up and goes to the wilderness road that stretches from Jerusalem to Gaza. Immediately, obediently, and swiftly, he follows the Spirit's direction to go over to the chariot—by running toward it (vv. 29–30). He opens the conversation with a simple question: "Do you understand what you are reading?" (v. 30). The eunuch reacts, "How can I, unless someone guides me?" (v. 31). Then he invites Philip into the chariot to talk further.

Note how Philip allows the conversation to unfold at its own tempo. The eunuch, not Philip, raises the question, "About whom, may I ask you, does the prophet say this, about himself or about someone else?" (v. 34). Philip honors the question and connects what they read in the Isaiah scroll to the good news about Jesus. He begins precisely where the eunuch is and deftly leads the conversation from the prophet Isaiah to Jesus Christ.

Philip does not take charge of anything in this story. He reacts eagerly to the Spirit's prompting to approach the chariot. Then, after asking a simple opening question, he responds to the eunuch's request. Philip's ability to respond rather than control the conversation appears especially clearly in the eunuch's request to be baptized. Without a word from Philip, the eunuch commands the chariot to stop; the two of them then head into the water together, where Philip baptizes him and leaves the eunuch to continue on his way rejoicing. What a story to inspire a responsive and supple approach to personal evangelism!

> Picture this pair sitting side by side, a black man and a (relatively) white man, a sexually crippled man (a eunuch) and a robust man with four daughters (Acts 21:9), bouncing along in a chariot on a desolate road, united solely by the scroll of Isaiah that is draped over their knees. It's a sight to behold. . . . An unexpected pair, a shared scroll, an out-of-the-way location, yet at the very center of God's work. One by unexpected one, the people of God grew. One by surprising one, the church of God was enriched. And why? Because Philip found himself in unexpected places, listened to the Spirit, was willing to take the initiative, open to questions and requests, and contented to sit and study scripture at another person's pace.[5]

and addresses their need for healing, restitution, or further learning; they respond in turn by bringing others to encounter Jesus.

5. Jack Levison and Priscilla Pope-Levison, *How Is It with Your Soul?* (New York: United Methodist Women, 2014), 71.

Theological Foundations

Personal evangelism finds its orientation in two theological foci: Christology and Pneumatology. The christological aspect to which advocates of personal evangelism primarily appeal is the incarnation, the full humanity and full divinity of Jesus. Jesus, the divine Word who from the beginning was God, was born as one of us fully and bodily. John 1:14 offers a lovely, earthy image of Jesus's pitching his tent (*skēnoō*) in humanity's midst: "The Word became flesh and lived [*eskēnōsen*] among us."[6] The related noun, *skēnē*, shows up in the Septuagint, the Greek translation of the Old Testament, where it refers to the tabernacle as the earthly place where God's presence dwelt.[7] As God's glory shone from the tabernacle, so Jesus shone forth God's glory: "The Word became flesh and lived among us, and we have seen his glory, the glory as of a father's only son, full of grace and truth" (v. 14). Through his incarnation, Jesus became "a visual aid" for the invisible God.[8] "Whoever has seen me has seen the Father" (14:9).

Jesus was sent into the world to make known the invisible God. He entrusted and commissioned his disciples with the same task: to make the invisible God known in the world. God sent the Son, who in turn sent his followers to communicate the good news of God's salvation in the person of Jesus Christ (John 17:18). As Rebecca Manley Pippert writes, "God didn't send a telegram or shower evangelistic Bible study books from heaven or drop a million bumper stickers from the sky saying, 'Smile, Jesus loves you.' He sent a man, his Son, to communicate the message. His strategy hasn't changed. He still sends men and women—before he sends tracts and techniques—to change the world."[9]

Devotees of personal evangelism also identify the Holy Spirit as the divine instigator and guide for personal evangelism. We read in the previous section how the Holy Spirit directed Philip to his encounter with the Ethiopian eunuch

6. The Greek verb *skēnoō* can mean "to live," "to dwell," "to shelter," or "to pitch a tent." For instance, *eskēnōsen* (in Gen. 13:12 in the Septuagint) possesses the meaning of pitching a tent: "Abram settled in the land of Canaan, while Lot settled among the cities of the Plain and moved his tent as far as Sodom." All English translations of the Septuagint are from *A New English Translation of the Septuagint*, trans. and ed. Albert Pietersma and Benjamin G. Wright (Oxford: Oxford University Press, 2007).

7. See Exod. 40:34–38 in the Septuagint.

8. Joseph Aldrich, *Lifestyle Evangelism* (Colorado Springs: Multnomah, 1993), 31.

9. Rebecca Manley Pippert, *Out of the Saltshaker and into the World: Evangelism as a Way of Life*, 2nd ed. (Downers Grove, IL: InterVarsity, 1999), 30.

(Acts 8:29–30). As with Philip, divinely ordained appointments can happen out of the blue. Years ago, during the last meal before Christmas break in a nearly empty college cafeteria, a friend of mine sat across the table from a fellow student whom he knew only in passing. He half-heartedly talked with her, hoping to finish his meal quickly to get on the road for home to relax after taking a slew of exams. Somehow the conversation veered to the topic of my friend's participation in a Bible study, and he ended up telling her about his yearlong pilgrimage to Christianity. After about fifteen minutes, my friend was startled to realize the student was actually interested in what he was saying. As they continued the conversation, my friend felt prompted to ask if she would like to pray to receive Christ. She said that she would. They prayed together, said goodbye, and never saw each other again. A wilderness road. A deserted college cafeteria.

Underlying this encounter is the conviction that the Holy Spirit inspires what to say, as my friend discovered. The evangelist is not on his or her own. A principal promise in the New Testament is that the Holy Spirit inspires testimony that points to Jesus. In Acts 1:8, for example, Jesus makes clear that the Holy Spirit will provide power to Jesus's disciples for their mission: "You will receive power when the Holy Spirit has come upon you; and you will be my witnesses in Jerusalem, in all Judea and Samaria, and to the ends of the earth." In a personal evangelism conversation, "the Spirit gives us both the words to say and the opportunity to say them. Our sensitivity to what to say and when to speak can be heightened by prayer and allowing ourselves to be led to those who are ready to hear the story of God's love."[10]

Equally foundational to this model is the belief that the Holy Spirit convicts people of their need for transformation. This is not something human beings can engender; transformation is left to the individual and the Holy Spirit. Our role is to help bring people to the point of decision, to accompany them through it, and to nurture them afterward. Think here of a progressive dinner: "Sharing the Good News of God's love at the point of conviction is like serving the last course of a progressive dinner. The Spirit has created the hunger. We simply serve the meal. . . . We are responsible for contacts, not for conviction. And even our contacts are made in response to the leading of the Holy Spirit."[11] Understanding the critical role of the Holy Spirit in personal

10. Duncan McIntosh, *The Everyday Evangelist* (Valley Forge, PA: Judson, 1984), 15.
11. D. McIntosh, *Everyday Evangelist*, 54.

evangelism encourages us to witness to Jesus Christ with the sure knowledge that we are not alone and that the task does not rest only on our shoulders. This partnership with the Holy Spirit allows us to relax—and even to enjoy speaking to people about Jesus.

Historical Foundations

One of the most renowned evangelists of all time, the influencer of American revivalism for successive generations—including those of Billy Sunday and Billy Graham—became a Christian through personal evangelism. What an evangelist he would go on to become! Estimates put the number at one million converted under his preaching. To prepare for his revivals, he set up an efficient evangelistic organization that visited one city after another for weeks at a time. He modeled this same efficiency during what some consider his apex, the 1893 World's Fair Campaign.[12] Each day of the campaign, his organization sponsored as many as five meetings in scores of venues that included ten churches, seven halls, two theaters, and five tents. Determined to "beat the World's Fair" with electrifying, crowd-pleasing events, he, along with his hand-picked team of evangelists and several hundred other workers, kept up a breakneck pace. On a day touted as the campaign's best, September 23, 1893, his evangelistic organization scheduled "sixty-four different meetings held in forty-six places, with an estimated attendance of from sixty-two to sixty-four thousand people."[13]

So how did Dwight L. Moody come to faith? Through the personal evangelism of his Sunday school teacher Edward Kimball. Moody had come to Chicago to work as a salesperson in his uncle's shoe store; the arrangement with his uncle included Moody's mandatory church attendance. After spending some time encouraging Moody to read the Bible and take it seriously, Kimball showed up at the shoe store on April 21, 1855. While Moody was putting away shoes in the back room, Kimball asked him point-blank to commit his life to Christ. He did and that very day Moody began sharing his faith with others. (Another wilderness road, by the way—the back room of a Chicago shoe store.)

Best known for his revivals, a model of evangelism we will explore in chapter 7, Moody also made a profound impact on young Christian leaders through Moody

12. Jean Miller Schmidt, *Souls or the Social Order: The Two-Party System in American Protestantism* (Brooklyn: Carlson, 1991), 99; Thekla Ellen Joiner, *Sin in the City: Chicago and Revivalism, 1880–1920* (Columbia: University of Missouri Press, 2007), 85.
13. Joiner, *Sin in the City*, 106.

Bible Institute, as well as through his annual summer school for college students. This summer program sparked in attendees a commitment to evangelism and mission. John R. Mott, who attended the first summer school in 1886, wrote to his parents about his experience: "Here are 225 young men all of whom are solid Christians and moreover who are all imbued, with the YMCA characteristic—*work for souls.* I know of no other such meeting in this country at least. They are all impressed with the feeling of responsibility also—I doubt very much if there is a fellow here but what will enter some active religious work."[14]

Personal evangelism to and by college students remains a backbone of campus ministry organizations like InterVarsity, Navigators, and Cru (Campus Crusade for Christ), to name a few. These organizations bolster personal evangelism by providing resources and training. One of the most widely used resources in personal evangelism, the Four Spiritual Laws, was developed in the mid-1960s by Bill Bright, founder of Cru.[15]

Fast-forward nearly a century to one of the most publicized conversions in the twentieth century, which occurred when a friend shared the gospel with Chuck Colson, former Special Counsel to President Richard Nixon. Colson described himself as a self-made man who found success in college and law school, in the Navy, and as a high-powered lawyer. After the presidential election in 1968, Nixon asked Colson to work at the White House, where they had offices next to each other. Four years later, after orchestrating a landslide victory for Nixon, Colson decided to return to his law practice, but his life took a dramatic detour at that point. He found himself feeling empty, "battle weary after being in the White House," and of course, Watergate was on the horizon.[16] Colson went to the home of his friend Tom Phillips, another self-

---

14. C. Howard Hopkins, *John R. Mott (1865–1955): A Biography* (Grand Rapids: Eerdmans, 1979), 26. Mott gave inspiration and leadership to the twentieth-century ecumenical movement and was awarded the Nobel Peace Prize in 1946.

15. The Four Spiritual Laws consist of these statements: (1) God loves you and offers a wonderful plan for your life (John 3:16; 10:10); (2) Humanity is sinful and separated from God. Therefore, we cannot know and experience God's love and plan for our lives (Rom. 3:23; 6:23); (3) Jesus Christ is God's only provision for our sin. Through him we can know and experience God's love and plan for our lives (John 14:6; Rom. 5:8; 1 Cor. 15:3–6); and (4) We must individually receive Jesus Christ as Savior and Lord; then we can know and experience God's love and plan for our lives (John 1:12; 3:1–8; Eph. 2:8–9; Rev. 3:20). Bill Bright, "Would You Like to Know God Personally?," Bright Media Foundation & Campus Crusade for Christ International, http://www.4laws.com/laws/englishkgp/default.htm.

16. The material for and quotations in these paragraphs, unless noted otherwise, come from a recorded speech Colson gave, which is available on YouTube. Chuck Colson, "Chuck Colson Gives His Testimony," Columbia University, 2008, YouTube video, 34:27, https://www.youtube.com/view_play_list?p=B7F7760E341D34BE.

made man and the CEO of a large corporation. Colson immediately noticed a change in Phillips's demeanor; Phillips seemed completely at peace. The reason? "I've accepted Jesus Christ," Phillips told Colson, "and committed my life to him." Phillips then read aloud a chapter from C. S. Lewis's *Mere Christianity*. The chapter he chose was "The Great Vice." "I listened to that and realized Lewis was writing about me," Colson said. "Everything I had done was all for me."

Colson left Phillips's home and tried to drive away but could not because he was weeping. Having grown up without any religious influence or "moral compass for the first 41 years of his life," he had never heard anybody talk like that about God.[17] He sat in the car for about an hour and called out to God for the first time in his life. The next morning, he quickly located a copy of *Mere Christianity* and read it through. He got out a yellow legal pad and made two columns, one headed by the statement "There is a God" and the other by "There isn't a God," and he thought carefully through the questions that confronted him. Then, he made his decision. "In the quiet of being on the Maine coast away from Watergate, before I was considered a target of the investigation, I simply quietly surrendered my life to Christ."

In 1974, Colson ended up in Alabama's Maxwell Prison, a "culture shock going from an office next door to the president of the United States to a prison cell." There he began a Bible study with seven men—a motley group composed of three people convicted of substance abuse, a swindler, a car thief, a moonshiner, and the president's former Special Counsel. After serving seven months of his four-year term, he was released. He founded Prison Fellowship in 1976, a ministry serving inmates, the formerly incarcerated, and their families. He also became a leading advocate for criminal justice reform. In recognition of his work among inmates, Colson received the prestigious Templeton Prize for Progress in Religion in 1993.[18]

Practical Foundations

There is a stark simplicity to personal evangelism. It requires no theological degree. It demands no need to control a conversation. It necessitates no

17. Jonathan Aitken, "Remembering Charles Colson, a Man Transformed," *Christianity Today*, April 21, 2012, https://www.christianitytoday.com/ct/2012/aprilweb-only/charles-colson-aitken.html.
18. "Our Approach," Prison Fellowship, https://www.prisonfellowship.org/about.

hyperspirituality. It certainly requires no sacred space. A cafeteria will do, as will a shoe store, a home, or a prison cell. At the same time, there are practical foundations that can enhance the practice of personal evangelism.

1. Begin with Lifestyle Evangelism

Lifestyle evangelism, a term coined by Joseph Aldrich, underscores the key point that for Christians, their lifestyle should communicate the gospel even before they speak a word. *Lifestyle* encompasses everything about us—what clothes we wear and what food we eat, where we live and work, whom we spend time with, and how we organize our day. Whether we recognize it or not, our lifestyle requires countless choices each and every day, and it communicates what we hold most dear, what we prioritize. Whether we recognize it or not, people notice our lifestyle and draw conclusions about us from it. This happens everywhere, including in the workplace. One bank employee relates how he started to watch Miles's life, who was one of the bank's vice presidents: "He asked Miles one day what made him so different. Miles invited him to meet him for breakfast and shared Jesus Christ with him."[19] This story illustrates Aldrich's claim that "Christians are to be good news before they share the good news. The words of the gospel are to be incarnated before they are verbalized."[20]

It goes without saying that integrity is key to a Christian's lifestyle. Actions and words on behalf of the gospel must be congruous with one's lifestyle, mutually enhancing and edifying. Hypocrisy communicates more loudly and forcefully than pious words, even the right pious words. Among those who reject Christianity, the reason most often given is that Christians are hypocrites; they act one way in public and another in private. The gospel is blunted by a lifestyle that lacks integrity. In North America, we have had the unfortunate and unwelcome opportunity to see this over and over again in the sexual misconduct and greed of prominent evangelists.

Hypocrisy does not belong only to the sphere of the famous and infamous. All Christians must be people of integrity. If our eye causes us to stumble, Jesus tells us, we should cut it out and throw it away (Mark 9:47). Hyperbole, to be sure, but to the point. Examples of hypocritical evangelists fill the pages of novels and the images of films. These are easy to spot and to

---

19. Stebbins, *Friendship Evangelism by the Book*, 153.
20. Aldrich, *Lifestyle Evangelism*, 19–20.

parade as public knowledge. But no less significant is the integrity that attracts unbelievers in the normal course of life, far from the roar of revival tents, television shows, and podcasts. We demonstrate the good news through our lifestyle, when we turn toward a neighbor who is from a different ethnicity, class, culture, country, language, or political party; when we demonstrate compassion; when we run toward chariots; when we oversee a bank or an office with honesty; and when we locate ourselves in the company of addicts, a swindler, a car thief, and a moonshiner. Integrity is an essential ingredient in a lifestyle that evangelizes.

2. Raise Your Evangelistic Temperature

"Every follower of Jesus has an evangelistic temperature," Harney explains. "It can be hot, cold, or somewhere in the middle. This temperature impacts the way we live and interact with those who are far from God."[21] The evangelistic temperature of many American Christians is cool and growing even cooler, according to a Barna Group study. When Christians were asked in 1993 about their agreement with the statement "Every Christian has a responsibility to share the gospel," 89 percent of respondents agreed. In 2018, the same statement received only 64 percent agreement, which indicates a 25 percent cooling off in evangelistic temperature over twenty-five years.[22] Blame for a downturn in evangelism often falls on the caricature of a hard-core, overbearing evangelist, but the reality is different—and more home grown. Evangelism is a topic and a practice that Christians want nothing to do with; they remain reluctant, even embarrassed, to talk about their faith to anyone.

How can we Christians move beyond this aversion to personal evangelism? One place to begin is with an honest assessment of your evangelistic temperature. Think numerically along a scale of one to ten, with one being "Ice Cold (personal evangelism is never on your radar screen, and you are extremely apprehensive about it)" and ten being "Sizzling Hot (personal evangelism is your daily default setting)."[23] Where are you currently on the scale? Being truthful at the outset, when it comes to personal evangelism, provides a baseline for gauging later on whether you have become warmer bit by bit, as you implement the practical foundations that follow.

21. Harney, *Organic Outreach*, 62.
22. Barna Group, *Spiritual Conversations in the Digital Age: How Christians' Approach to Sharing Their Faith Has Changed in 25 Years* (Ventura, CA: Barna Group, 2018), 18.
23. Harney, *Organic Outreach*, 63.

One way to warm up your evangelistic temperature is to invest more deeply in your own spiritual life by developing spiritual disciplines. Richard Peace explains: "Conscious spiritual formation as part of one's training to be an evangelist and as part of one's lifestyle as an evangelist would yield a depth of spirituality that would impact positively the work of evangelism."[24] Daily prayer. Daily Scripture reading. Participation in a community of faith that challenges you to be a Christian in less comfortable circumstances. Praying on a regular basis for the spiritually uninterested or disconnected people you know, with whom you cross paths. As a reminder to pray for these people, post a list someplace where you will see it throughout the day.[25] Pray especially that the Holy Spirit, as we discussed above, will prepare them—and *you*—for a faith-related conversation.

Another way to warm up your evangelistic temperature is to seek out those who have a high evangelistic temperature and listen to their stories. Perhaps accompany them on an errand or in a situation where they are engaged in personal evangelism. Become an informal protégé. Then be ready to act, because their encouragement and experience may be contagious.

3. Foster the Relationship

Building a relationship of trust, credibility, and communication through your presence is fundamental to personal evangelism. Through this relationship, you will be able to demonstrate your love, care, and respect for others by listening to them and getting to know them better. My mother-in-law cultivated relationships with many people through all sorts of venues, including "The Pajama League" at Mid-Island Bowl on Long Island, which in the 1960s consisted primarily of mothers who bowled while their kids were in school. In that league, she met Joan and Mary. They became friends. Friends for years to come. Mom invited them to a retreat at a rustic church camp in the Catskill Mountains. She invited them to join a Bible study of eight to ten women that met around her dining room table every Tuesday morning. She invited them to her daughter's wedding at a church where her family worshiped, and Joan and Mary were struck by its simplicity and authenticity. Finally, after years of friendship and hospitality, both Mary and Joan came to faith, becoming devoted Christians.

24. Richard Peace, "Evangelism and Spiritual Formation," *Theology, News & Notes* 51, no. 3 (October 2004): 11–12.
25. For a resource on prayer, see Levison and Pope-Levison, *How Is It with Your Soul?*, 7–27.

Then there were Doug and Helen, whom she met while selling Avon products. A knock on their door led to an invitation to her home and an evening Bible study. There were also Sallie and John, who would drive my father-in-law home from the train station after a long day in Manhattan. Mom invited them in for something cold to drink in the summer, something warm in the winter. This led to further conversations, friendship, and their lives transforming to follow Jesus Christ.

It may be tempting to shy away from personal evangelism in favor of keeping the relationship light and friendly. After all, discussing religion, like discussing politics, can be extremely thorny and tense, and we want to avoid making others feel awkward around us. Yet we must also recognize something else: often, this disquiet is our own and not our friend's at all. If this is a relationship in which we care about each other, then the other person may well want to hear about and understand what is most important to you.

If you feel discomfort, remember, too, that you have been praying for your friend and the presence of the Holy Spirit in their life—and in yours. You can, therefore, trust that the Holy Spirit is present and the ground plowed.

4. Share the Gospel

There comes a time, in this model, to share the gospel; at that point, there are many ways to proceed. We will consider a few here.

Ask questions. Begin with an open-ended question, like Philip's simple one with the Ethiopian eunuch: "Do you understand . . . ?" Questions alleviate the impression that you are preaching at someone or proselytizing.[26] Questions are invitational; they set up the conversation as a dialogue. These sorts of questions probe gently yet persistently: *What did religion mean to you as a child, and what does it mean now? What is your image of God? At what point are you in your spiritual pilgrimage?*[27] *What do you think about Christians and Christianity?* Your friend will in turn ask you questions, perhaps these

26. The ecumenical movement defines proselytism as "whatever violates the right of the human person . . . to be free from every type of physical coersion, moral restraint or psychological pressure which could deprive a person or a community of freedom of judgment and responsible choice." *Common Witness: A Study Document of the Joint Working Group of the Roman Catholic Church and the World Council of Churches*, WCC Mission Series 1 (Geneva: WCC, 1984), 24–25.

27. Aldrich calls this the "pilgrimage" question and claims that it works when other questions do not. Aldrich, *Lifestyle Evangelism*, 193.

same questions, and your conversation about the gospel will develop into a rhythm of asking and answering questions.[28]

Tell your faith story. Another way to engage in personal evangelism is to tell the story of how you have experienced God in your life and why you decided to follow Jesus Christ. Duncan McIntosh writes, "It is a good exercise for both our faith and our memories to recall how we realized and now realize our part in God's story. . . . Each of your answers may be a thread which could connect you to someone with similar ideas and images who may need to hear the gospel."[29] (This story is often called a *testimony*, but that's a churchy-sounding word that can put people off from the outset.) Be sure to emphasize God's actions in your story more than your own part so that you point to God as the trustworthy one. This approach to telling your story within God's all-encompassing story imparts a sense of humility because it is not all about you. At the same time, it is hard to refute or debate your story of God's saving grace, since it is peculiarly your own. As James Kennedy relates, "No one can argue with your own experience of Christ. It is your own story, told in your own words."[30] Because it is your story, you are its incarnation. In the words of Delos Miles, "You give flesh and blood and reality to the good news."[31]

Use a rubric. Different from and yet complementary to the first two approaches is to introduce the gospel in a brief, often prescribed format. Several popular condensations include the Romans Road,[32] the Four Spiritual Laws,[33] and the bridge diagram.[34] These programmatic formats provide helpful touchstones that can easily be expanded when there is time and openness. If these seem too canned or condensed or unpalatable, immerse yourself in the works

28. This has been called the "Socratic approach" to evangelism. George Barna stands by the Socratic approach to personal evangelism because it begins by asking others for their version of the answer to the meaning of life and the existence of God, it helps to develop a relationship between the conversation partners, and it acknowledges that evangelism will take time. For more on Barna on the Socratic approach to evangelism, see Ron Crandall, *The Contagious Witness: Exploring Christian Conversion* (Nashville: Abingdon, 1999), 158.

29. D. McIntosh, *Everyday Evangelist*, 17.

30. James Kennedy, *Led by the Carpenter: Finding God's Purpose for Your Life!* (Nashville: Nelson, 1999), 90.

31. Delos Miles, *Introduction to Evangelism* (Nashville: Broadman, 1983), 181.

32. The Romans Road presentation varies but generally includes these verses: Rom. 3:23; 6:23; 8:1; 10:9–10; 10:13; 12:1–2. See Harney, *Organic Outreach*, 230.

33. See note 15.

34. The diagram consists of a chasm bridged by the cross. Humanity is on one side of the chasm, and God is on the other, a picture that underscores the gulf between humanity and God. Jesus's cross fits across the gulf, enabling those who trust in Jesus to cross over to God's side. For a full discussion of this diagram, see Harney, *Organic Outreach*, 234.

of a substantive Christian writer, like Tom Phillips did with C. S. Lewis. You are not the first to travel this road, so find someone intelligent and faithful who can do the talking for you. This was key to Chuck Colson's conversion. Yet another format is to walk through a creed, like the Apostles' Creed, which presents God's salvation history from creation ("I believe in God the Father almighty, creator of heaven and earth") to new creation ("I believe . . . in the life everlasting. Amen").

When the opportunity presents itself to introduce the good news, resist the temptation "to unload the entire evangelistic dump truck the first time the conversation turns to spiritual things."[35] As you have been patient up to this point and invested time, energy, care, and prayer into the relationship, continue along the same vein.

5. Follow Up

Personal evangelism is a long-term endeavor. Chances are that the first time you verbalize the gospel won't be the last. Your friends may remain un-decided, unsure, uncertain. Follow up to hear their feedback, and in light of their response, rephrase, rework, or find another way altogether. Sometimes your friends will ask for further information on a specific point; be sure to look into it and get back to them. Sometimes your friends need reassurance that your love and care will continue, regardless of their faith or lack of it. Attending to these concerns will be persuasive in and of itself because it attests to an ongoing relationship. Think about the apostle Paul in this regard. He maintained contact with people who, in some way, responded to his message; he visited them again, wrote letters, and sent an ambassador in his place if he could not go in person. "Come, let us return and visit the believers in every city where we proclaimed the word of the Lord and see how they are doing," he counseled (Acts 15:36). We know, too, from his letters, how much he fol-lowed up with those whom he introduced to Jesus Christ.

Remember, too, that when your friends decide to follow Christ, your in-teraction with them is not done. They are not projects to be completed, a means to an end. An important part of following up includes connecting them with a church, a small group, a Bible study, or online resources to help them deepen and strengthen their fledgling faith. Another often overlooked aspect of following up is to mentor your friends in personal evangelism so they can become evangelists to others. In the early hours after such a momentous

35. Aldrich, *Lifestyle Evangelism*, 187.

transformation, they may be eager to share their experience with others, like the Samaritan woman was. Or consider the Gerasene demoniac. After he was healed, he wanted to stay with Jesus, but Jesus sent him back to his home with these words: "Go home to your friends, and tell them how much the Lord has done for you, and what mercy he has shown you." And the demoniac listens, "He went away and began to proclaim in the Decapolis how much Jesus had done for him; and everyone was amazed" (Mark 5:19–20). As Stebbins writes, "He [the demoniac] was to be a living letter for everyone to read. He was sane, not mad; holy, not unclean; gentle, not ferocious. Truly he was 'a new creation; the old [had] gone, the new [had] come!' (2 Cor. 5:17). His witness was to be among his old acquaintances where ofttimes it is most difficult to witness, but where our witness bears the most abundant and abiding fruit."[36]

Taking time to mentor in personal evangelism multiplies exponentially the number of evangelists—and, of course, the number of believers—in this world. This principle has been called by a variety of names, like "the multiplication principle" or "the Master Plan of Evangelism."[37] My spouse, Jack, recalls how, when he was a college freshman, an upperclassman named Kenny introduced him to the miracle of multiplication: "'If you mentor [Kenny called it *discipling*] someone for six months,' he'd tell me, 'and both of you mentor someone for six months and all four of you mentor someone for six months, by the end of ten years, you will have helped over a million Christians to be equipped to follow Jesus better.'" Yes, you read that right: over a million Christians active in evangelism. It's simple math. It's explosive math. It's math that all of us can do. Kenny would use a checkerboard to illustrate how this worked: the first square would have one penny, the second, two; the third, four; the fourth, eight; and so on. To help you fathom the miracle of multiplication, here is Kenny's chart:

	First Six Months	Second Six Months
Year 1	1 (mentor) + 1 (protégé) = 2	2 (mentors) + 2 (protégés) = 4
Year 2	4 (mentors) + 4 (protégés) = 8	8 + 8 = 16
Year 3	16 + 16 = 32	32 + 32 = 64
Year 4	64 + 64 = 128	128 + 128 = 256
Year 5	256 + 256 = 512 (total involved)	512 + 512 = 1,024
Year 6	1,024 + 1,024 = 2048	2,048 + 2,048 = 4,096

36. Stebbins, *Friendship Evangelism by the Book*, 82–83.
37. Robert Coleman, *The Master Plan of Evangelism* (Grand Rapids: Revell, 1993).

	First Six Months	Second Six Months
Year 7	4,096 + 4,096 = 8,192	8,192 + 8,192 = 16,384
Year 8	16,384 + 16,384 = 32,768	32,768 + 32,768 = 65,536
Year 9	65,536 + 65,536 = 131,072	131,072 + 131,072 = 262,144
Year 10	262,144 + 262,144 = 524,288	524,288 + 524,288 = 1,048,576

Such follow-up multiplies personal evangelism—and persons as evangelists.

Appraisal

Boiled down to its essence, personal evangelism is the simplest of the models in this book. Personal evangelism can take place anywhere—at work, on a plane, in a coffee shop, in a college cafeteria, at a shoe store, at home. This model doesn't need a distinctive location like the liturgical, revival, or visitation models do. Personal evangelism can take place anytime two people meet. No need for others to join in as with other models, like small group or church growth evangelism. Personal evangelism is free, except for the occasional cup of coffee purchased or meal served. No need for a budget as with other models, like media or revival evangelism. Personal evangelism can be done by anyone—a Sunday school teacher, a friend, a seatmate on an airplane. You don't need to prepare in advance like you do for visitation, liturgical, or small group evangelism. Personal evangelism needs no set place, no set time, no set form, and no set preparation; it demands no church, no cost, no organization.

At the same time, personal evangelism can be the hardest model in this book. Consider its nomenclature: *personal*. Strip every accoutrement away, and it's about me as an evangelist. I will bear the brunt of embarrassment; I will face the risk of rejection; I will be liable to the charge of ignorance; I will confront the reality that I am not yet a candidate for sainthood. Not surprisingly, then, in the rough-and-tumble, to-and-fro of daily life, I, like many who responded to the Barna survey, find dozens of other tasks to perform in order to avoid this one: simply sharing, sharing simply the good news of Jesus Christ with other people one-on-one.

How Can We Spark a Passion for Personal Evangelism?

Since motivation—or *lack* of motivation—is a key obstacle to this model of evangelism, let's consider a few modest ways to spark a passion for personal evangelism.

Remember that the primary mover in evangelism is the Holy Spirit. While it seems like it is all about *me* or *you* as an evangelist, in reality it is the Holy Spirit who prompts, leads, convicts, teaches, and transforms. The primary practice of an evangelist is not, surprisingly enough, to evangelize; rather, it is to pray for openness to the principal evangelist: the Holy Spirit. With this realization, Christians are back to the basics of prayer. We pray for all sorts of things—for healing, for a successful surgery, for reconciliation, for peace and justice—so why not pray for the Holy Spirit to lead us into meaningful conversations and the meaningful relationships that cradle them?

Something else you can do is to identify someone already motivated about evangelism and learn from him. Apprentice yourself informally to her. Ask questions about how they engage in personal evangelism, how they overcome fear or embarrassment. Ask them for an honest account of their worst and best experiences. Find out what they wish they had known at the outset. Let them encourage you, teach you, mentor you, pray for you.

And don't forget to be patient with yourself. If you feel discomfort about conversations with those who do not believe, then give yourself time and space to become comfortable. Begin perhaps by practicing with other Christians. This is not artificial. Every dancer or musician or athlete practices. Every student studies. Every actor rehearses. And who can imagine a comedian who has *not* told jokes standing at a mirror? An evangelist is the keeper—and giver—of great news, life-changing news, world-changing news. Learning to share that news intelligently and winsomely will take practice—like any other activity worth doing well.

Next, send up some test balloons. Call to mind those first invitations in the Gospel of John. *Come and see.* Remember Philip's opening question, "Do you understand what you are reading?" Simple enough. Send a text to someone, inviting them to coffee or to a church service or for a walk. Connect with an old friend on social media and see where it leads—remembering always that the Holy Spirit is at work in the world before you and around you, certainly in ways you cannot yet see.

Practice listening, too. When you begin a conversation about faith, open with a question, then listen intently. Most people want to talk. They will not find a listening ear offensive. After you offer someone an invitation—"come and see"—sit back and listen and pray.

Is the Church Irrelevant to Personal Evangelism?

From what you have read about personal evangelism, it may seem like the church, the body of Christ, is irrelevant. Where, after all, is the church in a cafeteria or a shoe store? This is the impression that one of the bestselling books on personal evangelism gives when it includes just one chapter—the *last* chapter—on Christian community. The author claims, "We are not called to be 'Lone Ranger' Christians," but the organization of the book and the short shrift given to the church says otherwise.[38] Not until the last three pages of the last chapter does the author even mention the church—and then does so largely to criticize what the church does wrong, such as door-to-door visitation evangelism. All in all, the church is depicted as forgettable and forgotten, except for what it does wrong.

This view of personal evangelism is misleading. Think again of the first chapter of the Gospel of John, where individuals were being brought into a tight-knit community of Jesus's followers. Or think of Philip, who was a servant in the church in Jerusalem (Acts 6:5–6) and the leader of a revival in Samaria, which the church in Jerusalem authorized (8:4–25), before he launched that conversation on a wilderness road. Think of Dwight Moody, too, how his personal interactions with Edward Kimball took place because he received a mandatory sentence of attending church! The church may not be on the edge of personal evangelism—that is the job of individuals—but it certainly provides sustenance and grounding and a community to bolster the evangelist. It is the source of spiritual disciplines such as prayer, Bible study, and worship. It catechizes Christians so they know how to respond to questions and comments. And it is the laboratory in which Christians learn to talk about faith and, more importantly, to listen carefully to others.

Reflection Questions

- How do you appraise personal evangelism?
- What implications does personal evangelism have for you? For your church?

38. Pippert, *Out of the Saltshaker*, 234.

- If you were to engage in personal evangelism, how would you share the gospel message?
- If your church were to promote personal evangelism, how should it begin?
- Which model do you think best complements personal evangelism? Why?

TWO

SMALL GROUP

Pause now for a moment to think through the small groups you've been involved in. Athletic teams. Confirmation classes. Science clubs. Neighborhood watch groups. Scout troops. Sunday school classes. Youth groups. Facebook groups. Bowling leagues. Bridge clubs. Fraternities and sororities. Political caucuses. Fantasy football leagues. So many small groups to join! A few decades ago, a major study in the United States found that four out of ten adults were active in a small group "that meets regularly and provides support or caring for those who participate in it." Directors of the study claimed that small groups had become an integral part of the American way of life, even more so than the most popular television programs at the time, with the exception of the Super Bowl.[1]

Small groups for religious purposes remain popular particularly among people currently involved in a church or seeking a church. Some megachurches recognize the importance of small groups; despite worship services seating thousands, they maintain a potent commitment to small groups. Take North Point Community Church outside Atlanta, Georgia. Its 2020 membership is nearly forty thousand across six campuses, yet the designated entry point remains a small group known as Starting Point. "If you're new to faith, just checking it out, or coming back to church after some time away, Starting Point

1. Robert Wuthnow, ed., *"I Come Away Stronger": How Small Groups Are Shaping American Religion* (Grand Rapids: Eerdmans, 1994), 369.

is a great first step. Starting Point is a short-term conversational small group environment where you can explore faith and experience community. It's a place where your beliefs and opinions are valued, and where no question is off limits."[2] Between January and October, the church launches a Starting Point small group every month.

Despite the preponderance of small groups in churches, it is uncommon for them to focus on evangelism. This is borne out in small group resources. One resource catalogs nine types of small groups divided under these four headings: education, Bible study, therapy, and mission groups. Only one of the nine types specifically focuses on evangelism.[3] Another resource lists four biblical goals for small groups: "Foster biblical love, promote fellowship and unity, build the body, and nurture spiritual gifts."[4] These are worthy aspirations, each of them, but evangelism is not listed as a primary or even a secondary biblical goal. This chapter will make up this gap by focusing on "the deliberate use of small groups for evangelistic purposes."[5] That in a nutshell is the small group model: taking a well-known and well-utilized format, the small group, and setting it up for evangelism.

Biblical Foundations

In one of his first public acts, Jesus convenes a small group of followers to send out "to fish for people" (Matt. 4:18–22; Mark 1:16–20). He focuses on this group, teaches them, negotiates group dynamics (such as who would be first or last and who was the greatest or the least), and launches them "to proclaim the good news, 'The kingdom of heaven has come near'" (Matt. 10:7). Upon them—and others who came alongside them—would rest the continuation of his life's work after his crucifixion, resurrection, and ascension. "Jesus changed human history through the process of forming an intentional small group of twelve persons."[6]

2. "Registration," Starting Point, North Point Ministries, Inc., https://www.startingpoint .com/northpoint.
3. Clyde Reid, *Groups Alive—Church Alive: The Effective Use of Small Groups in the Local Church* (New York: Harper & Row, 1969), 17–28.
4. Neal McBride, *How to Lead Small Groups* (Colorado Springs: NavPress, 1990), 26.
5. Richard Peace, *Small Group Evangelism: A Training Program for Reaching Out with the Gospel* (Downers Grove, IL: InterVarsity, 1985), 13.
6. Gareth Weldon Icenogle, *Biblical Foundations for Small Group Ministry: An Integrational Approach* (Downers Grove, IL: InterVarsity, 1994), 14.

Along with the twelve recorded male disciples, Luke points out that women were also part of a small group around Jesus (Luke 8:1–3). Luke 10:38–42 shows Jesus at the home of Mary and Martha—with Mary taking on the role of a disciple sitting at a rabbi's feet to hear his teaching. Women also compose the small group that accompanied Jesus at his death (Matt. 27:55–56, 61; Mark 15:40–41, 47; Luke 23:27–31, 49; John 19:25b–27), and they were the first to find the empty tomb (Matt. 28:1–10; Mark 16:1–8; Luke 24:1–11; John 20:1–2, 11–18). They continued, after his resurrection and ascension, to be among those in the upper room who waited and prayed together in Jerusalem (Acts 1:14). From these accounts, it is clear that women, too, were part of the small group that accompanied Jesus during his life and at his death and continued as post-resurrection followers.

In the book of Acts and the letters of the New Testament, we can discern a cluster of small groups. The book of Acts contains, almost as an aside, the detail that "on the sabbath day we went outside the gate by the river, where we supposed there was a place of prayer; and we sat down and spoke to the women who had gathered there" (Acts 16:13). Apparently, followers of Jesus sought out small groups—in this case, a small group of faithful women—that were already gathering for worship and prayer. Small groups also met in house churches. There were house churches in the house of Mary, mother of John Mark (12:12); the house of Priscilla and Aquila (Rom. 16:3–5; 1 Cor. 16:19); the house of Philemon (Philem. 2); and the house of Nympha (Col. 4:15). House churches were places for galvanizing communal activities like worship, teaching, and fellowship. Despite appearing to be insular gatherings for believers to be nurtured and discipled, house churches were also evangelistic, serving as the "primary arena and vehicle for Christian ministry in a hostile world."[7] In that regard, let's take a closer look at what went on in the home of Priscilla and Aquila.

Priscilla and Aquila were refugees in Corinth who had been thrown out of Rome because of an imperial persecution of Jews. Though away from home themselves, they still managed to host Paul for more than a year (Acts 18:1–3). The next time we see Priscilla and Aquila, they have moved to Ephesus; even in this new city, they utilized a small group setting in their home to advance the gospel by evangelizing and training Apollos, a Jew and a native of Alexandria, who was eloquent and well versed in Scripture. We see their small

7. Icenogle, *Biblical Foundations for Small Group Ministry*, 14.

group evangelism in three verbs in one verse: "He [Apollos] began to speak boldly in the synagogue; but when Priscilla and Aquila heard him, they took him aside and explained the Way of God to him more accurately" (v. 26).

First, Priscilla and Aquila *listened* to Apollos as he spoke "boldly" in the synagogue in Ephesus. How many times they heard him speak, we do not know, but we do know that they listened intently enough to ascertain that Apollos had more to learn. At some point, they *took him aside*. The translation "took aside" is too bland a description of what Priscilla and Aquila did. (It misleadingly suggests scolding: they pulled him aside.) They most likely took him home and showed him hospitality. The Greek verb *proslambanō*, translated as "take aside," is used in the book of Acts of eating, of taking nourishment into bodies (27:33, 36).[8] It can be translated as "to welcome," as in Acts 28:2, where it depicts warm hospitality after a shipwreck: "The natives [of Malta] showed us unusual kindness. Since it had begun to rain and was cold, they kindled a fire and welcomed all of us around it." They welcomed cold and wet guests by taking them in and perching them around a warm fire. And that's what Priscilla and Aquila offered Apollos. Think a home-cooked meal, a warm fire, and a convivial atmosphere. There in the warmth and welcome of their home, Priscilla and Aquila *taught* Apollos "more accurately." Luke phrases it perfectly: Apollos taught the people "accurately"; Priscilla and Aquila taught him "more accurately." The result was stunning: Apollos profited the early church's mission in Achaia when he "powerfully refuted the Jews in public, showing by the scriptures that the Messiah is Jesus" (18:28).

This scenario sounds like it would fit better with the previous model. Small group evangelism is a more structured, less spontaneous, more collaborative mode of personal evangelism. What occurred among Priscilla, Aquila, and Apollos was deeply personal, but there was a community of believers that surrounded them. Notice the next encounter after Priscilla and Aquila have taught Apollos more accurately. When Apollos "wished to cross over to Achaia, the believers [in Ephesus] encouraged him and wrote to the disciples to welcome him" (Acts 18:27). Clearly, Priscilla and Aquila were not alone, so when Apollos readied to leave Ephesus, it was not Priscilla and Aquila who authorized him but the believers as a whole. They were the encouragers

8. Acts 27:33 reads, "Just before daybreak, Paul urged all of them to take some food, saying, 'Today is the fourteenth day that you have been in suspense and remaining without food, having eaten [*proslabomenoi*] nothing.'" Acts 27:36 reads, "Then all of them were encouraged and took food [*proselabonto trophēs*] for themselves."

and the letter writers. This is true to the form of the small group evangelism model. Someone takes the lead, but in the best practice, small group evangelism will occur in conjunction with a believing community.

Theological Foundations

Small group evangelism captures an aspect of God's nature to be in community, not to exist in isolation. God created community along with the heavens and the earth, the fish of the sea and the birds of the air. Right at the start of Scripture, the language of creation is communal:

> Then God said, "Let us make humankind in our image, according to our likeness." . . .
>
> So God created humankind in his image,
> in the image of God he created them;
> male and female he created them. (Gen. 1:26–27)

"Small groups are microcosms of God's creation community. Wherever two or more persons come together, they become an actual reflection of the image and likeness of God," as Gareth Icenogle contends.[9] God then instructs the first man and woman to be stewards of the rest of creation and blesses them for the task ahead. In this creation text, with man and woman in relationship with each other and with God, we see how "the human community exists foundationally as *small group*."[10]

A pastor friend who lived in Kansas City in the 1980s was fond of saying, "God is a small group." There is a strong measure of truth to this quip. The Trinity—God in three persons—reveals God's inclination to be in relationship, in community. A particular view of the Trinity, known as the Social Trinity, comes closest to describing God-as-community. The gist of the Social Trinity is that the Christian God exists as three persons (*hypostases*) who are reciprocally interdependent such that they constitute a single essence (*ousia*).[11] If that

---

9. Icenogle, *Biblical Foundations for Small Group Ministry*, 20–21. A similar refrain sounds in Matt. 18:20: "For where two or three are gathered in my name, I [Jesus] am there among them."

10. Icenogle, *Biblical Foundations for Small Group Ministry*, 22–23.

11. See Avery Dulles, "Problems of Ecclesiology," *First Things* 87 (November 1998): 52.

sounds too stilted, then another way to grasp the Social Trinity without the Greek words is to picture the Trinity as a community, as a small group "who love each other and live together in harmony."[12] Eastern Orthodox bishop Kallistos Ware employs the understanding that "God is triunity: three equal persons, each one dwelling in the other two by virtue of an unceasing movement of mutual love."[13] The emphasis in the word *person* is on relationality; *person* is a relational concept.[14] To explain the dynamism of the relationality between the three persons of the Trinity (*perichoresis*), theologians turn to the illustration of three dancers (the three persons) holding on to each other as they move in a dynamic, circular motion.

An image (*ikon*) of the Trinity as community was created in the fifteenth century by Anton Rublev. Icons, which are religious works of art, serve as windows to a deeper connection with and understanding of God. Every brushstroke of color, every symbol, and every figure is bathed with prayer and secures a holy significance. In this particular icon, aspects of the story of community and hospitality from Genesis 18:1–15 serve as the iconic framework. In the background stands a tree representing the "oaks of Mamre" where "the LORD appeared to Abraham" (v. 1). Front and center sit the three strangers who unexpectedly visit Abraham and Sarah (v. 2); in the icon, they represent the three persons of the Trinity. The way they are seated gives the sense of their inclining toward each other in a circular fashion, yet "the circle is not closed."[15] None of the three display their back to the viewer. The arrangement evinces an open circle into which others are welcomed: "One has the distinct sensation when meditating on the icon that one is not only invited into this communion but, indeed, already a part of it. A self-contained God, a closed divine society, would hardly be a fitting archetype of hospitality."[16]

The icon's centerpiece—the chalice on the altar—epitomizes the gracious hospitality of the Triune God, who welcomes us into their loving relationship as honored guests and nourishes us with eucharistic bread and wine.

---

12. Shirley Guthrie, *Christian Doctrine* (Louisville: Westminster John Knox, 1994), 92.

13. Kallistos Ware, *The Orthodox Way* (Crestwood, NY: St. Vladimir's Seminary Press, 1995), 27.

14. Stanley J. Grenz, *The Social God and the Relational Self: A Trinitarian Theology of the Imago Dei* (Louisville: Westminster John Knox, 2001), 4, 9.

15. Catherine Mowry LaCugna, ed., *Freeing Theology: The Essentials of Theology in Feminist Perspective* (New York: HarperSanFrancisco, 1993), 84.

16. LaCugna, *Freeing Theology*, 84.

In similar fashion, small groups reflect this bond of mutual love when they welcome, nourish, and invite others into relationship with the Triune God. A stanza from the beloved hymn by John Fawcett encapsulates this mutuality:

> Blest be the tie that binds our hearts in Christian love;
> The fellowship of kindred minds is like to that above.[17]

Historical Foundations

During the eighteenth century, Oxford don John Wesley (1703–91), founder of Methodism, along with his brother Charles (1707–88) established a tiered system of small groups whose entry point was the class meeting. Class meetings consisted of a dozen or so people who helped each other to work out their salvation; membership was open to anyone expressing a desire to flee from the wrath to come.[18] Many conversions happened in class meetings because, as John Wesley recognized, "the beginnings of faith in a man's heart could be incubated into saving faith more effectively in the warm Christian atmosphere of the society than in the chill of the world."[19] Week by week, Methodists, according to Wesley, would "speak, each of us in order, freely and plainly the true state of our souls."[20] The format provided for sharing spiritual fellowship within the group, prompted by the class leader's weekly inquiry of each member, "How is it with your soul?" In order to assess the soul's state, Wesley developed three categories of what he called "searching questions":

Have you carefully abstained from doing evil?

Have you zealously maintained good works?

Have you constantly attended on all the ordinances of God?[21]

---

17. See Grenz, *Social God and the Relational Self*, 336.

18. John Wesley, *The Nature, Design, and General Rules of the United Societies*, in Rupert E. Davies, *The Works of John Wesley*, vol. 9, *The Methodist Societies: History, Nature, and Design* (Nashville: Abingdon, 1989), 69–70. The biblical basis for the idea of helping each other "work out their salvation" lies in Phil. 2:12.

19. Glenn Gould, *Healing the Hurt of Man: A Study in John Wesley's "Cure of Souls"* (Kansas City, MO: Beacon Hill, 1971), 65.

20. John Wesley, "Rules of the Band Societies, Drawn Up Dec. 25, 1738," in Davies, *Works of John Wesley* 9:77.

21. John Wesley, "Directions Given to the Band Societies, Dec. 25, 1744," in Davies, *Works of John Wesley* 9:79.

The fusion of mutual affection, accountability, and spiritual growth is expressed in this prayer composed for class meetings:

> Help us to help each other, Lord,
> Each other's cross to bear;
> Let each his friendly aid afford,
> And feel his brother's care.
>
> Help us to build each other up,
> To help each one improve;
> Increase our faith, confirm our hope,
> And perfect us in love.[22]

Class meetings were the basic building block of the early Methodist movement and a fervent forum for evangelism. In the classes, "members were assimilated, voices were found, spiritual experiences were shared, and communities of faith were built. . . . At their best they were the spaces in which the message became flesh."[23] Class meetings in Methodism had all but disappeared until the late 1980s, when concerted efforts breathed new life into these small groups. David Lowes Watson, for example, developed Covenant Discipleship Groups patterned after early Methodism's class meetings. The purpose of these groups, like class meetings, is to form its members "into faithful disciples of Jesus Christ who live as his witnesses in the world."[24] The renaissance of Wesleyan class meetings coincided with a 1988 Gallup survey titled "The Unchurched," which forecast that small groups would become a key evangelistic methodology of the decade.[25]

Sociologist Robert Wuthnow, who produced a major small group study in the early 1990s, vividly compared small group proliferation in North America to the "mood of early Christianity or that of the Israelites during

22. Charles Wesley, "Help Us to Help Each Other Lord," *The Hymnal of the Evangelical United Brethren Church*, #275 (Dayton: Board of Publications of the Evangelical United Brethren, 1957), 260–61.

23. David Hempton, *Methodism: Empire of the Spirit* (New Haven: Yale University Press, 2005), 79.

24. "Getting Started in Covenant Discipleship Groups," Discipleship Ministries, United Methodist Church, July 13, 2010, https://www.umcdiscipleship.org/resources/getting-started-in -covenant-discipleship-groups. See also David Lowes Watson, *Covenant Discipleship: Christian Formation through Mutual Accountability* (Nashville: Discipleship Resources, 1991).

25. George Gallup, *The Unchurched American: 10 Years Later* (Princeton: Princeton Religious Research Center, 1988), 4.

their sojourn in the wilderness." He explained that "home meetings were preferred over public spectacles. Tabernacles were favored over temples. Faith was portable." Wuthnow pointed out that this move toward small groups cut against the grain of American Christianity. "Throughout much of American history," he noticed, "the course of events has run in the other direction. Bigger was better. Religious leaders tore down small meeting houses and built larger ones. More advanced degrees were required in order to preach. Services required more elaborate planning, larger choirs, more expensive organs, and thicker padding on the pews."[26] Small groups, in contrast, returned Christians to a more portable, pliable faith to be shared with others in a more intimate setting.

Even some megachurches—designated attractional churches because they are designed to attract to their large worship settings those who do not yet adhere to Christianity[27]—recognized that bigger is not necessarily better, and several, including Willow Creek Community Church in north suburban Chicago, Saddleback Church in Southern California, and North Point Community Church in Atlanta, championed small groups. The limitations of megachurches, such as the lack of intimacy and the tendency toward anonymity, as Wuthnow framed it, "necessitated a countertrend toward small groups."[28] North Point Community Church, as we saw earlier, views small groups, not as something to join once a person has participated in a worship service for a while, but as a point of entry.

In Seoul, South Korea, small group evangelism advanced the exponential growth of what would become the largest church in the world, the Yoido Full Gospel Church, founded in 1958 by David Yonggi Cho. In the mid-1960s, Cho implemented a plan for small group evangelism in Seoul's neighborhoods with the goal of transforming each small group into the focal point of revival in its neighborhood. "I like to describe Full Gospel Central Church as the smallest church in the world as well as the biggest church in the world," commented Cho. "It is the biggest [and] it is also the smallest church in the

26. Wuthnow, "I Come Away Stronger," 350–51.

27. "An attractional church is one that is centered on attracting people into the church building and programs, with the worship gathering being the centerpiece and most important activity of the week. . . . The 'seeker' churches that became very popular in the 1990s were premier examples of the attractional church." Elaine A. Heath and Larry Duggins, *Missional, Monastic, Mainline: A Guide to Starting Missional Micro-Communities in Historically Mainline Traditions* (Eugene, OR: Cascade Books, 2014), 40.

28. Wuthnow, "I Come Away Stronger," 350–51.

world—because every member is part of a home cell group."[29] These groups became the dynamic core of a vital evangelistic strategy aimed at reaching an entire city. Both Cho and John Wesley, even though separated by centuries, language, and culture, nevertheless grasped the genius of the small group and its potential for evangelistic outreach.

Practical Foundations

As we've just seen in this brief historical sketch, small group evangelism can take place in a variety of ways and contexts. Nevertheless, in the process of implementing this model, a few shared elements rise to the surface.

1. Invite Participants

People to invite to a small group cross your path regularly. They are among those you know at work, in your neighborhood, or at places you frequent, like the gym or a favorite coffee shop. They are friends on your Facebook page, or they follow you on other social media sites. Still, it will most likely require a concerted effort on your part to find people to invite to an *evangelistic* small group. Those most likely to be interested in a small group of this kind will already possess some initial level of interest, though without identifying as Christian. "Small group meetings can be an effective venue for *seekers* (−4 [Positive Attitude toward the Gospel] to −1 [Repentance and Faith in Christ] on the Engel Scale) to have some of these conversations."[30] Launching an evangelistic small group, therefore, requires being inventive, creative, and persistent.

As you get to know people and start to invite them, be honest about yourself and your faith. Be candid in your invitation by asking a question like, "Would you like to take an hour this Saturday evening to see what the Bible really says about Jesus?"[31] Hospitality begins the moment you explain *in full disclosure* what the group's focus will be. Otherwise, imagine what the reaction might

---

29. David Yonggi Cho, *Successful Home Cell Groups* (Alachua, FL: Bridge-Logos, 1981), 50.
30. M. Scott Boren, *Missional Small Groups: Becoming a Community That Makes a Difference in the World* (Grand Rapids: Baker Books, 2010), 159. For the full Engel Scale, see James F. Engel and Wilbert Norton, *What's Gone Wrong with the Harvest?* (Grand Rapids: Zondervan, 1975).
31. Ada Lum, *How to Begin an Evangelistic Bible Study* (Downers Grove, IL: InterVarsity, 1971), 8.

be if your invitees thought they were coming over to enjoy dinner or to meet new people, then when they arrive, they come face to face with Christians eager to talk with them about Jesus. The disparity between invitation and event, between expectation and reality, may actually engender mistrust and be counterproductive to an honest, engaging discussion.

Transparency also extends to letting people know in advance how many meetings are on the docket. To invite people to a small group meeting for four weeks, for instance, sets out from the beginning the length of the commitment. Keep in mind, too, that it is easier for people to commit to a short series. Combined with a transparent statement that this is in fact a small group intended for people who do not adhere to the Christian faith, a realistic description of time and duration will go a long way to encourage people to make a commitment to something entirely new.

Practicing honesty and hospitality can facilitate an initial buy-in from all who accept the invitation to the small group. Complement these qualities with continued honesty, giving participants the freedom to decide not to continue if they find the group to be unsafe or uninteresting—or if they simply lack the time to maintain their commitment. Transparency, integrity, and honesty, as we saw in the personal evangelism model, remain at the core of this model of evangelism as well, because these virtues are essential to being a hospitable and winsome witness to Jesus, who himself invited people into a small group.

2. Decide on the Format

A range of formats suits small group evangelism. One is an evangelistic Bible study. Given that the Bible is the primary text for Christians, it is important for seekers to read the Bible and see for themselves what it says. Stress that prior knowledge of the Bible is not necessary. All a person needs to bring to the Bible study is an openness to consider it, a willingness to take it seriously. One small group leader began her evangelistic Bible study with this statement of the group's purpose: "This is for people who are interested in discovering who Jesus is and what the Bible has to say. . . . This study doesn't assume you already believe in Jesus or that you accept the Bible as true. Rather, it's to help you make up your own mind once you know what the Bible actually says."[32]

---

32. Rebecca Manley Pippert, *How to Lead a Seeker Bible Discussion* (Downers Grove, IL: InterVarsity, 2003), 9, 37. Pippert suggests three key parts to an inductive Bible study: observe, interpret, apply.

An excellent way into an evangelistic Bible study is to lead with an open-ended question that grounds the discussion in people's experiences, then pair this question with a relevant biblical text. One small group leader offers an example of this strategy: "What are common complaints people have against religious institutions such as the church?" Following a discussion of the question by participants, the leader responded, "It was no different in Jesus' day. We are about to read a story in which Jesus takes on these very issues: hypocrisy and religious leaders making a buck off people in the name of religion. You may be surprised to see how Jesus responds."[33] The small group leader then turned their attention to John 2:13–25, the story of Jesus cleansing the temple from unjust practices, which opened a discussion of the possible faults of established religious institutions—a common port of entry for many people. It is important to allow participants to clear out the ugly underbrush; it is also important then to lead the conversation back to the good news of the gospel.

Another format is a directed dialogue on a topic through which the gospel can shine forth. In this format, the facilitator introduces a topic that many people relate to, like loneliness, relationships, or ambition. A film clip, a TED talk, the Voke app,[34] or a magazine article can be utilized as an engaging way to introduce the topic. The task of the leader in this sort of evangelistic small group is to integrate the good news of the gospel into the discussion.

Yet another option is to utilize an established small group curriculum, like the Alpha course, which walks seekers through the basics of Christianity. Alpha's promotional video emphasizes its purposeful design toward exploring meaning and asking questions: "If you've ever wondered if there's more, you're not alone in that. We all explore every day, in small ways and big. . . . For all our searching, it's rare to find time to think, to talk about the big questions of life. About faith and reason and God and meaning. But exploring is good. We're built for it."[35] Each Alpha session begins with food and fellowship, followed by a twenty- to thirty-minute talk on a question related to Christianity: Who is Jesus? How can we have faith? Why and how do I pray? How does God

33. Pippert, *How to Lead a Seeker Bible Discussion*, 9–10.

34. The Cru website explains Voke as follows: "Voke is a video-sharing app that offers compelling, short videos that will help you kickstart deeper conversations." The website also suggests how to use Voke effectively: "Select a short film from our unique video library and share it with a friend you would like to start a deeper conversation with." "Apps & Tools: Voke," Cru, https://www.cru.org/us/en/digitalministry/apps-tools/voke.html.

35. "What Is Alpha?," Alpha International, video, 2:26, https://alpha.org.

guide us?[36] Afterward, there is ample time for conversation, raising questions, and further discussion. A structured curriculum like Alpha, complete with a topical video from an established teacher, takes pressure off the convener to develop something unique for every meeting of the small group.

3. Convene the Meeting

Boiled down to its essence, each small group meeting consists of four parts:

- welcome (with food and drink)
- a word about the format of the meeting
- a brief presentation
- interaction

Always begin with food and general conversation to help people feel at ease. Hospitality is key to small group evangelism and provides the best sort of welcome for strangers and friends alike. Then explain how the meeting will proceed so that everyone fully understands what to expect. Again, this puts people at ease and eliminates surprises. What follows next is a brief introduction (five to seven minutes) to the topic or biblical passage, unless you are using Alpha or other curricula with a longer presentation. Focus these introductory comments on provoking interest by connecting the topic or biblical text to a contemporary context or situation.

Following the presentation, ease into the discussion with several application questions that encourage substantive interaction with the presentation beyond a simple thumbs-up or thumbs-down:

What in the presentation resonated with you?

What disturbed or frustrated you?

What helped you better understand a particular situation?[37]

Keep in mind that in a small group "you have the chance to discuss a topic that is worthwhile and important with a handful of others, each of whom is an interesting and unique person. Such conversation is lively; it builds relationships,

36. "What Does an Alpha Session Look Like?," Alpha International, https://alpha.org.
37. Peace, *Small Group Evangelism*, 134.

and it results in personal growth. *Life changing group conversation around important issues—this is the genius of small groups.*"[38]

Close the meeting with a brief time for feedback about what people experienced. Welcome all comments, including those that are not fully positive. Warmly invite everyone to return, and announce the date, time, topic, and place. This general invitation should be followed up by a personal contact from the small group convener before the next meeting.

The initial meeting is the most important because it often determines whether someone decides to remain in the group. For that reason, emphasize building connections among the participants and developing a safe atmosphere for statements and questions without invoking judgment or a lecture. (A Barna Group study found the following: "One of outsiders' most significant concerns about present-day Christianity: Christians are judgmental."[39]) To that end, consider setting ground rules for the group:

- Eliminate theological jargon or insider language, which excludes newcomers. As one small group expert put it, "Such terminology is biblical but unfamiliar to seekers, and it might scare them away, because they will feel like they don't fit in the group."[40]
- Minimize controversy and petty disagreements over nonessentials, like infant or adult baptism.
- Rather than catching up with friends, spend the evening helping everyone feel welcome.
- Avoid giving advice or offering bland platitudes, such as the false assurance that everything will work out well if only one trusts in Jesus.
- Take each person seriously, which means listening to them to find out who they are and how the group can best serve them, and be honest in return, candid about both faith and unfaith, joy and grief. "This is the nature of an authentic Christian group—a holy people who have faced their dark sides, found forgiveness in Christ and from one another, and are able therefore to live transparently honest lives. A

38. Richard Peace, "Reflections on Small Group Process and Interactive Bible Teaching," e-mail correspondence with the author, May 17, 2019.

39. David Kinnaman and Gabe Lyons, *Unchristian: What a New Generation Really Thinks about Christianity . . . And Why It Matters* (Grand Rapids: Baker Books, 2007), 182.

40. Bill Donahue, *Leading Life-Changing Small Groups* (Grand Rapids: Zondervan, 2002), 166.

non-Christian entering such a group finds the experience virtually irresistible."[41]

4. Plan Now for the Future

The vision of small group evangelism consistently looks outward toward sharing the gospel. To that end, once the small group meetings have concluded, launch a new evangelistic small group with those who responded to the gospel in the first round. They take the lead on inviting their acquaintances and friends to this new group. And so on. Cho adopts a useful metaphor to describe the multiplication of small groups—what he calls "home cell groups"—in biological terms. "The home cell groups are living cells," writes Cho, "and they function much like the cells in the human body. In a living organism, the cells grow and divide. Where once there was one cell, there become two. . . . Cells are not simply added to the body; they are multiplied by geometric progression."[42]

This is a proven and effective strategy. Alpha, for instance, enlists new converts to lead a small group in the next go-round.[43] In this way, new converts transition quickly from invited participants to leaders. It is difficult to grow inward when every round of small groups is directed outward—and led by those who have just made the transition from invitee to convener. This, of course, is the genius of a clear strategy, undergirded by a hospitable invitation and a generous spirit of inquiry.

Keeping in mind that the focus of this small group is evangelism, set up in advance an avenue for moving those who express ongoing interest in Christianity, or those who make a faith commitment, into a Christian community once the initial set of meetings comes to an end. To facilitate this, it is essential to partner with a congregation that is eager to embrace newcomers. This partnership enhances both the effectiveness of the small group and also the church's ability to integrate seekers. Evangelistic small groups provide a perfect entry point for visitors who show up at church. Too often, churches lack a specific venue for people on the fringes of faith who, though they actually make the effort to visit a worship service, get lost in the shuffle of an

41. Peace, *Small Group Evangelism*, 68.
42. Cho, *Successful Home Cell Groups*, 65.
43. George G. Hunter III, *The Celtic Way of Evangelism: How Christianity Can Reach the West . . . Again* (Nashville: Abingdon, 2000), 114.

unfamiliar environment, never to return. An evangelistic small group provides a set strategy for welcoming and evangelizing church visitors.

Appraisal

People's prior experience with small groups of any sort, whether a collaboration at work or a neighborhood watch group, provides entrée to evangelistic small groups. So the idea of joining a small group is not threatening; it feels more comfortable from the outset. The face-to-face interaction with a handful of people can increase intimacy, which appeals to the desire many people have for connection, for knowing others and being known by them. Small groups provide a means for "*intensive* evangelism, that is, concentrating on one or two or three seekers in a *sustained* way. . . . Here we can invite our friends who show confusion, vagueness or a fragmented knowledge of the gospel. Here none of us will feel rushed or pressured but can calmly examine the facts about Jesus Christ."[44]

On the other hand, the notion of joining a small group focused on evangelism can be downright intimidating, prompting many people to turn down the invitation. That is why initial practical steps, especially offering a winsome and welcoming invitation with clear goals and a set schedule and duration, are so important. People will then know they are not being asked to join an offbeat cult; they will know the invitation is genuine, the Christian goal is transparent, and the duration is limited. Each of these elements, when carefully executed, will increase the likelihood of people accepting the invitation.

How Do Small Groups Retain an Evangelistic Emphasis?

Still, a major obstacle remains: despite a goal of evangelistic outreach, many small groups do not in fact engage in evangelism. A study by Wuthnow corroborates this assessment. Even the small groups who claim to be evangelistic are often not overtly so but opt instead for a quieter approach, which relies less on evangelism than on an attractive spirituality.

Group members do say they are sharing their faith, but they are not drawn to the formal programs of evangelism that many clergy advocate (knocking on neighbors' doors, inviting their friends to church, or perhaps eavesdropping

44. Lum, *How to Begin an Evangelistic Bible Study*, 8.

to find poor troubled unbelievers they can help). They are not trying to learn techniques for talking to the unconverted or even to gain logical arguments to use in defense of their faith. Rather, they are trying to incorporate some sense of spirituality into their lives so that it will shine through naturally. . . . Thus, convinced that their faith is authentic, they feel that other people will be attracted to it naturally.[45]

Wuthnow also says that small group spirituality can exhibit a tendency to promote a "me-first religion." This happens when participants focus on how faith meets their personal needs rather than keeping the attention on seekers and their faith journey. "Group members are encouraged to think about the ways in which spirituality can help them, to apply faith concepts to their personal problems, and to share these problems with the group. In the process, it is easy for these practical, personal applications of faith to take precedence over everything else."[46] This explains why many churches representing every theological stripe provide opportunities for discipleship, marriage support, friendship, outreach, and a slew of other things, but evangelistic small groups are few and far between.

In order to keep the focus on evangelism rather than revert to a support group or a group of Christians only—this is always the risk—it is essential to adhere to the practical strategies set out in this chapter and to the purpose of this model: to convene a short-term small group of religious seekers, introduce them to the gospel, set up those who respond in an environment where they continue to grow in their faith, spawn another small group, and so on. If the goal of evangelism is blunted or obscured and the clear directions for conducting small groups forgotten, it is unlikely that small group evangelism will take place. It is more likely that members of the group will choose the comfort of other Christians, with whom they share common values and vocabulary, rather than facing the challenge of discussing the faith with those who do not believe. Perhaps, then, it is important to remember that small group evangelism is not for everyone. It is not for settlers; it is for explorers and pioneers willing to do the hard labor of traversing the good news of the gospel with seekers.

45. Robert Wuthnow, *Sharing the Journey: Support Groups and America's New Quest for Community* (New York: Free Press, 1994), 246.
46. Wuthnow, *"I Come Away Stronger,"* 356.

How Does a Trinitarian Foundation Correspond to the Temporary Nature of These Groups?

This is a reasonable question given that the Triune community is eternal, while these small groups are by design short lived. Appealing to this theological foundation, therefore, may not be particularly helpful. Still, the trinitarian foundation can be of use in one respect: it centers on relationality. Relationships are a key component of this model, especially relationships that offer support without judgment of a participant's opinion and with a willingness to be hospitable to strangers. If "the mystery of God as Trinity, as final and perfect sociality, embodies qualities of mutuality, reciprocity, cooperation, unity, [and] peace in genuine diversity,"[47] then a small group may be the perfect place to exhibit these virtues and, as a consequence, reflect the Triune God, not only in the content of what is said but in the character of its openness, its mutual cooperation, and its peaceful acceptance of diverse points of view. By embodying these relational qualities, this kind of small group mirrors the community of the Trinity.

Reflection Questions

- How would you appraise the small group evangelism model?
- What materials would you utilize for the small group meetings?
- Who would you invite to an evangelistic small group? If no one comes to mind, why is that the case?
- What would it take for your church to venture into small group evangelism?
- Which model do you think best complements small group evangelism? Why?

47. Anne Carr, *Transforming Grace: Christian Tradition and Women's Experience* (New York: Continuum, 1996), 156–57; quoted in Grenz, *Social God and the Relational Self*, 5.

THREE

VISITATION

There you are, sitting contentedly in your own home, when a pair of nicely dressed people toting pamphlets rings your doorbell. Evangelists at your door. Such a pair appearing uninvited at your doorstep is why this model—visitation evangelism—raises our hackles. I am with you on this. A few years back, when I saw such a pair dressed to the hilt and knocking on a neighbor's door down the block, I quickly sprinted inside from the front garden. When they came to our house, I tiptoed quietly on the other side of the door until the doorbell stopped ringing.

Last autumn, it was my turn to experience this scenario from the opposite perspective when my husband and I canvassed for a congressman in our Dallas district. There *we* were, armed with pamphlets, ringing doorbells up and down the block. We saw people head inside, just as I had. We noticed people indoors, tiptoeing, just as I had. We even heard parents order their children not to open the door. Clearly, people did not welcome uninvited guests bearing pamphlets and a "vote-for-our-candidate" spiel on a blue-skied Sunday afternoon.

Because many of us have this reaction to such uninvited guests, evangelism professor Len Sweet pronounces visitation evangelism dead on arrival. "Home is now a hiding place, not a gathering place. Doorbell rings bring anxiety, not anticipation. We run from, not to, knocks at the door. People do not welcome unsolicited or uncontrolled intrusions into their postmodern castles."[1] Add

1. Leonard I. Sweet, *FaithQuakes* (Nashville: Abingdon, 1994), 32.

to this the inescapable reality that few church members want to make visits of any sort. In his mammoth study of small groups, referenced in the previous chapter, sociologist Robert Wuthnow asked small group participants to rank the activities they had done in their church in the past year in terms of enjoyment. Parish visitation came in at the bottom, alongside nursery duty and babysitting.[2]

Certainly, there are notable obstacles to the visitation model of evangelism, which a proponent defined as a "planned approach, when one or more persons, unannounced or by appointment, enter a home for the purpose of sharing the gospel and inviting response."[3] Still, and not to be dismissed easily, there are notable biblical, theological, historical, and practical foundations for visitation evangelism that warrant a second look and may even alter our perception. This is what happened to me as I delved into this model, despite my initial resistance to it.

This chapter, like the others, presents the fruit of research garnered from various proponents over the years. With this model, however, I had to work especially hard to gather those insights into a contemporary approach to visitation evangelism. I am glad I did. What I discovered—and I hope you will, too—are invigorating possibilities offered to Christians willing to visit outside the church walls, to meet people in their neighborhoods and beyond. In an age of anonymity and isolation, this in itself could be an extraordinary achievement.

Biblical Foundations

Proponents of visitation evangelism enlist a diverse set of biblical materials. The basic meaning of the Greek word *episkeptomai* is "to visit."[4] In the Septuagint, the Bible used by the early church, *episkeptomai* can connote deep concern.[5] Sometimes that concern is punitive: God visited the Israelites with

---

2. Robert Wuthnow, *Sharing the Journey: Support Groups and America's New Quest for Community* (New York: Free Press, 1994), 331.

3. Nelson E. Kauffman, "Personal and Visitation Evangelism," in *Probe for an Evangelism That Cares*, ed. James Fairfield (Scottdale, PA: Herald, 1972), 139.

4. It is important to point out that there is no direct relationship between biblical conceptions of visitation, represented by the verb *episkeptomai*, and the visitation model of evangelism, in which one visits, unprompted, people whom one has not yet met. Yet this verb, translated at base as "to visit," provides the context in which visitation can be regarded as an act of care, concern, and encouragement.

5. Hermann W. Beyer, "*episkeptomai*," in *Theological Dictionary of the New Testament*, ed. Gerhard Kittel (Grand Rapids: Eerdmans, 1964), 2:602.

punishment after they worshiped golden calves (Exod. 32:34). More often, God visited in order to comfort, help, and show favor as in God's visitation of the children of Israel when they screamed in agony during their experience of slavery in Egypt (4:31). Sometimes this is apparent in the verbs with which *episkeptomai* is paired: God remembers and visits people (Pss. 8:4; 106:4; Jer. 15:15); God seeks people out (Ezek. 34:11). The essence of care is captured in Ezekiel 34:11: "For this is what the Lord says: Behold, I will search for my sheep and watch over [*episkeptomai*] them."[6]

This same depth of care continues through the uses of *episkeptomai* in the New Testament, where "it never implies merely 'to visit' them in the usual sense, or for selfish ends, but always 'to be concerned' about them, with a sense of responsibility for others."[7] In a speech leading to his martyrdom, Stephen, an early church leader, declares that "when [Moses] was forty years old, it came into his heart to visit his relatives, the Israelites" (Acts 7:23). This desire arises in Moses's heart out of concern for his fellow Israelites. "[Moses] seeks them out because he belongs to them and shares responsibility for their destiny."[8] Later in Acts, this same penchant for visitation emerges when Paul suggests that he and Barnabas "return and visit the believers in every city where we proclaimed the word of the Lord and see how they are doing" (15:36). Paul's underlying motive for the visit was to follow up with those to whom he had preached previously, "to see how they are doing."

Visitation meant company for the sick and those in difficult straits, like widows and orphans (James 1:27). Jesus told his disciples to visit prisoners as if they were visiting him (Matt. 25:36). Several verses later, he underscored this responsibility when he pronounced judgment on those who refused to visit prisoners (25:43–46). The verb *episkeptomai*, as interpreted by Richard Armstrong (a proponent of visitation evangelism), "is not a question of isolated acts but of a fundamental attitude. One has to realize that one does not exist of and for oneself, but of and for the other. This is to be expressed in one's actions."[9]

---

6. *A New English Translation of the Septuagint*, trans. and ed. Albert Pietersma and Benjamin G. Wright (Oxford: Oxford University Press, 2007).

7. Beyer, "*episkeptomai*," 2:603–4.

8. Beyer, "*episkeptomai*," 2:603–4.

9. Richard Stoll Armstrong, *The Pastor-Evangelist in the Parish* (Louisville: Westminster John Knox, 1990), 25–26.

Another proponent points to the model of Jesus, who "set the pattern of visitation evangelism"[10] when he traveled "through cities and villages, proclaiming and bringing the good news of the kingdom of God" (Luke 8:1). He did not, of course, knock on doors, but he did go to where people lived—their towns and villages—rather than expecting them to come to him.

Still another biblical foundation is the mission on which Jesus sent his disciples (Mark 6:7–13; Matt. 9:35–10:23; Luke 10:1–24). According to Mark, the earliest Gospel, Jesus "called the twelve and began to send them out two by two" (6:7). The disciples head out two by two into new territories ahead of Jesus—preparing the way for him. Jesus gives specific instructions to those who would visit ahead of him, such as telling them not to carry too much or stay too long in inhospitable towns.

Matthew and Luke tell the story differently—in Matthew's Gospel, only twelve go out and the mission is only to Israel, while in Luke's Gospel, seventy go out on a far more widespread mission—yet both Gospels contain this saying of Jesus verbatim: "The harvest is plentiful, but the laborers are few; therefore ask the Lord of the harvest to send out laborers into his harvest" (Matt. 9:37–38; Luke 10:2). In a book published nearly a century ago, A. Earl Kernahan describes Jesus's model as the foundation for visitation evangelism: "Send a number of laymen, two by two, out into any community to visit about Jesus with the people for whom your church is responsible, and there will be others like Andrew [and] Peter . . . who will accept the invitation to meet Jesus."[11]

Proponents of this model are quick to point out that it lifts up the primacy of the laity (*laos*, translated "people" in the NRSV) in the church.[12] The word *laos* occurs in 1 Peter 2:9 as a metaphor for the church: "But you are a chosen race, a royal priesthood, a holy nation, *God's own people*, in order that you may proclaim the mighty acts of him who called you out of darkness into his marvelous light." Lying behind the phrase "God's own people" is a verse in Isaiah:

> The people whom I formed for myself
> so that they might declare my praise. (43:21)

10. Arthur C. Archibald, *Man to Man: Ten Sermons on Visitation Evangelism* (Nashville: Broadman, 1955), 42.

11. A. Earl Kernahan, *Visitation Evangelism* (New York: Revell, 1925), 46. See also Arthur C. Archibald, *New Testament Evangelism: How It Works Today* (Philadelphia: Judson, 1946), 42.

12. Kennedy's first chapter in *Evangelism Explosion* is "Equipping Laypeople." D. James Kennedy, *Evangelism Explosion: Equipping Churches for Friendship, Evangelism, Discipleship, and Healthy Growth*, 4th ed. (Carol Stream, IL: Tyndale, 1996), 1–18.

The people as a whole, not just clergy or professors of religion, are the engine that powers visitation evangelism. Visitation by the laity rather than the clergy brings with it the added benefit of being perceived as less threatening because the good news comes from an ordinary person rather than a "religious specialist." Len Sweet, despite his comment that visitation is dead on arrival, applauds visitation when done by the laity; he write that it is "most dynamic and growing where it is a lay movement."[13] He further suggests that a more suitable place for laity to show up for visitation evangelism is at a person's workplace. Whether this place is in fact more suitable than a home is up for debate.[14]

Theological Foundations

Ekklēsia—the church—was a well-used word long before the apostle Paul wrote it in his letters. It referred to "the regular assembly of citizens in a city to decide matters affecting their welfare."[15] In Paul's letters, *ekklēsia* came to refer to the actual assemblies of Christians meeting together for a religious purpose. *Ekklēsia* is a dynamic composite word, made up of the preposition *ek*, which means "out of" or "from," and the verb *kaleō*, which means "to call." This suggests an assembly of people called together. The word is dynamic rather than static; it represents both the gathered community and the act of gathering as a community. In other words, without the regular meeting together, there is no *ekklēsia*.[16] From *ekklēsia* comes the theological term *ecclesiology*, which refers to the doctrine of the church. Ecclesiology lies at the heart of visitation evangelism. Even though the locus of visitation lies *outside* the church building—in neighborhoods, across streets, around the block—the church community is essential to its practice.

Few would argue that the practice of visitation evangelism is an easy one. Jesus himself gave clear instructions about what to do when his disciples experienced rejection while visiting. For this reason, the church is pivotal to

13. L. Sweet, *FaithQuakes*, 33.

14. This *Huffington Post* blog writer disagrees with Leonard Sweet concerning evangelism in the workplace: John Shore, "10 Reasons It's Wrong to Evangelize in the Workplace," *HuffPost*, June 17, 2016, https://www.huffpost.com/entry/10-reasons-its-wrong-to-evangelize-in-the-work place_b_7597602.

15. Robert Banks, *Paul's Idea of Community: The Early House Churches in Their Cultural Setting* (Grand Rapids: Baker, 1994), 34.

16. Banks, *Paul's Idea of Community*, 41, 51.

sponsoring and undergirding visitation by training those who are visiting, sustaining them with ongoing prayer, and welcoming with open arms those who respond favorably to the visit. Before visitation begins and as it progresses, the church is to be an active, engaged presence.

This action by the church corresponds to two of Avery Dulles's influential five models of ecclesiology: the church as herald and the church as servant. As herald, the church communicates the gospel message. "This ecclesiology goes with a strong evangelistic missionary thrust," notes Dulles. "The preaching of the gospel is related to salvation, because it summons [people] to put their faith in Jesus as Savior. It announces the day of salvation that is at hand for believers."[17] Though Dulles and proponents of Evangelism Explosion[18] may be strange bedfellows, the first question posed in the Evangelism Explosion script has the same sense of urgency in announcing the day of salvation: "Have you come to a place in your spiritual life where you know for certain that if you were to die today you would go to heaven?"[19] The tone is different and the tenor dissimilar, but the urgency is the same.

The church as servant—another of Dulles's models—enters into solidarity with humanity to offer hope and healing. As the church responds tangibly to the needs of those who answer the knock on the door, it demonstrates through its service the good news of the gospel. The beneficiaries of the church as servant are primarily those beyond the church's walls; they are those who need to "hear from the Church a word of comfort or encouragement, or who obtain from the Church a respectful hearing, or who receive from it some material help in their hour of need."[20] Visitation from the church as servant entails more than a rote message for those on the other side of the door with crumbling marriages, broken families, financial shortfalls, or physical challenges. It demands service, deeds that accompany words.

These encounters in turn strengthen the church. While pastoring an inner-city church during a time of changing demographics in the neighborhood in the 1960s, Richard Armstrong observed the impact on those who participated in a visitation evangelism program called Operation Doorbell. At the heart of this program were those doing the visitation, who were known as the Monday

---

17. Avery Dulles, *Models of the Church*, expanded ed. (New York: Doubleday, 1987), 84.
18. For more on Evangelism Explosion, see the end of the next section "Historical Foundations."
19. Kennedy, *Evangelism Explosion*, 32–33.
20. Dulles, *Models of the Church*, 97.

Night Callers. Armstrong noted that this group's spiritual growth deepened along with their sense of social responsibility. "It was reflected in their giving. It was reflected in their increased ability to articulate their faith. It was reflected in their sensitivity to the challenges presented by a racially changing neighborhood. And as their pastor I could point to the fact that the Monday Night Callers as a group could be counted on to support whatever worthwhile project, whatever important cause, the church undertook."[21]

Those who engage in visitation evangelism, then, are extensions of the church as herald and the church as servant. They have a message of good news, of the day of salvation. They have, too, a sensitivity to human needs—and a keen awareness of what the church, the *ekklēsia*, can do to welcome people with such needs.

Historical Foundations

The practice of evangelism through visitation has a long and auspicious history. Dwight L. Moody (1837–99) incorporated visitation into the advance publicity for his renowned citywide revival meetings. During the 1893 Chicago World's Fair revival, a massive visitation program supplemented revival preaching. Particularly active in visitation were women from Moody Bible Institute, who "combed Chicago neighborhoods, knocking on doors [and] handing out Bible tracts."[22] These urban evangelists often engaged in what was referred to as "rescue work" because those who inhabited these neighborhoods had physical as well as spiritual needs. As late nineteenth-century urban areas grew exponentially in population, crime, and congestion, lay evangelists regularly visited brothels, saloons, and gambling houses to initiate contact with people on the margins and to help them build a new life, physically and spiritually. In short, they embodied the models of the church as herald and the church as servant, which Avery Dulles identified nearly a century later.

Emma Ray (1859–1930), a Free Methodist evangelist, visited prostitutes, inmates, and drug addicts in downtown Seattle and along its wharves. Her

21. Richard Armstrong, *The Oak Lane Story: The Renewal of a City Church Which Started Ringing Doorbells* (New York: Division of Evangelism, Board of National Missions, United Presbyterian Church in the USA, 1971[?]), 31.

22. Thekla Ellen Joiner, *Sin in the City: Chicago and Revivalism, 1880–1920* (Columbia: University of Missouri Press, 2007), 91.

regular practice of visitation created opportunities to hold evangelistic meetings in the brothels and, on Sunday afternoons, in the Seattle jail. Emma and others stood before the inmate's bars, handed out songbooks, led the singing, and then preached. A bathtub doubled as an altar.[23]

At the same time and on the other side of the country in New York City, visitation evangelism brought Delia, a twenty-three-year-old with facial bruises and patches of missing hair, to faith in Christ. Delia had at least three nicknames at the time of her conversion: "the Mystery," because the police could never find her; "the Mulberry Slum Bummer," because she frequented the slum neighborhood along Mulberry Street; and "Blue Bell," because she always wore a blue dress. During a night of visitation by rescue mission founder, Emma Whittemore (1850–1931), Delia trailed her from door to door, announcing, "I'm neither afraid of man, God nor the devil, and so can go *anywhere.*" Before the night ended, Whittemore handed Delia a pink rose with the parting invitation to meet the next night at the mission. Eventually Delia, still clutching her rose, landed at Whittemore's Door of Hope rescue mission, where she was "so wondrously rescued of God out of one of the worst dives on Mulberry Street."[24] Thanks to Whittemore's visitation evangelism, Delia became a Christ follower. Delia would never have first come to a church, a steepled building, a community at worship. Yet she did meet Whittemore, who visited her in her own neighborhood.

For the next eleven months, until her death in 1892, Delia spent her days and nights alongside her former Mulberry Street companions, telling them about her conversion. Her funeral, the largest in New York City other than President Ulysses S. Grant's, also served an evangelistic purpose. In a letter to Whittemore afterward, a handful of men from Mulberry Street made this pledge: "We *promise* here that we shall at least try and become different men, and do something for ourselves and for our God. We don't say *everyone* will keep his promise, but we *know* there will be a good many who *will* change their lives owing to Delia's sweet happy face that they seen [in her casket] Tuesday."[25]

23. Emma J. Ray, *Twice Sold, Twice Ransomed: Autobiography of Mr. and Mrs. L. P. Ray* (Chicago: Free Methodist Publishing House, 1926), 72–77.

24. Emma Whittemore, "Snatched as a Brand from the Burning," *The Christian Alliance and Missionary Weekly*, July 1891, 10. See also Emma Whittemore, *Delia: Formerly the Blue-Bird of Mulberry Bend* (New York: Door of Hope, 1893).

25. Emma Whittemore, "Out of Darkness into Light," *The Christian Alliance and Missionary Weekly* (December 1892): 377–78.

After World War I, an increasing number of urban churches in America invested in visitation evangelism as a means of canvassing and evangelizing their neighborhoods.[26] A. Earl Kernahan (1888–1944), a Methodist minister in the Boston area, became convinced that visitation evangelism provided the key to reaching America for Christ, so he subsequently resigned from the pastorate and opened a Washington, DC, office in 1925 as headquarters for his full-time operation. He wanted to demonstrate "what laymen can do towards winning the fifty million or more people in our country who are now outside of the Roman Catholic, Jewish, and Protestant Churches to friendship with Jesus Christ and membership in some body of His followers."[27]

Kernahan developed a neighborhood survey to be used in visitation to ascertain the religious status of a neighborhood's population. From the survey, a list was compiled of contacts to be visited. Then, Kernahan and his associates came to town to train the pastor and especially the laity in visitation evangelism. Kernahan claimed that—all over North America— "two Christian disciples can win an average of sixteen people in one Sunday afternoon and six evenings during the week to Christian discipleship and church membership."[28] Over the next several decades, mainline Protestant denominations, one after another, adopted this method as an official part of their evangelism outreach. The ecumenical list of denominations signing on included the American Baptist Church, the African Methodist Episcopal Church, the Methodist Church, the Church of the Nazarene, the Presbyterian Church (USA), the Lutheran Church–Missouri Synod, and the United Lutheran Church in America. By the 1950s, even the Federal Council of Churches, the forerunner of the National Council of Churches, supported visitation evangelism.[29] In the ensuing decades, however, interest in visitation evangelism among these denominations waned and now has largely disappeared—with one exception.

In the 1960s, D. James Kennedy (1930–2007), pastor of the newly founded Coral Ridge Presbyterian Church in Fort Lauderdale, Florida, developed a visitation evangelism training program called Evangelism Explosion (EE).

26. See William G. McLoughlin Jr., *Modern Revivalism: Charles Grandison Finney to Billy Graham* (New York: Ronald Press, 1959), 456–62.

27. Kernahan, *Visitation Evangelism*, 25.

28. A. Earl Kernahan, *Adventures in Visitation Evangelism* (New York: Revell, 1928), 14.

29. A. Karl Boehmke, "Visitation Evangelism in American Churches," *Concordia Theological Monthly* 28, no. 9 (September 1957): 669.

EE is a highly scripted approach that opens with two famous diagnostic questions:

- "Have you come to a place in your spiritual life where you know for certain that if you were to die today you would go to heaven, or is that something you would say you're still working on?"
- "Suppose that you were to die today and stand before God and He were to say to you, 'Why should I let you into My heaven?' What would you say?"[30]

Through EE, the church Kennedy led grew exponentially in a decade to over ten times its original size; for fifteen years it grew faster than any other Presbyterian church in the country.[31] EE flourished beyond the United States, as well. By 1994, Kennedy estimated that approximately one hundred thousand churches in over two hundred countries used the program to train people in visitation evangelism. EE's current global reach is staggering, including nearly two thousand leadership training events annually, thirty-eight thousand churches implementing the EE program (with more than six thousand added in 2017), and more than half a million children in Explorer's Club, EE's discipleship training for new believers.[32]

Practical Foundations

If Wuthnow's numbers still ring true—regarding visitation ranking as church members' least favorite activity, alongside nursery and babysitting—this is a difficult model of evangelism for American Christians to embrace. Yet it is an extremely doable model, one that requires the ability to approach a door—whether of a house, an apartment, a hospital room, or a prison—greet someone, and initiate a conversation. What follows are some practical guidelines that can be culled from the writings of those who champion this model of evangelism.

30. Kennedy, *Evangelism Explosion*, 32–33. For more explanation and analysis of the intent of these diagnostic questions, see Kennedy, *Evangelism Explosion*, 75–85.
31. "History of Coral Ridge: 1959–1966," Coral Ridge Presbyterian Church, 2020, http://www.crpc.org/1959-1966.
32. "Annual Results," Evangelism Explosion International, 2017, https://evangelismexplosion.org/about-us/annual-results.

1. Prepare the Congregation

Given the central role of the church—the *ekklēsia*—in visitation evangelism, it is imperative to enlist the congregation's buy-in from the outset. Presentations in public gatherings—Sunday school classes, the worship service,
an evening event—accompanied by blogs or church newsletter articles, are
integral to galvanizing interest in and commitment to visitation evangelism.
In these public sessions and written materials, the importance, and even the
responsibility, of every Christian engaging in evangelism should be front and
center. Here is an opportunity to utilize the biblical, theological, and historical
foundations of visitation evangelism.

In the preparation phase, alert the congregation to the many ways they can
participate. Richard Armstrong reflects on the wide-ranging support required
of a visitation program:

> We need people to help in the office, preparing the calling lists, summary reports
> and records of calls; we need people to provide refreshments for the callers and
> people to help in the kitchen; we need people to help recruit callers; we need
> young people to babysit for couples who want to take part and for parents who
> want to attend our membership classes. . . . If you can't do any of these things,
> you can at least undergird the program with your prayers, which more than
> anything else will ensure its success.[33]

It is important for those who are unable or who prefer not to visit to know
they can contribute in other ways. Not least of which, they can be enlisted as
a prayer partner for a team of visitors; such a daunting task demands devoted
people of prayer.

2. Train the Visitors

Practitioners of visitation evangelism advise that training sessions focus
on two primary topics: faith sharing and best practices. During sessions on
faith sharing, integrate chapter 1 of this book on personal evangelism. In
these sessions, allow ample time for soon-to-be visitors to narrate their own
experience of coming to faith. Verbatims, case studies, and role playing are
important learning tools to use in this training.[34]

---

33. Armstrong, *Oak Lane Story*, 15.
34. See Kernahan, *Visitation Evangelism*, 76–83, and Richard Stoll Armstrong, *Service Evangelism* (Philadelphia: Westminster, 1979), 114–27.

Sessions on best practices should cover a range of topics concerning the visit itself. These should include:

- stating up front and honestly the reason for the visit
- listening well to concerns and criticisms, *not* becoming defensive
- showing courtesy and care even in a difficult situation
- anticipating the questions that might be asked, especially antagonistic ones about Christianity or the church
- dealing with distractions during the visit[35]

Overall, these sessions will provide strategic skills for visitors to become better neighbors to their community. They will help "develop and refine [visitors'] listening and caring skills, skills [they] need everywhere—in [their] homes, workplaces, neighborhoods, communities, and church community. . . . What could be more important for disciples of Jesus the Christ?"[36] Equally important, participants will begin to see their faith become stronger through visitation. They will learn more about God, particularly by trusting God for each encounter. They will have the opportunity to change the lives of those in their neighborhood for the better. They may even experience a reawakening of their own faith, as they see others discover the joy of Christian faith.

3. Launch the Visitation

The visitation program's launch should be marked in some way, perhaps through a guest speaker or a special worship service during which the visitors are commissioned. This public staging gives the program visibility and prominence. The optimal stretch of a dedicated visitation evangelism program, practitioners suggest, is six to eight weeks in the fall or spring. One

35. Even in the 1950s, visitors expressed concern over how to handle a radio or television set playing loudly. The suggested response may seem comical to someone living in the twenty-first century: "It has been suggested that the visitors might hang their coats over the television set but this is not usually the best procedure! Normally it will be enough either to speak very quietly until someone thinks to turn down the volume, or to ask, 'I'm sorry, it's difficult to hear. I wonder if we could have the radio turned down a bit?'" (Lewis Misselbrook, *Training in Visitation: Talks to Those about to Take Part in Visitation Evangelism* [London: Carey Kingsgate Press, 1957], 21.) Today, the challenge of technology is even more intense and pervasive so that adopting a measured approach is essential to effective visitation evangelism.

36. Shirley F. Clement and Susanne G. Braden, *Caring Evangelism: A Visitation Program for Congregations, Leader's Guide* (Nashville: Discipleship Resources, 1994), 7.

approach is to set up the program for visitation one night a week during this time period. Another approach is to launch the program with a special week of visitation for a four-evening stretch, preferably Monday through Thursday. Then the program continues with one night of visitation for each week of the remaining time frame. Every night of visitation can follow this schedule:

6:00   dinner for those who will go on the visit

6:45   final instructions

7:00   visitation assignments handed out, followed by prayer

7:15   visitors depart for their visits

9:00   finish the visits and return to the church to debrief

Ideally, during the weeks of the visitation program, every church group should be praying for the visits, even if they are not specifically involved.

Because the visitation assignments are usually constructed geographically around where the church meets, it is essential to chart the area to be visited. This involves creating a large map of the surrounding community. In an urban or suburban area, the map will consist of ten to fifteen blocks, with each street named. Assign each pair of visitors to a certain number of blocks.[37] In a rural area, the map will be labeled with main roads and landmarks, and each pair of visitors will be instructed to visit a bounded area on the map.

As Kernahan commended, visitors may find it beneficial to bring a brief survey as a natural conduit for the visit. The survey asks, among other questions, about the religious affiliation and degree of involvement of each family or individual and their spiritual interests. When the surveys are compiled, they offer in-depth data about the community which, if well utilized, can help the congregation serve its neighbors more effectively. One pastor described the importance of the questionnaire: "Six months before the Mission began, the people in my parish were strangers to me. I knew nothing about them—the size of the family, the conditions under which they were living, their church

37. When Jack and I canvassed for our aspiring congressman, the organization provided us with an app that allowed us to track each home we visited, what their prior response was, whether they had voted, and whether they would tend to be amenable to our visit. Without this app, our visits would have been inefficient and haphazard. With this app, we knew exactly which houses we needed to visit and, at least in part, what we might expect. Tapping a technologically savvy person in your congregation to develop such an app would be a great benefit to the visitation evangelism program.

affiliations—all this was unknown territory. At the end of the Mission a new situation existed. I had a record of every home in the parish."[38]

4. Engage in Conversations

When someone opens the door, do the following in your opening statement:

a. *Identify* who you are and what church you represent.

b. *Explain* why you are on their doorstep.

c. *Acknowledge* the intrusion.

d. *Ask* to come in.

e. *Promise* to be brief.[39]

From this point on, follow the best practices listed above, as well as the suggestions under the heading "Share the Gospel" in chapter 1.

Visitors return to the church afterward for light refreshments, compile a brief report on every visit made, and debrief each visit, noting particularly where follow-up is needed. Debriefing provides the opportunity for visitors to learn from each other's experiences. Some proponents regard it as "the heart of our on-going training program." They explain: "We learned from one another how to tackle most any kind of situation, from how to talk with a television set blaring away and how to cope with an over-friendly mutt that thinks he's a lap dog and isn't, to what you say to a nuclear physicist who cordially informs you he is an atheist or to a distraught widow whose husband has just died of cancer. . . . There were hundreds of human dramas unfolding behind the doors whose bells we rang, and we became part of them."[40]

5. Integrate Newcomers

Vital to a successful visitation evangelism program is the timely and seamless integration of newcomers into a church poised to welcome them into its midst. All the hard work, time, effort, and friendliness of the visitor can be dismantled instantaneously if the congregation closes itself off from strangers who show up because they were intrigued by the visit. (This is often done

---

38. Tom Allan, *The Face of My Parish* (London: SCM, 1956), 25.
39. This list is from Armstrong, *Service Evangelism*, 83.
40. Armstrong, *Oak Lane Story*, 19.

without thinking, like when church members use Sunday mornings only to catch up with their friends. Newcomers are then left on the margins to observe silently as conversations flow around them.) A congregation that has been trained in advance of the visitation evangelism program on how to integrate newcomers can assist with hospitality, including transportation to and from the worship service, a get-acquainted coffee time, or a home-cooked or restaurant meal afterward.

Deeper assimilation of newcomers can occur in a Sunday school class or, better yet, in a new small group set up for the purpose of initiating newcomers who were called on during the visitation evangelism program. With this dedicated small group in place, even on their initial visit, people will find a place specifically prepared for them. The welcome they received during the visitation evangelism program continues, in other words, without a hitch.

Without a hospitable response from the congregation, newcomers may quickly disappear and become hardened toward Christianity; the momentary openness they once felt will become a scar. One pastor saw this happening when the visitation evangelism program brought new people to church, but they never found a place where they belonged. Sometimes the message was communicated through something as flippant as asking a newcomer to move to a different seat because they happened to sit down in a spot normally occupied by a longtime member. Sometimes people sitting next to visitors never said hello; they simply got up after the service and turned their backs to the newcomers. Sometimes they buried themselves in reviewing the church bulletin before the service rather than greeting a visitor sitting next to them. The pastor reflected, "Tragically we had to watch many of these people drifting away as the months passed from a church which appeared to have nothing for them and which was incapable of assimilating them into its life." He continued, "It is a plain fact that a great number of the newcomers are simply chilled out of the church by the attitude of the old members."[41] Hospitality, again and again, is at the heart of yet another model of evangelism.

6. Serve the Neighborhood

Knocking on doors will help the congregation get to know the neighborhood in a deeper way than it did previously. A well-managed, ongoing visitation program provides an avenue for a congregation to extend Christ's

41. Allan, *Face of My Parish*, 33–34.

compassion to its neighbors. Oak Lane Presbyterian Church became such a congregation. Visitation evangelism led to neighborly compassion, as the church was led to demonstrate love in tangible ways. To serve the needs discovered as they knocked on doors, the church "acquired hospital beds, wheelchairs, and other equipment and made them available to families who could not afford them otherwise. They helped find suitable retirement homes for the aged and infirm with no one to care for them, visited the sick and lonely, provided emergency food and clothing for the indigent, sought jobs for the unemployed."[42]

In turn, Oak Lane organically grew into a more diverse church that reflected the changing demographics of its neighborhood. While visiting residences across the street and down the block, for instance, they met Cuban refugees, and the church became a sponsor for their citizenship. They helped several of those formerly incarcerated get back on their feet. Thanks to the church's intervention, one went on to study for ministry at Princeton Theological Seminary and another became president of a men's Bible class.[43]

While teaching at Perkins School of Theology, Elaine Heath took her evangelism class to meet with several Missionaries of Charity sisters in one of the poorest neighborhoods in Dallas. One of the sisters explained that they would visit two by two throughout the neighborhood. They knocked on doors, offered to pray with people, and found out what needs they might have. She said, "Sometimes they don't want to talk to us or let us come in. It's always because they think we want something. A donation or money. We tell them no, we are just there to pray for them and get to know them. That is how we basically do our ministry."[44] The students reacted to their visitation with concern that the sisters would come across as "coercive toward those they help" because "this is, after all, a pluralistic world."[45] The sister countered that their visitation was not coercive at all. Then she told a story about a man who refused her offer to pray with him because he wasn't religious. Her response: "That's okay. I need prayer for myself so you can just listen while I pray for both of us."[46]

42. Armstrong, *Oak Lane Story*, 26.

43. Armstrong, *Oak Lane Story*, 25.

44. Elaine Heath, *The Mystic Way of Evangelism: A Contemplative Vision for Christian Outreach*, 2nd ed. (Grand Rapids: Baker Academic, 2017), 112.

45. Heath, *Mystic Way of Evangelism*, 113.

46. Heath, *Mystic Way of Evangelism*, 113.

Appraisal

It is not surprising that visitation evangelism is rarely practiced these days. Critics claim it is too mechanical, too scripted. This critique reflects the image from an earlier era of door-to-door salesmen, who rang the doorbell to sell a vacuum cleaner or an encyclopedia set. This critique also reflects the tendency of James Kennedy's Evangelism Explosion to choreograph visits meticulously from start (asking the two diagnostic questions) to finish (calling for commitment). The visit is to be managed in such a way as to compel a decision for Christ.

This critique, while understandable, is not entirely valid. Return for a moment to the word *visit*, which suggests attention and carefulness, conjuring visions of a cup of coffee and a chat about important matters. In an era of short sound bites, is it possible that a visit could be welcome? Someone to listen. Someone to care, even for a few moments. Someone to offer an invitation. Someone with genuinely good news.

Remember, too, the history of visitation evangelism, during which evangelists visited slums and mud flats, brothels and prisons, bearing a word of good news and a measure of hope. This is not a matter of conscripting converts; it is a matter of welcoming strangers.

Think as well about the impact this outreach could have on churches, which often exist as islands of homogeneity in seas of diversity. The neighborhood changes, but the church does not. Visitation is an opportunity for the church to engage its neighborhood and for its neighbors to engage the church. Churches can be changed by visitation evangelism—and made to look more like their neighborhood. Heading out to change their world, they can be changed themselves. Perhaps, then, it is time to discard caricatures and consider visitation evangelism as a means of integrating the church into its neighborhood, of finding out firsthand what the real needs of its neighbors are, and of offering them the opportunity to participate in a supportive, thoughtful, compassionate community of faith.

Where Does the Holy Spirit Fit in Visitation Evangelism?

A surprising gap in this model of evangelism is its very few references to the Holy Spirit. Practitioners, like Kennedy, rely on training and strategy. In his book, which outlines in full detail the EE program, there is one brief section on the Holy Spirit in the first chapter. Kennedy explains that "our witnessing must always be a 'trialogue' rather than a dialogue. . . . The witness should be taught from the very beginning to depend not on his own persuasiveness but upon the power of the Holy Spirit, or else he is witnessing in the flesh and not in the Spirit."[47] Then, curiously, the Holy Spirit disappears for the remaining two hundred pages. Even in the outline of the gospel presentation, the Holy Spirit is not mentioned; only God and Jesus Christ are considered part and parcel of the good news. The bulk of the book confronts the tactical issues of screening contacts, developing leaders, asking diagnostic questions, and handling objections.

In evangelism, no matter the model or approach, reliance on the Holy Spirit is essential. Jesus understands this. In his final teaching on the Holy Spirit in the Gospel of John, he declares to his disciples that the Spirit will "remind you of all that I have said to you" (John 14:26). The Spirit will "glorify me, because he will take what is mine and declare it to you" (16:14). Talking about Jesus to people in our neighborhoods requires the presence of the Holy Spirit, which teaches us, by way of reminder, what Jesus himself taught, what Jesus himself did, how he died, and that he was raised from the dead. It is important to be as knowledgeable as we can be in the Scriptures, but it is the Holy Spirit who provides the connecting link between the life of Jesus and the lives of people around us. Sensitivity to the Holy Spirit, while remembering what we have learned, makes us supple, malleable, responsive, and faithful to the person on whose behalf we are taking a breath, saying a prayer, and knocking on a neighbor's door.

As we saw in personal evangelism, it is the Holy Spirit who guides the encounter, who inspires the visitor with what to say and do, and who convicts the conversation partner with their need for transformation. The same is true in visitation evangelism. This fundamental aspect of evangelism cannot be overlooked. It is the presence and power of the Holy Spirit that is needed during the visitation; this should be the focus of the congregation's prayers while the visitors knock on doors and engage in conversation.

Is Visitation Evangelism Relevant for the Twenty-First Century?

Evangelism professor Jack Jackson notes the difficulty of the visitation model of evangelism: "Visitation is most often seen as a time-consuming relic of a previous age with no relevance to contemporary Christian communities.

47. Kennedy, *Evangelism Explosion*, 11.

Therefore, not surprisingly, when United Methodist candidates for ordination are asked as a group by their bishop the historic Wesleyan question, 'Will you visit from house to house?' the response is often a communal sheepish 'Yes,' accompanied by smiles and chuckles."[48] You may not have read the notes to this chapter, but if you did, you will have noticed that the publication dates of books and articles on visitation evangelism were mostly between 1920 and 1950, which suggests that visitation evangelism is a relic best left in the past.

Not so. Permit me to point out that many people in contemporary society, like myself (and perhaps especially urban dwellers), do not know their neighbors. Currently, in our twelve-unit townhome complex, we barely see our neighbors because we hit the automatic garage door opener, park the car inside, and close the door behind us. Rarely do we see anyone out and about because we have little common space and certainly no front porches. And this reality is increasing, as thousands of townhomes just like ours are under construction in Dallas. We are giving ourselves fewer and fewer opportunities to meet our neighbors. This, of course, is nothing new. A few decades ago, Robert Putman's pivotal book, *Bowling Alone*, held up a mirror to Americans' increasing isolation. Since its publication, we have become even more distant from those around us because now our communities are often virtual; we are increasingly dependent on connection through electronic devices rather than face-to-face encounters. Most of us have had the experience of coming up to someone we know, then just as we are about to greet them, we notice they are busy sending a text. Our response is to head in another direction so that we do not interrupt them.

This is not an effort to offer a wholesale critique of American society, but it is an attempt to point out the increasing isolation in our society, which is fueled in part by social media and virtual communication. Investing time and energy to visit people in person where they live, in the physical spaces they inhabit, speaks volumes about a church's desire to go outside itself and to greet its neighbors firsthand. It is the difference you feel between walking into a big box store, where no one can help you find a particular nail or wrench, and entering a local hardware store, where someone greets you and asks how they can help. So, consider adapting the visitation evangelism model in a way that suits your church and neighborhood. Begin with the verb *episkeptomai*

48. Jack Jackson, *Offering Christ: John Wesley's Evangelistic Vision* (Nashville: Kingswood Books, 2017), 158–59.

and the understanding it evokes of visitation as a show of concern for some-one, like Jesus telling his friends to visit the sick and those in prison as if they were visiting him. Or like the people of Oak Lane Presbyterian Church in Philadelphia, who not only changed their neighborhood but were changed by it, by the Cuban refugees, the elderly people, and those formerly incarcerated who lived next door or across the street. Or like Emma Ray in the mud flats of Seattle. Or like Emma Whittemore, three thousand miles away in New York City, who was willing to find a Delia, to face her, and to give her a pink rose.

Reflection Questions

- How would you appraise the visitation evangelism model?
- In what context—rural, urban, small town, apartment complex—is visitation evangelism most applicable?
- How would you construct the format of a visitation evangelism program in your church?
- Would you volunteer to be a visitor? Why or why not?
- Which other model of evangelism best complements visitation evange-lism? Why?

FOUR

LITURGICAL

*L*iturgy and *evangelism* at first glance seem out of step with each other. *Liturgy* evokes images of Gothic cathedrals with pointed arches, ribbed vaults, saints carved in stone, and flying buttresses; inside a golden chalice rests on an ornate altar with censers streaming incense, as a robed figure processes regally down the aisle and bells chime (hence the shorthand expression "smells and bells"). *Evangelism* conjures images of anything but liturgy. A sweaty-browed charlatan with a toothy smile, peddling a sleazy, heavy-handed appeal to repent and believe the gospel *now*. A well-dressed pair knocking on a door. Even an earnest conversation in a cafeteria. *Anything* but liturgy.

Who would think to fuse liturgy with evangelism? Pomp with commonplace circumstances? Pageantry with the seemingly pedestrian? Grandeur with the gritty? Robert Webber did in the 1980s when he used the term *liturgical evangelism* to lift up liturgy as a means to communicate the gospel. Through regular participation in the church's liturgical life, argued Webber, a person would be evangelized. Liturgical evangelism at its core is "a conversion experience regulated and ordered by the liturgical rites of the church. These services order the inner experience of repentance from sin, faith in Christ, conversion of life, and entrance into the Christian community."[1] In liturgical evangelism,

1. Robert Webber, *Celebrating Our Faith: Evangelism through Worship* (San Francisco: Harper & Row, 1986), 1.

conversion happens over time in the cradle of the church's liturgy, as it moves through God's story of salvation.

The irony—and genius—of liturgical evangelism is that it returns to an era two thousand years ago to discover afresh how to communicate the gospel in our era. It dials back the clock to the context of the early church, where the essentials of Christianity were taught to those living in a culture not yet familiar with this faith. Liturgy was, at its core, evangelism. Fast-forward to today. Liturgical evangelism recognizes that familiarity with the essentials of Christianity can no longer be assumed for current generations, especially Millennials and Generation Z. In this so-called post-Christian context, liturgy can be a winsome, welcoming venue for evangelism.

You may be tempted, if you are part of a tradition that avoids pomp and shuns pageantry, to skip this chapter. What could you possibly do, you might wonder, with a model that incorporates hymns and written prayers? Do not jump, I would ask you, to the next chapter because you have jumped to conclusions about this one. Liturgical evangelism is rooted in Scripture, rich with history, and overflowing with theology. You may be surprised to learn that you are not only uncovering a great deal about the origins of your faith and church but also discovering how the liturgical life of the early church, which was inherently evangelistic, can revitalize your own church and your own faith through the slow burn of the ancient—and ever contemporary—model known as liturgical evangelism.

Biblical Foundations

Proponents of liturgical evangelism find biblical grounding for this model in Jesus's upbringing, as Jesus himself was immersed in Jewish liturgical practices and places. Jesus's parents brought him as a newborn to the temple to fulfill the prescribed Jewish rites of passage, including the offering for a firstborn son (Luke 2:22–24). At Jesus's dedication, Simeon blesses the baby (2:25–38). When Jesus turns twelve, he accompanies his parents to the temple for the Passover festival and remains behind to engage there with Jewish scholars (2:41–50).

Jesus's life as a teacher takes him at times to synagogues, which were the center of Jewish teaching, worship, and community, apart from the temple in Jerusalem. The first instance of Jesus's extended teaching takes place

in his hometown synagogue, where he proclaims the fulfillment of God's
good news:

> The Spirit of the Lord is upon me,
>> because he has anointed me
>>> to bring good news to the poor.
> He has sent me to proclaim release to the captives
>> and recovery of sight to the blind,
>>> to let the oppressed go free,
> to proclaim the year of the Lord's favor. (Luke 4:18–19; cf. Isa. 61:1–2)

In the synagogue in Nazareth, Jesus first proclaims that God anointed him
to bring good news. Small wonder, then, that the synagogue provided the
space and the worship setting for the gospel message of the life, crucifixion,
resurrection, and ascension of Jesus. Time and again, early church evangelists speak in synagogues. Even in Jerusalem, Stephen, a leader in the early
church, argues with men who belong to the synagogue of the Freedmen so
fiercely that they stone him (Acts 6:9–7:60). When Paul and Barnabas begin
journeying into the Mediterranean basin, they (with the help of John) sail
first to the island of Cyprus, where "they proclaimed the word of God in the
synagogues of the Jews" (13:5).

They continue on to Pisidian Antioch, where they again go to the locus
of worship, learning, and prayer—the synagogue. Cyprus is the home of
Barnabas, so the leader of the synagogue invites them to speak, which they
do, reciting the acts of Jesus's life, death, and resurrection (Acts 13:14–43).
Jealousy leads to conflict with Jewish leaders on the island, so Paul and Barnabas begin to preach to the gentiles—non-Jews—who also come to believe.
This is a remarkable first venture for Paul and Barnabas, the result of which
is that "a great number of both Jews and Greeks became believers" (14:1).
They continue, too, to head first to synagogues, where Jews gathered around
the study of Torah, prayed, worshiped, and listened to Paul and Barnabas
(though the Jews did not always agree with what they heard). Luke writes that
Paul, at one point, entered Thessalonica, "as was his custom, and on three
sabbath days argued with them from the scriptures" (17:2).

It is important to recognize that Judaism provided these evangelists with
a living tradition in which the earliest followers of Jesus learned, lived, and
prayed. In the first sermon in the book of Acts, Peter includes little more than

Old Testament texts strung together to illuminate the life, death, and resurrection of Jesus, as well as the later gift of the Holy Spirit (Acts 2:14–36). When the sermon is over, Peter offers the opportunity of repentance—expressed in the language of the Old Testament as a gift to those near and far[2]—and the invitation to water baptism, with which Jewish hearers would have been familiar (vv. 38–39). Those who came to follow Jesus then entered into a living and practicing community (here, too, the practices would have been known in Judaism and adopted by Jesus's followers): "They devoted themselves to the apostles' teaching and fellowship, to the breaking of bread and the prayers" (v. 42). The elements of catechesis and community life, which shaped the earliest followers of Jesus, took place in the context of regular disciplines: study, eating together (possibly the sacred meal in memory of Jesus), and prayer.

Evangelism in this instance is the first step to a rich life of worship, learning, and prayer. This, at least, is how proponents of liturgical evangelism understand the experience of that first Pentecost. "The first step proclaims the mystery of the gospel and awakens faith, cutting the listeners 'to the heart' and prompting them to ask 'what shall we do?' When the listeners come to faith, they are invited to take the second step—to repent and be baptized."[3] The fruits of Pentecost are rooted in learning from the Scriptures (the apostles' teaching throughout Acts, like Peter's sermon, is rooted in the Old Testament), expressed in bodily activities such as baptism and eating together, and exercised through regular activities such as the practice of prayer—and all this in the context of a living, worshiping community.[4]

Consider, too, the fledgling church at Antioch, which spent an entire year of study before they received a word of the Holy Spirit instructing them to set apart Paul and Barnabas "for the work to which I [the Holy Spirit] have called them" (Acts 13:2; see also 11:25–26; 13:1–3). The church at Antioch was not an established church; it grew as it learned and learned as it grew—so much so that this was the first group of people to be identified explicitly with the moniker "Christian": "For an entire year [Paul and Barnabas] met with the church and taught a great many people, and it was in Antioch that the

2. See Joel 2:32 (Joel 3:5 in the Septuagint and the Hebrew text). See also Isa. 57:19.
3. Webber, *Celebrating Our Faith*, 18. For others who commend this twofold process, see Tory Baucum, *Evangelical Hospitality: Catechetical Evangelism in the Early Church and Its Recovery for Today* (Lanham, MD: Scarecrow, 2008), 32–38; and Michel Dujarier, *A History of the Catechumenate: The First Six Centuries* (New York: Sadlier, 1979), 19–20.
4. Webber, *Celebrating Our Faith*, 18.

disciples were first called 'Christians'" (11:26). This regular, yearlong devotion to gathering, learning, and worshiping—this is what ultimately makes up the biblical roots of liturgical evangelism.

Theological Foundations

One theological foundation to which proponents of this model appeal is Christology, particularly Jesus as *Christus Victor*. In his ministry, Jesus as *Christus Victor* disarmed the powers of darkness through healings and exorcisms. As he testified in Matthew 12:28, "But if I throw out demons by the power of God's Spirit, then God's kingdom has already overtaken you."[5] Through his crucifixion and resurrection, he conquered the kingdom of darkness and established once and for all the kingdom of light. This dimension of Jesus's ministry comes to life in the Methodist baptismal liturgy, when the new believer "renounces the spiritual forces of wickedness and rejects the evil powers of this world" (kingdom of darkness) and confesses Jesus Christ as Savior and Lord (kingdom of light).[6] In essence, the baptismal liturgy is evangelistic, a proclamation of the good news that Jesus has and will—ultimately and completely—vanquish the powers of darkness in this world. Still, it is up to Jesus's followers to continue the battle against the kingdom of darkness until Jesus returns as *Christus Victor* in final victory. Paul seems to have understood this when he encouraged Christians to arm themselves for this ongoing battle between light and dark. "Put on the whole armor of God," he urged, "so that you may be able to stand against the wiles of the devil. For our struggle is not against enemies of blood and flesh, but against the rulers, against the authorities, against the cosmic powers of this present darkness, against the spiritual forces of evil in the heavenly places" (Eph. 6:11–12).

While Christology provides an important theological foundation for liturgical evangelism, the heart and soul of this model rests in the church, in ecclesiology. Liturgical evangelism "is not mass evangelism, para-church evangelism, or even one-on-one evangelism. While each of these models of evangelism may feed into liturgical evangelism, liturgical evangelism takes place in the context of the local church, of the mystery of faith that is experienced and

5. Michael Grant, trans., *Jesus* (New York: Scribner's Sons, 1977), 34, quoted in William J. Abraham, *The Logic of Evangelism* (Grand Rapids: Eerdmans, 1989), 27.

6. "The Baptismal Covenant I," *The United Methodist Hymnal* (Nashville: United Methodist Publishing House, 1989), 34.

modeled by a local spiritual family."[7] The church is the primary evangelist in this model, both within its walls (as the gathered community through its liturgy, catechesis, and sacramental life) and beyond its walls (as the scattered community when it proclaims the gospel in the world through words and actions).

In liturgical evangelism, the church, at its best, provides catechetical expertise and experience, along with communal support, in the context of public worship and liturgy. In its fullest sense, liturgical evangelism extends from pre-catechism to full participation. To emphasize the church's role in helping to birth belief in seekers and provide them with soul-enriching food so that eventually they come to full maturation in the body of Christ, some proponents of liturgical evangelism identify the church as Mother as a central metaphor. This metaphor draws on some early church writers who portrayed the church as "the womb in which God's children are born," nurtured, and held together.[8] Liturgy is like a womb, in which seekers, alongside believers new and old, receive the nutrients of faith; they absorb new life, breath, and all those elements that will bring them to birth and, eventually, maturity.

As we turn to Avery Dulles's ecclesiological models, we see two models are well represented in liturgical evangelism: the church as sacrament and the church as herald. As sacrament, the outer workings of the church reveal an inner grace available to those who participate in its worship life: "As believers succeed in finding appropriate external forms by which to express their commitment to God in Christ, they become living symbols of divine love and beacons of hope in the world."[9] This conception of the church as sacrament spills over into the church as herald. We have already encountered the church as herald before (in personal evangelism, small group evangelism, and visitation evangelism), but the conception in liturgical evangelism is slightly different. Here it is the *church's* lifestyle that witnesses rather than an individual's, since the emphasis in liturgical evangelism rests on the integrity and witness of the community. The church presents Jesus Christ to the world by its ongoing liturgical life of worship, by its integrity, and by the justice it enacts. The church is an evangelist, whether it is aware of it or not. People watch what

7. Webber, *Celebrating Our Faith*, 8.

8. Webber, *Celebrating Our Faith*, 6. Webber lists examples of this imagery in the writings of Tertullian, Clement of Alexandria, Cyprian, Justin Martyr, and Augustine. Webber, *Celebrating Our Faith*, 7–8.

9. Avery Dulles, *Models of the Church*, expanded ed. (New York: Doubleday, 1987), 73.

the church does and listen to what it says from afar, especially with today's pervasive media coverage. The church as herald, therefore, must be vigilant about the message it communicates in both word and deed.

It is not difficult to become a skeptic, given this vaunted view of churches that, in reality, are often plagued by dissensions, divisions, and injustices. Still, this is the reality churches must deal with honestly; if they do not face it themselves, those who do not believe will certainly point this out. Renowned theologian Henri Nouwen, when giving advice to his teenage nephew, puts the matter simply but profoundly. "First of all, listen to the church," advises Nouwen. He continues,

> I know that isn't a popular bit of advice at a time and in a country where the church is often seen more as an obstacle in the way than as the way to Jesus. Nevertheless, I'm deeply convinced that the greatest spiritual danger for our times is the separation of Jesus from the church. The church is the body of the Lord. Without Jesus there can be no church; and without the church we cannot stay united with Jesus. I've yet to meet anyone who has come closer to Jesus by forsaking the church.[10]

Historical Foundations

Apart from the Bible, the primary source for liturgical evangelism is an early third-century document called *The Apostolic Tradition*. It was a key text—a primer of sorts—for Christian worship practices at the time.[11] Hippolytus (170–235), generally considered the author of *The Apostolic Tradition*, was a presbyter, perhaps even a bishop, in Rome. Eventually he became a martyr who died in the Sardinian salt mines. Hippolytus is alleged to have written the document before Christianity became a legal religion, when Christians were being persecuted, as even he himself would be. It was intended to provide extensive instructions for teaching, or catechizing, converts from paganism to Christianity and integrating them into the liturgical tradition that Christians practiced.

These converts were pagans; they were not Jews, as in the earliest years of the nascent church, when the Jewish synagogue was the foremost locus of preaching

10. Henri Nouwen, *Letters to Marc about Jesus* (San Francisco: Harper & Row, 1988), 83.
11. Gregory Dix claims it was written within two years of 215 CE. Gregory Dix, ed. *The Treatise on the Apostolic Tradition of St. Hippolytus of Rome* (London: Alban, 1992), xxxvii.

and evangelism. Catechism for pagan peoples aimed "to deconstruct their old world, and to reconstruct a new one, so that they would emerge as Christian people."[12] In that context, the combination of evangelism and catechesis took time; it was a lengthy process—from one to three years—during which pagans with no prior knowledge of the gospel were initiated into the Christian fold.[13] *The Apostolic Tradition* sets out in illuminating detail distinct stages for the catechetical and liturgical process, from the first stages of evangelism (pre-catechism) to full membership in the community, marked by baptism and communion.

This lengthy evangelistic, catechetical, and liturgical process slowly disintegrated and nearly disappeared, due in large measure to Christianity's increasing legitimization as an official religion of the Roman Empire during the fourth-century CE reign of Constantine (272–337). The church, in turn, increasingly streamlined the formation process.[14] Still, proponents of liturgical evangelism point to times and movements over the centuries when it resurfaced, never fully disappearing, until it came to life again in the wake of the Second Vatican Council (Vatican II) of the Roman Catholic Church (1962–65). Vatican II set in motion profound changes in the Catholic Church, including a vast liturgical renewal that incorporated—again—an unbreakable link between catechesis, formation, and evangelism.[15] In 1972, drawing inspiration from *The Apostolic Tradition* as well as Vatican II debates and decrees, the Catholic Church published the Rite of Christian Initiation of Adults (RCIA) for evangelizing, catechizing, nurturing, and welcoming into full membership people beyond the age for infant baptism. RCIA recognizes four stages of evangelism and initiation; three rites mark the transition from one stage to the next.

12. Alan Kreider, *Worship and Evangelism in Pre-Christendom* (Cambridge: Grove Books, 1995), 23.

13. Baucum, *Evangelical Hospitality*, 4.

14. For Webber's discussion on this point, see Robert E. Webber, *Ancient-Future Evangelism: Making Your Church a Faith-Forming Community* (Grand Rapids: Baker Books, 2003), 25–26.

15. Aidan Kavanagh emphasizes the rapidity and thoroughness of liturgical reform in this statement, "Of first importance here is the necessity of remembering just how unprecedented the recent process of liturgical reform in the Western church has been. As Robert Taft never tires of pointing out, what has been done with the liturgy of the Western churches in the last twenty years has no parallel in the history of religions." (Aidan Kavanagh, "Life-Cycle Events and Civil Ritual," in *Initiation Theology*, ed. James Schmeiser [Toronto: Anglican Book Centre, 1978], 12.) The importance of Vatican II cannot be overestimated. "There is scarcely an element in the Catholic Church's internal life or in its relationship with others that has been unaffected by the Second Vatican Council. . . . It is no exaggeration, then, to say that the Catholic Church has changed more in the twenty-five years since Vatican II than it had in the previous two hundred." Joseph A. Komonchak, "1962: The Second Vatican Council," Christian History Institute, https://christianhistoryinstitute.org/magazine/article/second-vatican-council.

1. Pre-catechumenate: "A time for evangelization, for inquiry and introduction to the gospel, a time for the beginnings of faith"
   Rite of Acceptance
2. Catechumenate: "A time for catechesis and formation"
   Rite of Election
3. Purification and Enlightenment: "An intense time of spiritual growth, a kind of retreat in preparation for the celebration of the sacraments"
   Rite of Initiation
4. Postbaptismal Catechesis or Mystagogy: "A time for deepening the Christian experience and entering more fully into the life of the faithful"[16]

This is conceived as a seamless process in which evangelism is an essential first step leading eventually to full participation in the life of the church. Notable in this process is the role of the church—the priority of ecclesiology—as the locus of every phase of a person's life of faith.

In his first book on liturgical evangelism, published in 1986, Robert Webber (1933–2007), a longtime professor of historical theology at Wheaton College, adopted these four stages and three rites verbatim and presented them as a model for the local church's liturgical evangelism. Fifteen years later, he cast the four stages in more user-friendly—though still ancient—terms: *seeker, hearer, kneeler,* and *faithful.* In between each stage, a public rite of passage occurs in the church: a rite of welcome after the first stage, the enrollment of names after the second stage, and baptism after the third stage.

1. A time for Christian inquiry, known as the *seeker* period
   Rite of Welcome
2. A time of instruction, when the converting person is known as a *hearer*
   Enrollment of Names
3. An intensive spiritual preparation for baptism, when the candidate is known as a *kneeler*
   Rite of Baptism

16. Lawrence E. Mick, *RCIA: Renewing the Church as an Initiating Assembly* (Collegeville, MN: Liturgical Press, 1989), 55–56.

4. A time after baptism for incorporating the new Christian into the
full life of the church, when the newly baptized person is known as
faithful[17]

Epiclesis, a nondenominational church in Sacramento, claims to be the
first church founded on this ancient-future foundation. Epiclesis integrates
church members through the four stages of seeker, hearer, kneeler, and
faithful. In its vision statement, the church as sacrament and the church as
herald, the two ecclesiological models mentioned earlier, can be glimpsed:
"In line with Scripture, creed, and tradition, it is our deepest desire to embody God's purposes in the mission of the Church through our theological
reflection, our worship [church as sacrament], our spirituality, and our life
in the world, all the while proclaiming that Jesus is Lord over all creation
[church as herald]."[18]

Practical Foundations

There is a rich coherence to this model that arises from its historical underpinnings. Rooted in Scripture, delineated in Hippolytus's *Apostolic Tradition*,
refined in the RCIA, and adapted for Protestants by Robert Webber, the basics
of liturgical evangelism are clear and precise—and, therefore, they can be
readily applied, with various modifications of language and practice, to the
life of a local church.

1. Invigorate Public Worship

Worship is the wellspring, the lifeblood of the church, the *ekklēsia*, the
gathered community. Worship is a public activity that happens when believers
come together for any reason: to offer praise to God; to celebrate the mighty
acts of God past, present, and future; to confess the ways the community has

17. Robert E. Webber, *Journey to Jesus: The Worship, Evangelism, and Nurture Mission
of the Church* (Nashville: Abingdon, 2001), 11. The Ancient-Future Faith Network (AFFN)
continues in Webber's trajectory to foster church life and liturgy around these principles.
AFFN is a nonprofit, cross-denominational association of like-minded Christian individuals
and churches—evangelicals of all kinds with a longing to return to classic Christian orthodoxy
and practice, and a deep hunger for renewal in the worship and spirituality of the church. For
more on AFFN, see their website: https://www.ancientfuturefaithnetwork.org.
18. "About Our Church," Epiclesis, https://www.epiclesis.org/about-our-church.

fallen short of God's desires; to listen to God's word in Scripture and sermon; and to receive food for the journey into the world as vital witnesses to the person of Jesus Christ. "Through participation in worship—in the word read and proclaimed, in intercession, in praise, thanksgiving, and communion—the church's members offer themselves anew and are empowered anew for what Henri Nouwen has called 'service and prayer in memory of Jesus Christ.'"[19] Celebrating a weekly worship service that "does God's story" with these elements is essential to liturgical evangelism.[20]

Along with these elements, invigorating public worship requires paying particular attention to welcoming visitors in every way possible. This entails explaining insider language and actions in worship—and even eliminating what is unnecessary—that keep visitors from fully participating in worship. There is a great deal in Christian worship—actions and words insiders know but visitors do not—that can actually blunt the evangelistic impulse of liturgy. I remember hearing someone say that he was absolutely alarmed when he heard someone standing before an altar covered in cloths and declaring, "This is my body." He actually thought there was a corpse underneath the cloths rather than glasses of grape juice and loaves of bread.

Insider actions and language do not pose an insurmountable challenge; in fact, they create an evangelistic opportunity. Consider as a church creating a welcoming glossary of terms and actions in which you clarify for visitors, first of all, that they are welcome and, second of all, that you want them to feel at home despite some strange terms and activities. In the glossary, include definitions of terms such as *hymn*, *narthex*, *doxology*, and *creed*, and explain actions that may seem strange. Also include FAQs (Frequently Asked Questions) such as: Why do Christians bow their heads in prayer? Why do they collect money in small baskets or tins? Why do they "pass the peace"? Why does a priest or pastor dress up in robes? Why do so many churches have pews rather than chairs? If you do this well, you will make visitors feel welcome, *and* you will communicate essential ingredients of the gospel. This invigorates public worship for all.

19. Joe G. Burnett, "Christ Has Died, Christ Is Risen, Christ Will Come Again: Toward a Liturgical Evangelism," *Journal for the Academy of Evangelism in Theological Education* 1 (1985–86): 47–48. The quotation from Nouwen comes from his book *The Living Reminder: Service and Prayer in Memory of Jesus Christ* (New York: Seabury, 1981).

20. I am grateful to Chris Alford, pastor of Epiclesis and founder of AFFN, for this phrase.

2. Integrate Evangelistic Preaching

An effective means of intensifying evangelism before and during the inquiry stage (the initial phase of liturgical evangelism) is to preach a series of evangelistic sermons. While this sort of preaching looks primarily toward seekers and the unchurched, it also serves to remind believers of who they are in light of the good news of the gospel. Sermons like these "remind them of their citizenship. They help them remember who they are and to what they have been called and commissioned. . . . Evangelistic sermons rekindle the gospel mandate within believers."[21]

Evangelistic sermons are not the work of sleazy or slick salespeople. They are the product of thoughtful efforts to pare the Christian message down to basics; they are attempts to drill down to the bedrock of what is essential to the Christian faith. They are meant to meet head on the searching gaze of inquirers, who may have little familiarity with the Christian tradition but who may, too, have more than their share of interest and intellect.

Evangelistic sermons keep Christology, particularly Jesus's death on the cross, central. Evangelist Billy Graham appealed repeatedly and effectively to Paul's words in 1 Corinthians 2:2: "For I decided to know nothing among you except Jesus Christ, and him crucified." We could do worse than to cover Graham's fourfold outline of this message in the context of an evangelistic sermon:

- everyone has sinned and fallen short of God's glory (Rom. 3:23);
- salvation through Christ's death on the cross is accessible for everyone;
- everyone must respond in repentance with a change of life and priorities;
- there is a cost for coming to Christ: the cost of discipleship.[22]

These points can certainly be adapted. I, for example, would include in this list a stronger emphasis on the bodily resurrection of Jesus and the gift of the Holy Spirit. Still, Graham's outline provides an apt starting point for a short series of sermons intended to be especially inviting to those who do not yet claim the Christian faith as their own.

21. Craig Loscalzo, *Evangelistic Preaching That Connects: Guidance in Shaping Fresh and Appealing Sermons* (Downers Grove, IL: InterVarsity, 1995), 73.
22. Billy Graham, *A Biblical Standard for Evangelists* (Minneapolis: World Wide Publications, 1984), 51–52.

While these sermons are directed to inquirers, they also offer the entire community gathered in worship a time to respond in repentance, in a change of perspective and priorities. Repentance comes with the simple admission of heading in the wrong direction, of missing the mark (which is the essential meaning of the verb *hamartanō* typically translated as "to sin"). As Peter says in Acts 2:38, "Change your hearts and lives" (CEB). Such a change—from death to life, from brokenness to healing, from life apart from God to life with God for eternity—comes through the power of the simple but stunning message of the cross (1 Cor. 1:18). This can occur through a public statement of confession of sin or perhaps a time for individuals to consider their sins in silence. In whatever way it takes place, repentance involves an acknowledgment of sin and a pledge to proceed differently, with a keen eye for the cross of Jesus Christ, his resurrection, and his eventual victory over darkness and death.

3. Utilize the Liturgy of the Church Year for Conversion and Initiation

Liturgical evangelism "brings the converting person into Christ and the church through periods of increasing intensity and commitment."[23] The church's liturgy throughout the church year moves people from initial inquiry to conversion to full participation along these stages: inquiry, rite of entrance, catechumenate, rite of election, purification and enlightenment, rite of initiation, and mystagogia.[24]

Inquiry. In this stage, the whole church (clergy and laity) is to engage in gospel-talk and gospel-deeds with neighbors, friends, family, and acquaintances, to encourage initial interest in and inquiry into the Christian faith. This is precisely the point where other models of evangelism can accompany liturgical evangelism. Pray for opportunities for conversations in personal evangelism. Set up small groups for evangelism. Send people into the neighborhood for visitation evangelism. These and other models—presented in subsequent chapters—can function in harmony during this phase of evangelism. This is not so much a time of convincing as a time of inquiry, not so much a period of conversion as a period of invitation.

Rite of Entrance. This first rite of passage marks publicly the inquirer's decision to advance deeper in the Christian faith, to enter a more formal

---

23. Webber, *Celebrating Our Faith*, 38.
24. Webber, *Celebrating Our Faith*, 109. See also Frank C. Senn, *The Witness of the Worshiping Community: Liturgy and the Practice of Evangelism* (New York: Paulist Press, 1993), 146–47.

relationship with the congregation. This can be physically—and liturgically—enacted by beginning the rite in the narthex or gathering place. The inquirers then walk into the sanctuary and sit among the worshipers. If it is not too off-putting, this rite offers the opportunity for inquirers to state their name, their reason for making this decision, and their renunciation of their old life as they seek to live into new life in Christ. This is a rite that can also invigorate those who have been celebrating the liturgy week by week; the insight and enthusiasm of newcomers to the faith often has that impact.

The Catechumenate. This is the period of substantive instruction into the mysteries of the Christian faith. Its depth is such that it cannot possibly be covered in an hour on a Sunday after church, complete with lunch, as often happens prior to admitting someone to full membership. What can possibly be covered in any depth in sixty minutes, beyond asking people to introduce themselves and do a quick read-through of membership vows? An hour or two on a Sunday afternoon is a long way from the one to three years that the early church expected of converts.

Recent studies and surveys have pointed out that biblical illiteracy is on the rise and, with it, there is a growing lack of familiarity with the Christian faith. In this respect, modern culture is not far from pre-Constantinian culture, in which people knew almost nothing about Christianity. In our world, where many have little or no Christian memory, the catechumenate provides the perfect time to deepen and expand instruction for Christian faith and living. Without this intentional period of learning, it is all too easy for a new convert to drift away from their initial commitment or enter a world of dangerous alternatives.

This happened to an Irish farmer who theologian Billy Abraham led to Christ: "It was a kind of textbook conversion. The person concerned had been searching for God for weeks and was ripe to come to repentance and faith in Jesus Christ. It was a moving experience to see him find liberty and joy in the Holy Spirit." When Billy came back to the area for a visit several years later, he asked about how the farmer fared. Billy was told that, shortly after the man's conversion, he was taken "under the wing of a group of bigoted, political, anti-Catholic Christians who proceeded to initiate him into a form of Christianity which was profoundly inadequate and deeply hostile to vital dimensions of the kingdom of God."[25]

25. William J. Abraham, *The Art of Evangelism: Evangelism Carefully Crafted into the Life of the Local Church* (Sheffield, UK: Cliff College Publishing, 1993), 74.

A straightforward proposal for organizing the catechumenate is to delve deeply into the Apostles' Creed or the Nicene Creed, taking one section per teaching session. A creed has a long-standing tradition in the church as a catechetical, or teaching, document. It offers "a map that lays out the fundamental contours of how the Christian thinks about God, about Christ, and about the Holy Spirit. As such, it is particularly well suited to meet the needs of the beginner who is seeking to grasp the theological essentials of the community that he or she is called to join in baptism."[26] While a creed supplies the intellectual substructure of faith, it is essential, too, to introduce new believers and inquirers to the disciplines of the faith. These can include regular worship, fasting, prayer, methods of Bible study, and generosity in giving.

Another approach is an in-depth study of Jesus's Sermon on the Mount (Matt. 5–7), which enjoys a long, rich, catechetical history that includes church leaders such as Augustine, John Wesley, and Dietrich Bonhoeffer, all of whom adopted it as the basis for their instruction.[27] The Sermon on the Mount contains Jesus's wonderful—and extraordinarily challenging—teaching about what a follower of Jesus looks like (in the Beatitudes), what it means to fulfill the demands of God's teaching or torah in daily life, how to pray, how to forgive, how to avoid hypocrisy, how to build a life on a rock-solid foundation rather than on sand—and other topics that are essential to the life of faith.[28]

The Rite of Election. In this rite of passage, which generally takes place on the first Sunday of Lent, catechumens come before the congregation to be examined. The catechumen's sponsor, enlisted as a spiritual mentor to walk alongside, attests to the catechumen's learning, transformation, and personal conduct. If all is as it should be, she is then set apart for the next stage of purification and enlightenment. The congregation, who has witnessed this public assessment of the catechumen's faith, promises to pray for her.

Purification and Enlightenment. During the next six weeks, intensity and commitment ramp up. Catechumens and their sponsors meet more frequently in proximity to the rite of initiation, when the catechumens will renounce the principalities and powers of the kingdom of darkness and enter the kingdom

26. Abraham, *Logic of Evangelism*, 150–51.

27. Jaroslav Pelikan, *Divine Rhetoric: The Sermon on the Mount as Message and as Model in Augustine, Chrysostom, and Luther* (Crestwood, NY: St. Vladimir's Seminary Press, 2001), 101. Bonhoeffer, for instance, used it as the framework for his classic exposition on what it means to follow Christ. Dietrich Bonhoeffer, *The Cost of Discipleship* (New York: Macmillan, 1963).

28. According to Baucum, *Evangelical Hospitality*, 110, Jesus intended this teaching to provide an "ethical center" for his followers.

of light. This is the time, then, to discern the sin that resides within and to develop armor for the ongoing struggle against its manifestation.[29] This period offers "a time for reflection, a time to enter the desert and be alone. . . . The image of the desert has always represented going to the heart of a conflict."[30] This was true for Jesus. Following the beauty and grace of his baptism, when he heard God's reassuring voice and saw the dove descend through the broken clouds, Jesus was driven (the verb is a harsh one, *ekballō*) into the wilderness for forty days, during which period he was tempted by Satan (Mark 1:12–13).[31] Jack Levison writes, "No sooner does he have this moment of clarity than it is torn from him, because the truest measure of clarity emerges for Jesus not in the singular confines of a moment's revelation—however idyllic it may be—but in the dogged days of testing in the desert. Jesus is not entitled to a lifetime supply of perfect springtimes; he is destined to endure late summer as well. Those are the dog days, the desert days, that test his mettle."[32] In the same way, following Jesus's model, this time of purification and enlightenment tests the catechumen's resolve for following Jesus's path to death and, after death, to new life.

The Rite of Initiation. This rite happens during a two- to three-hour vigil on the Saturday night preceding the dawn of Easter. The liturgical timing underscores Jesus as *Christus Victor*, who conquered the kingdom of darkness

---

29. Patrick Keifert, *Welcoming the Stranger: A Public Theology of Worship and Evangelism* (Minneapolis: Fortress, 1991), 105.

30. Webber, *Celebrating Our Faith*, 78.

31. Regarding the verb *ekballō*, Jack Levison writes,

This is an explosive verb—*ekballein*—related to the English word *ballistic*. The Holy Spirit drives Jesus out in the same way that Jesus *drives out* demons (Mark 1:34, 39), *drives out* mourners from the room of a dead child (5:40), and *drives out* the money changers from the temple precincts (11:15). With this powerful verb Jesus even communicates how high the stakes are as he commands his disciples, "If your eye causes you to stumble, *drive it out*; it is better for you to enter the kingdom of God with one eye than to have two eyes and to be thrown into hell" (9:47 alt.). The word also surfaces in Jesus's story about the owner of a vineyard who sent a series of slaves to receive payment from recalcitrant tenants, who just as repeatedly rejected them. The tenants beat the slaves and eventually killed one, so the owner sent his son, thinking that the tenants would respect him at least. They did not. The mutinous vineyard workers recognized the owner's son and "seized him, killed him, and *drove him out* of the vineyard" (12:8 alt.). The verb *ekballein* could not be more violent than in this story. The gentleness of a dove following Jesus's baptism has been left behind by the violent force of the Spirit, driving Jesus out into the battlefield of Satan. (Jack Levison, *An Unconventional God: The Holy Spirit according to Jesus* [Grand Rapids: Baker Academic, 2020], 62–63)

32. Levison, *Unconventional God*, 62.

and established the everlasting kingdom of light. Here, as we remember Christ's crucifixion and celebrate his resurrection, catechumens are baptized with water in the midst of the congregation, who join the catechumens in the renewal of their own baptismal vows. Together they celebrate the Lord's Supper.

On the eve of Easter, new believers come into full participation in the community of faith; in turn, the community is refreshed by the presence of new and earnest believers in their midst. This is the genius of liturgical evangelism. Two words, two worlds, two realities that, at the start of this chapter, seemed as if they could hardly be farther apart, are joined at the hip. Liturgy cradles the good news of evangelism, while evangelism revitalizes the worshiping community—year after year after year.

Mystagogia. This deeper stage of learning provides the opportunity for the ongoing nurture and instruction of the newly initiated. It also sets the stage for a turn toward the world to be salt and light, recalling Jesus's words in the Sermon on the Mount (Matt. 5:13–16). During this phase, the evangelized become the evangelizers. It is an especially appropriate time, therefore, for enlisting the newly initiated, while they are in the throes of enthusiasm for their faith and new life, into the practice of evangelism. Proponents of liturgical evangelism are not the first to adopt this practical strategy. The Salvation Army had converts immediately get up on an overturned barrel to narrate their salvation to the gathered crowd, many of whom had recently been their comrades with a shared bottle or at a gambling table. Evangelists Emma and L. P. Ray recalled how, while they still basked in their conversion during a Sunday morning church service in 1890, they headed straight to the downtown Seattle saloon they had frequented to locate acquaintances with whom they "had danced, drank beer, and played cards, and they sang, prayed, and shared their experience."[33] The newly initiated, with the fires of faith brightly burning, can be valuable and winsome evangelists for enlisting new seekers for the inquiry stage. Liturgical evangelism is not a one-time event; it is a circular occurrence, a perennial source of outreach and renewal. Just as the church calendar repeats itself year after year, the church can discover new resources of renewal year after year through liturgical evangelism.

---

33. Emma J. Ray, *Twice Sold, Twice Ransomed: Autobiography of Mr. and Mrs. L. P. Ray* (Chicago: Free Methodist Publishing House, 1926), 53.

Appraisal

Liturgical evangelism provides churches, especially those that observe the church year, that adopt a highly structured weekly service, and that embrace ancient Christian traditions, a way to merge worship with evangelism. Often, such churches may be inclined to shy away from evangelism because its stereotypical revivalistic flavor conflicts with their more formal worship pattern and theological outlook. Like oil and water, liturgy and evangelism simply do not mix.

This chapter, I hope, has put the lie to that superficial claim to incompatibility. The power of liturgy opens up unique possibilities for evangelism week by week and year by year, possibilities rooted in public worship and attuned to the church season. This model embeds evangelism in the long-standing tradition of the church's preaching, worship, and catechesis. This model takes seriously the strength of mentoring, as it pairs inquirers with mature believers, both of whom benefit from this relationship. All the threads come together—worship, catechesis, evangelism, fellowship—in this weekly event so that people who participate regularly will be brought to conversion, catechized, and integrated into the body of Christ in all its fullness.

The incorporation of the evangelistic dimension of the faith can bring unbelievers to faith, of course, but it can also invigorate believers, who rediscover, through communion with new believers, the good news of Jesus Christ. The good news is always proclaimed in the liturgy, but it is easily taken for granted without the continual influx of new believers, who receive this news as good, who embrace this message with vigor, and who stand (especially in their fledgling days of faith) in need of the grace and wisdom of the community of faith.

How Evangelistic Is Liturgical Evangelism?

Integrating evangelism into a weekly liturgical service and the church-year cycle may appear to diminish the significance of evangelism in its own right; evangelism can easily get lost in the mix. Evangelism could also be reduced by its limitation to a particular period each year; the only targeted time of evangelism in this model takes place in the inquiry period—typically during the summer months—when church members are encouraged to strike up gospel-related conversations with friends, neighbors, family members, and acquaintances. Still, for many churches, focusing on evangelism at *any* point of the year would constitute an increase over their current practice.

To ensure that liturgical evangelism remains evangelistic, consider several ways to amplify evangelism. One simple way is to preach evangelistic sermons on a more regular basis, perhaps the first or last Sunday of the month, rather than only during the inquiry period. This pattern reminds the local church of its ongoing responsibility to share the gospel in every season of the year, and it has the practical impact of letting church members know on which Sundays it is best to invite those who express interest in the faith. Other ways of elevating evangelism throughout the year include the integration of other evangelism models in this book, such as regular training sessions in personal evangelism, setting up small groups for inquirers whose interest occurs outside the inquiry phase, and maintaining a relationship with the neighborhood through visitation evangelism. Supplementing liturgical evangelism with personal, small group, and visitation models of evangelism—as well as others we will discuss in the chapters ahead—will strengthen every model and create a robust cycle of growth in the church.

Is Liturgical Evangelism Too Time Consuming?

Liturgical evangelism is not intended to generate instantaneous conversions. Nor is it a quick fix to stem declining church membership. Therefore, it may seem too time consuming, too cumbersome, too focused on perfecting the saints rather than converting the seeker to be of much use. To devote an entire year to progress from conversion to initiation to full participation may seem impractical and over the top.

This objection can be countered by the realization that we live in an era when Christendom no longer dominates culture. We live in a culture much closer to the cultures surrounding the early church, in which paganism abounded. This gives us all the more reason and necessity, therefore, to approach evangelism as a deeper, more thoughtful, more time-intensive endeavor, which goes hand in glove with learning and worship. With so little familiarity with the faith, it is important to give inquirers an honest awareness of the world they are entering. No surprises. No hidden agendas. As much as possible, the Christian mysteries are laid bare in this evangelistic model.

This lengthy devotion to learning, we should also point out, is not mechanical. This is not an online course but a relationship—with the community as a whole but also with a mentor in the faith. Building in continual nurture decreases the chance that new converts will drift away once their initial enthusiasm wanes. Eugene Peterson, translator of *The Message*, puts the matter poignantly in his book *A Long Obedience in the Same Direction*:

> It is not difficult in such a world [of speed] to get a person interested in the message of the gospel; it is terrifically difficult to sustain the interest. Millions of people in our culture make decisions for Christ, but there is a dreadful attrition rate. Many claim to have been born again, but the evidence for mature Christian discipleship is slim. In our kind of culture anything, even news about God, can be sold if it is packaged freshly; but when it loses its novelty, it goes on the garbage heap. There is a great market for religious experience in our world; there is little enthusiasm for the patient acquisition of virtue, little inclination to sign up for a long apprenticeship in what earlier generations of Christians called holiness.[34]

A patient acquisition of virtue. A long apprenticeship. A long obedience in the same direction. These are what liturgical evangelism offers by situating the good news of Jesus Christ in the ongoing life of the church as it worships and serves (both *worship* and *service*, by the way, can be a translation of the same Greek word, *leitourgia*).

Where Does the Kingdom of God Fit in Liturgical Evangelism?

Writings about liturgical evangelism make almost no mention of the kingdom of God. The church evangelizes. The church tells the gospel story. The church receives the inquirers. The church catechizes. The church provides the rites and sacraments to initiate the converts. The church is all in all for liturgical evangelism. Full stop.

However, while the church and the kingdom of God are closely aligned, they are not the same. The church remains a primary witness to God's kingdom. The church points the way to the kingdom, invites all to enter it, and teaches people how to align their priorities with it, but the church is not, ultimately, the full embodiment of the kingdom. The church must always, like John the Baptist, point beyond itself to God's kingdom. The church's role in evangelism is, in fact, akin to John the Baptist, who famously said, "He must increase,

---

34. Eugene Peterson, *A Long Obedience in the Same Direction: Discipleship in an Instant Society*, 2nd ed. (Downers Grove, IL: InterVarsity, 2000), 16.

but I must decrease" (John 3:30). This is a reality of which the church must never, ever lose sight. It is the kingdom of God, launched by the life, death, resurrection, and ascension of Jesus, and culminating in his coming again in final victory, that must be the end all and be all of liturgical evangelism. Of evangelism, full stop.

Reflection Questions

- How would you appraise liturgical evangelism?
- Do you see cooperation between liturgy and evangelism?
- How might your church integrate liturgical evangelism? If not all of it, what aspects might be most applicable?
- How can the laity engage in liturgical evangelism when it tends to emphasize clergy tasks, like liturgy, worship, and preaching?
- Which other model of evangelism best complements liturgical evangelism? Why?

FIVE

CHURCH GROWTH

T he founder of the church growth movement, Donald McGavran, once told the story of his encounter with a minister from a small town in the Ohio cornfields. The story illustrates church growth's goal, which is to establish "a living church of Jesus Christ in every segment of society."[1] It also illustrates the pushback that talk of church growth often meets. McGavran writes,

> Some years ago when I was speaking at a church growth seminar held in an Ohio town, one of the influential ministers in the town said to me, "I shall attend the seminar, but I am not really convinced that it is needed. Surely we have plenty of churches in this town, and every church is very cordial to all those who come. Most churches will see that visitors are called upon by either the minister or members of the evangelistic committee. We do not need to increase the number of congregations in this town. There are too many already."
>
> In preparation for the opening session I spent the next two days assembling some data—the population of the town, the number of churches, the seating capacity of each. At the first session of the seminar, without referring to this minister at all, I said, "In this town you have thirty thousand residents. There are sixty-one churches. Less than six thousand men and women are to be found in these churches on Sunday; twenty-four thousand will not be in church. Granted

1. Donald A. McGavran and Winfield C. Arn, *Ten Steps for Church Growth* (New York: Harper & Row, 1977), 21.

that church members number somewhat more than six thousand, it nevertheless seems perfectly clear that at least half and possibly two-thirds of the people in this town have yet to become genuine followers of Christ. This is the reason why you should emphasize church growth."[2]

Let's unpack this story. Notice first the resistance of the minister, who expresses the reluctance many Christian leaders feel about adopting church growth strategies. Notice second that church growth strategies incorporate real data and keen analysis, the likes of which many church leaders are unaware of or apprehensive about. Such data can often be disappointing, even unpalatable, because they shed light on whether churches are growing numerically or not. Notice third that McGavran does not talk about discipleship, intensity of commitment, or depth of theological awareness. He talks primarily about who is *not* in church on any given Sunday. This third element gives the church growth model its quick pulse. Church growth advocates believe that the church grows fastest when the focus of evangelism is conversion growth, or "winning the lost," as opposed to biological or transfer growth—that is, having babies and baptizing them or offering something new and different in order to draw people to your church from one down the street.[3]

What is the engine, then, that drives the church growth model of evangelism? Certainly not brick and mortar—impressive buildings with cafés and the latest technology. Definitely not committees and bylaws. What fuels a growing church is captured in the Greek word for church: *ekklēsia*. As we saw in chapters 3 and 4, this is a dynamic word referring to an assembly of people called out and together by the gospel message in order to call others into their local *ekklēsia*.

Biblical Foundations

Biblical inspiration for the church growth model of evangelism can be summarized in two texts: Matthew 28:18–20 and Acts 1:8. Jesus's words to his disciples at the end of Matthew's Gospel are essential to this model:

2. Donald A. McGavran, *Effective Evangelism: A Theological Mandate* (Phillipsburg, NJ: Presbyterian and Reformed, 1988), 42.
3. For more on the different kinds of growth, see McGavran, *Effective Evangelism*, 43. See also Donald A. McGavran, *Understanding Church Growth*, 2nd ed. (Grand Rapids: Eerdmans, 1980), 98–100.

And Jesus came and said to them, "All authority in heaven and on earth has been given to me. Go therefore and make disciples of all nations, baptizing them in the name of the Father and of the Son and of the Holy Spirit, and teaching them to obey everything that I have commanded you. And remember, I am with you always, to the end of the age." (Matt. 28:18–20)

Jesus's Great Commission, the magisterial conclusion to Matthew's Gospel, contains the seeds of two distinct but related tasks. Discipling, the first stage of evangelism for McGavran, appears in verse 19: "Go therefore and make disciples of all nations . . ." Discipling encompasses bringing the good news of the gospel to nonbelievers with the intention of "winning the lost" for Christ. "Faithfulness to God implies doing our part, empowered by the Holy Spirit, to persuade all men and women to become disciples of Jesus Christ and responsible members of his church."[4] This definition is different from what many Christians mean by discipling; they understand it as a second stage of faith following conversion, with a growth in spiritual disciplines and practices. It evokes the image of a mentor-protégé relationship, in which one individual guides another deeper into the disciplines of faith. Not for McGavran. Discipling is evangelism.

The most effective discipling takes place within a people movement, when an entire people converts to Christianity. McGavran translates the next phrase of the Great Commission ("all nations [*ethnē*]") as "all *people* or *peoples*." By "people," he means a closely interrelated group, which functions together as a unit—that is, as something more unified than an aggregate of individuals. The ideal, then, is to disciple a people together, not individual by individual, as in personal evangelism, and to launch a people movement that turns *en masse* to Christianity.

McGavran sees evidence for such people movements in the book of Acts: three thousand Jews at Pentecost (2:41), many Samaritans (8:5–12), and the entire villages of Lydda and Sharon (9:35). McGavran applauds these group conversions because they leave intact existing social structures and familiar surroundings. Proceeding even further, McGavran cautions against baptizing a convert or two immediately and suggests that evangelists wait until more are ready to make a decision for Christ. Then they proceed to baptism together. "Ostracism is very effective against one lone person," he argues.

4. Donald A. McGavran, *Understanding Church Growth*, 3rd ed. (Grand Rapids: Eerdmans, 1990), 9.

"But ostracism is weak indeed when exercised against a group of a dozen. And when exercised against two hundred it has practically no force at all."[5]

If making disciples is the first stage in church growth, perfecting is the second. This stage, which follows discipling, emerges in Jesus's words in the final verse of Matthew's Gospel: ". . . and teaching them to obey everything that I have commanded you" (28:20). *Perfecting* focuses on teaching converts about the Christian life, helping them to cultivate their spiritual practices in adherence to holy living and equipping them to develop appropriate ethical convictions. In this stage, the new Christian grows into what McGavran calls a "responsible member" of the church.[6]

Perfecting, while indispensable for Christian formation, plays second fiddle to discipling. McGavran even assigns a sequence to each stage: first, disciple as widely as possible when people are especially receptive to the gospel message and only then, as enthusiasm wanes, devote time to fostering a more perfect life of faith in new believers. Receptivity to the gospel message always takes precedence over refining Christian behavior and practice. In the tension between discipling and perfecting, the priority goes to discipling.

Jesus's command in the second indispensable text, Acts 1:8, is strategic for this vision of church growth: "But you will receive power when the Holy Spirit has come upon you; and you will be my witnesses in Jerusalem, in all Judea and Samaria, and to the ends of the earth." These words, spoken to the disciples gathered in Jerusalem forty days after Jesus's resurrection and just prior to his ascension, supply proponents of church growth with a concrete strategy for extending the gospel from familiar (Jerusalem) to unfamiliar territories (all Judea and Samaria, and to the ends of the earth). Missiologist Ralph Winter labels these concentric circles in Acts 1:8 as E-1, E-2, and E-3 evangelism.[7] In E-1, or "near-neighbor evangelism," no cultural or linguistic barrier is crossed, though the evangelist still has the hard task of crossing the

---

5. Donald A. McGavran, "A Church in Every People: Plain Talk about a Difficult Subject," *Journal of the American Society for Church Growth* 9 (Fall 1998): 46.

6. McGavran, *Understanding Church Growth*, 3rd ed., 9.

7. Ralph D. Winter, "The Highest Priority: Cross-Cultural Evangelism," in *Let the Earth Hear His Voice: International Congress on World Evangelization, Lausanne, Switzerland*, Official Reference Volume: Papers and Responses, ed. J. D. Douglas (Minneapolis: World Wide Publications, 1975), 213–25. George Hunter refines Winter's enumerations into a sevenfold typology of evangelism that expands E-1 into four parts: E1-A through E1-D. (See McGavran, *Understanding Church Growth*, 2nd ed., 69–72.) Martha Grace Reese articulates a similar progression from easiest to hardest to reach by adopting a bandwidth metaphor. See Martha Grace Reese, *Unbinding the Gospel: Real Life Evangelism* (St. Louis: Chalice, 2006), 87–91.

frontier between faith and nonfaith—what McGavran, taking his cue from Paul's letter to the Corinthians, refers to as "the offense of the cross."[8] E-1 evangelism for Jesus's disciples would have taken place first in and around Jerusalem, among those who shared a common language and customs. Similarly, in our day, E-1 evangelism summons us to seek out acquaintances, friends, and family and to share with them the good news of the gospel. As we saw in personal evangelism, "the gospel spreads most effectively across an existing network of trust relationships."[9]

The next concentric circle, E-2, is more difficult to reach with the gospel. E-2 evangelism engages people whose culture and social class, language and geographical location, or some combination of these factors are different from the evangelist's. Consider Jesus's followers in Acts, who had to flee from Jerusalem; this E-2 phase of evangelism did not come naturally, even to those in the earliest church. After the persecution that drove Jesus's followers from Jerusalem, Luke recalls, "Those who were scattered because of the persecution that took place over Stephen traveled as far as Phoenicia, Cyprus, and Antioch, and they spoke the word to no one except Jews. But among them were some men of Cyprus and Cyrene who, on coming to Antioch, spoke to the Hellenists also, proclaiming the Lord Jesus" (Acts 11:19–20). Only *some* of Jesus's followers dared to speak to Hellenists, to those who spoke Greek.[10]

Winter differentiates between the first two circles in this way: he likens E-1 evangelism to the apostle Paul's work among the Jews, his own people. After all, his Jewish pedigree is undeniable—"circumcised on the eighth day, a member of the people of Israel, of the tribe of Benjamin, a Hebrew born of Hebrews; as to the law, a Pharisee; as to zeal, a persecutor of the church; as to righteousness under the law, blameless" (Phil. 3:5–6). E-2 evangelism, then, compares to Paul's work among the Greeks, a different people group both culturally and theologically. This distinction echoes the phrase in Paul's letters "to the Jew first and also to the Greek" (Rom. 1:16). In many cosmopolitan neighborhoods all over the world today, where different cultures, social classes, and linguistic groups live alongside each other, E-2 evangelism does

---

8. McGavran, *Understanding Church Growth*, 3rd ed., 168. See 1 Cor. 1:17–25.

9. Tom Stebbins, *Friendship Evangelism by the Book: Applying First-Century Principles to Twenty-First-Century Relationships* (Camp Hill, PA: Christian Publications, 1995), 72.

10. The manuscript tradition of the Greek text is tortured here; it seems best to suggest that the Greeks or Hellenists in this passage are *not* Jews.

not require a long-distance move; it can happen as people—and churches—cross the street or the backyard to engage in conversations about the gospel.

The third phase, E-3, expands these differences exponentially—"to the ends of the earth"—to people who "live, work, talk, and think in languages and cultural patterns utterly different from those native to the evangelist."[11] These people are considered "unreached" because there is not a church in their midst that can engage in E-1 or E-2 evangelism. E-3 evangelism requires a massive commitment of time and resources to invest in learning the language, culture, and customs of a very different context, with the ultimate aim of being able to engage in E-2 evangelism, then eventually in E-1 evangelism. E-1 and E-2 evangelism will keep most of us reading this book fully occupied. At the same time, we can financially and prayerfully support people and ministries tackling E-3 evangelism.

Theological Foundations

Church growth is grounded in what McGavran calls "harvest theology."[12] Think here of an actual harvest in a garden or in a farmer's field. *Harvest* as a noun refers to the time when the crops are ready; it is also a verb referring to the process of gathering in the crops. These are the two uses to which practitioners of this model put the word *harvest*.

At the heart of harvest theology is a God who has always reached out, found people, and brought them in. God finds Israel in Egypt, for instance, and binds them as God's people through a covenant—an agreement—at Sinai. This God, quick to search and quicker still to find, sends Jesus Christ, Lord of the Harvest, into the world to ready the harvest. Jesus himself recognizes the need for harvesters and reapers to gather the lost. Jesus instructs his disciples to pray that God will send people willing to work, laborers, into the harvest (Matt. 9:37–38; Luke 10:2). Jesus taught in parables about finding what is lost—the lost sheep (Matt. 18:12–14; Luke 15:3–7), the lost coin (Luke 15:8–10), the lost son (15:11–32). Jesus told the story, too, about a master who

11. Winter, "Highest Priority," 218.
12. "Harvest theology" contrasts with what is known as "search theology," a prevalent theological perspective undergirding many mainline and ecumenical mission and evangelism organizations in the mid- to late twentieth century. Church growth proponents criticize search theology, charging it with an aversion to numerical results and with a nebulous form of Christian witness, often practicing philanthropic work but not the kind of evangelism that results in conversion growth. For a robust discussion of search theology, see McGavran, *Understanding Church Growth*, 2nd ed., 23–40.

kept issuing invitations to more and more people until enough were found to come to the banquet and fill all the places (14:15–24).

From this parable we also learn that the master did not return again and again to invite those who were disinterested or resistant. The master adopted another strategy, and he extended the invitation until the banquet was full. Along a similar vein, Jesus encourages his disciples not to stay too long with those who refuse to respond to the gospel. The disciples, the harvesters, should instead "shake off the dust" from their feet and move on to more receptive people (Matt. 10:14). Paul and Barnabas's adoption of this symbolic practice in Acts suggests a familiarity with Jesus's saying. Religious leaders in Antioch "incited the devout women of high standing and the leading men of the city, and stirred up persecution against Paul and Barnabas, and drove them out of their region. So they shook the dust off their feet in protest against them, and went to Iconium" (Acts 13:50–51).

The view of the church—the ecclesiology—at the heart of this model of evangelism, if we refer again to Avery Dulles's models, is the church as herald because of its emphasis on the proclamation of the gospel. "The mission of the Church [as herald]," explains Dulles, "is to proclaim that which it has heard, believed, and been commissioned to proclaim. . . . [The Church] receives an official message with the commission to pass it on."[13] A church centered on harvest theology will be missional in its outlook, with a passion for the Great Commission (Matt. 28:16–20) as its bedrock. It will, in partnership with the God of the harvest, continually and constantly move outside itself, transcending familiar boundaries (Acts 1:8) to encounter receptive peoples and establish new local churches among every people group. McGavran believes that "the God Who Finds is now and always will be in charge of His mission" until everyone on earth has heard the gospel from someone who speaks their own language and "whose word is unobstructed by cultural barriers. . . . Thus [this person] speaks a theology of harvest."[14]

Historical Foundations

The church growth movement cultivated a research-based, tactical approach to growing churches that evolved from McGavran's prototype, which he

13. Avery Dulles, *Models of the Church*, expanded ed. (New York: Doubleday, 1987), 76.
14. McGavran, *Understanding Church Growth*, 2nd ed., 39.

developed while he worked with churches in India. The child of missionary parents in India, McGavran (1897–1990) went on, in the 1930s, to serve as superintendent of the Disciples of Christ work in Central India, where he honed his analytical skills. As he analyzed annual membership reports from 145 congregations, he discovered that 134 churches had stagnated or declined, while only 11 churches grew at a rate of 20 percent yearly or more. As he visited various churches, he asked the obvious question, "Why is/isn't your church growing?" He received inconclusive answers and sometimes the same answer for both why the church was declining and why it was growing. Regarding a church's growth, church leaders responded, "Because we preach the pure Word of God." Regarding a church's decline, they responded, "Because we preach the pure Word of God!" Clearly something had to give, so, on the basis of these encounters, McGavran did substantial research into why churches grow or why they decline. According to George Hunter, who relates this story, McGavran also developed "reproducible principles" for growth that would be applicable in other contexts.[15]

McGavran's work was pioneering, though not unprecedented. He built his own work on J. Waskom Pickett's field research classic, *Christian Mass Movements in India*. Pickett (1890–1981), a Methodist missionary who served in India for forty-six years, utilized field research—questionnaires, interviews, observations, and cultural analysis—to understand how and why churches grow. McGavran claimed he "'lit [his] candle at Pickett's fire,' mastered [Pickett's] research methods, added [his] own and took up where Pickett left off."[16]

Then in 1961, McGavran set up the Institute of Church Growth in North America at Fuller Theological Seminary in Pasadena, California. Originally, he referred to the missiological insights he had discovered as "evangelism," but the word *evangelism*, even in the sixties, proved difficult for many to accept, so he adopted the moniker *church growth* instead. "To McGavran, church growth, or evangelism, simply meant the process of winning people to Christ and incorporating them into a local church to grow in their new-found faith. Toward the end of his life, he began using a new term—effective evangelism—to reference what he was advocating."[17] He titled his autobiog-

---

15. George G. Hunter III, *To Spread the Power: Church Growth in the Wesleyan Spirit* (Nashville: Abingdon, 1987), 21–22.

16. Hunter, *To Spread the Power*, 23.

17. Gary L. McIntosh, "The Roots of Donald A. McGavran's Evangelistic Insights," *Journal of Evangelism & Missions* 7 (Spring 2008): 67.

raphy, published in his ninety-first year, *Effective Evangelism: A Theological Mandate*.

Fuller Theological Seminary no longer houses the Institute of Church Growth; however, several graduate theological programs continue to offer courses and degrees related to church growth, including Asbury Theological Seminary, Talbot School of Theology, Wheaton College, and several seminaries associated with the Southern Baptist Church. McGavran's legacy also includes the Church Growth Network, founded in 1987 and led by Gary McIntosh.[18] This network offers coaching, consulting, workshops, and seminars based on church growth methodology.

Practical Foundations

The church growth model of evangelism offers a coherent approach grounded in clear principles. These principles, in turn, are based on observations. The upshot of this model is a well-organized sequence of strategies, which includes the following:

- identifying bridge people
- finding receptive people
- multiplying homogeneous units
- developing new ports of entry
- planting new churches

Together, these elements make up the church growth model of evangelism.

1. Identify Bridge People

In a survey of church members in the United States, when asked, "What person was it that led you to faith in Christ?" they overwhelmingly identified a bridge person—a connector within a defined social network. For 43.2 percent of the respondents, a family member acted as the bridge person; for 15.7 percent, a friend; for 2.9 percent, a neighbor; and for 1.8 percent, a work colleague. Add these together and nearly 64 percent of people identify as having a bridge

18. "History of the Church Growth Network," McIntosh Church Growth Network, https://www.churchgrowthnetwork.com/welcome-to-home-test2.

person who introduced them to the gospel.[19] These statistics highlight a key church growth strategy—that bridge people are among the most valuable communicators of the good news. McGavran illustrates the importance of bridge people by drawing attention to what lies at each end of a bridge spanning a river. People gravitate there, settle down, and build towns and cities. Those who live nearest the bridge cross over the water easily because everything from ideas to groceries passes most conveniently there. It requires much more energy and ingenuity to cross a river where a bridge does not exist. Bridge people in a social network facilitate communication and connectivity.[20] In this model of evangelism, the initial task is to identify bridge people, cultivate in them an eagerness for evangelism, and equip them to carry it out. This can be done through their engagement with any of the evangelism models in this book.

2. Find Receptive People

Church growth advocates contend that at all times, in every season—in keeping with the harvest imagery—some people, some groups, some cultures are particularly open to hearing and responding to the gospel message. Identifying receptive people involves more than a hunch. Church growth strategists have developed a scale to provide markers for where individuals and people groups might fall on a *receptivity continuum* (see fig. 5.1).[21] People on the right end of this scale are more likely to be receptive to the gospel message; people on the left are less so.

Particularly during experiences of transition people become more receptive to the good news of Jesus Christ. Receptive people can often be found in

Figure 5.1
Resistance/Receptivity Scale

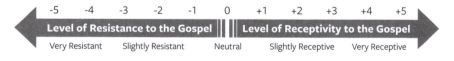

19. Gary L. McIntosh, *Growing God's Church: How People Are Actually Coming to Faith Today* (Grand Rapids: Baker Books, 2016), 95.
20. McGavran, *Understanding Church Growth*, 3rd ed., 253.
21. This scale appears in McGavran, *Understanding Church Growth*, 3rd ed., 189, though it originated in Edward R. Dayton's book *That Everyone May Hear: Reaching the Unreached*, 3rd. ed. (Monrovia, CA: MARC, 1983), 47.

new housing developments, among first-generation immigrants, among first-time visitors to church, and among those who find themselves in the middle of major life changes, such as a move, a new job, a divorce, an illness, or the death of a loved one. These are "the church's greatest apostolic opportunity"; for this reason, the second key to evangelism, along with identifying bridge people, is "to identify and reach receptive people while they are receptive."[22]

The consequences of this observation? The employment of resources, from people to finances, should be allocated to those on the right-hand side of the scale because maximal church growth occurs when receptivity is high. This strategy, which gives priority to making disciples, has a consequence for the second stage as well, the phase of perfecting believers. "One thing is clear—receptivity wanes as often as it waxes. Like the tide, it comes in and goes out. Unlike the tide, no one can guarantee when it goes out that it will soon come back again."[23] In other words, from a strategic standpoint, there will come a time later on when disciples can be perfected, but that happens on another day, when receptivity has lessened.

The strategy for those who are initially resistant to the gospel is also set out. They should not be entirely neglected; in other words, unlike in the biblical foundations cited above, we shouldn't "shake off the dust" and never return. Rather, the initially resistant should be prayed for and provided a Christlike presence until their receptivity grows. Then, once they've become more receptive, resources should be allocated to them.

3. Multiply Homogeneous Units

A basic principle of church growth—yet another one borne out by observation—is that people naturally connect with others who are similar to them. Social networks for the most part are homogeneous. Hence the adage "Birds of a feather flock together." This reality is applied, in church growth terms, in the *homogeneous unit principle*, which says that "people like to become Christian without crossing racial, linguistic, or class barriers."[24] We see this,

22. Hunter, *To Spread the Power*, 64.
23. McGavran, *Understanding Church Growth*, 3rd ed., 181.
24. McGavran, *Understanding Church Growth*, 3rd ed., 163. McGavran defines a homogeneous unit as a "section of society in which all the members have something in common." See David Britt, "From Homogeneity to Congruence: A Church-Community Model," in *Planting and Growing Urban Churches: From Dream to Reality*, ed. Harvie Conn (Grand Rapids: Baker, 1997), 136.

proponents point out, in the opening chapters of the book of Acts, in which the early church grew exponentially among Jews who stayed in Jerusalem, who remained within Judaism, and who maintained Jewish customs. This growth slowed dramatically, church growth advocates argue, when other cultures, especially the gentiles or Greeks, entered the church in large numbers.

Based on this principle, the multiplication of homogeneous units remains the most efficient and effective way to disciple all varieties of people groups, which together make up the human mosaic. This method is not intended to exclude anyone. On the contrary, the ultimate goal of the church growth movement is to reach all of humanity with the gospel. The most effective means of reaching all people, according to church growth observation and analysis, is through the establishment of homogeneous units around the globe. McGavran describes this as "a cluster of growing, indigenous congregations, every member of which remains in close contact with his kindred." He observes that "this cluster grows best if it is in one people, one caste, one tribe, one segment of society."[25]

This principle does not undermine the creation of heterogeneous, diverse congregations. Nor does it suggest that homogeneous churches are somehow of more worth than heterogeneous ones. Rather, it arises through observation and analysis, which leads McGavran to conclude that, for the purpose of rapid evangelism and church expansion with the aim of reaching the entire human race as quickly as possible, homogeneous units are highly effective.[26]

4. Develop New Ports of Entry

Another key strategy is to multiply the new groups. Why? Because new groups, which lack the baggage of established groups, grow more quickly than existing ones. These new groups offer unencumbered spaces where visitors can enter the church more easily. When the group structure and relationships within it are still in the works—when everything about it remains undetermined—people tend to feel safer to join; they can come in comfortably and find a way to fit in among others who are similarly new to the group. The group is free from insider language, from insider practices, and from insiders who communicate with each other more deeply than they do with newcomers. This strategy is rooted, like so much else in the church growth model, in

---

25. McGavran, "Church in Every People," 45.
26. McGavran, *Understanding Church Growth*, 3rd ed., 170.

the observation that once a period of newness and expansion tapers off, so do newcomers.

Ports of entry should arise from a church's awareness of its neighborhood and the needs and opportunities it presents, which can be identified through visitation evangelism. A church's caring and outreach ministry can play an important role in recognizing a group of people in a similar situation and developing an appropriate port of entry for them. One church found such a group when they began hosting a fun event on a monthly basis for children with special needs. Eighty children and their parents came the first night. During these events, church members began to realize that the parents also needed a group, so the church launched a program specifically geared to parents of children with special needs, which met during the children's event. This program resulted in many families being discipled.[27]

These children—and their parents, too—needed a port of entry geared for them, which this church provided. Through a thoughtful application of the homogeneous unit principle and an awareness of a community's needs, a church can consider how to provide new ports of entry (such as these groups for children with special needs and their parents), which are essential for reaching as many people in as many different circumstances as possible.

5. Plant New Churches

One final observation: "Churches after 15 years typically plateau. After 35 years, they typically can't even replace those [members] they lose. New congregations reach a lot more pre-Christian people."[28] With this statistic in mind, the effort to develop new ports of entry extends to the planting of new churches. Not just new ports of entry in established churches but new churches altogether are promoted by the church growth model of evangelism.

27. Hunter, To Spread the Power, 142.
28. George Hunter, quoted in Tim Stafford, "Go and Plant Churches of All Peoples," Christianity Today, September 2007, 69. A study from the Hartford Institute for Religion Research also confirms this to be true. "Typically, it is the early years of a congregation's life where the most rapid growth occurs. . . . In all areas, suburban, rural or urban, younger congregations are more likely to grow than older congregations. . . . After 15 to 20 years, the window of opportunity closes up and the 'adult' congregation does not grow as much, on average, as it did when it was more 'youthful.'" C. Kirk Hadaway, Facts on Growth: 2010 (Hartford, CT: Hartford Seminary, 2011), https://faithcommunitiestoday.org/wp-content/uploads/2019/01/FACTs-on-Growth-2010.pdf, 4.

There is a vast amount of literature on church planting; here I will briefly present only a few approaches for consideration. One approach occurs when an established church plants within itself, so to speak, one or more congregations, each made up of a different people group. This happens when bridge people intentionally cross racial, ethnic, linguistic, or class barriers to set up new, homogeneous congregations within these populations, which are then incorporated as separate churches within the established church. Examples of this model abound. First Baptist Church of Flushing, New York, for instance, describes itself as "a multiethnic, multicultural, multilingual, and cross-generational family serving in three congregations (English, Spanish and Chinese), all under one church."[29]

Another approach to church planting, frequently referred to in mother-daughter terms, takes place when an established church sends out a team from among its membership to begin a new church. Logistically, it is ideal for the mother church to launch the daughter church nearby to facilitate the transfer of personnel and resources. Eventually, the daughter church can become a fully independent church and then reproduce itself by setting up its own church plant and so on. This can also happen, without consideration of geography, through online media.[30] In 2006, Life.Church, a brick-and-mortar church with thirty-four campuses spread over ten states, launched an online daughter church called Church Online. It "meets" in every country in the world, with over ninety online services every week.[31] In this iteration of church planting, the mother church planted an online daughter church.

29. "About Us," First Baptist Church of Flushing, https://fbcflushing.org/welcome. Rodney Woo is critical of this approach because it has been used as a way to maintain homogeneity while appearing to embrace diversity. He cites the example of Wilcrest Baptist Church in Houston, Texas, which "originally established ethnic mission churches in the early 1980s in order to separate the African-Americans and the Chinese from the primary white congregation" (Rodney M. Woo, *The Color of Church: A Biblical and Practical Paradigm for Multiracial Churches* [Nashville: B&H, 2009], 51). Woo's book in its entirety sets out the vision and plan by which Wilcrest became a fully multiracial church. For more on Wilcrest Baptist Church within the larger context of multiracial churches in the US, see Michael Emerson with Rodney Woo, *People of the Dream: Multiracial Congregations in the United States* (Princeton: Princeton University Press, 2006).

30. Planting an online church can also proceed, and has done so for nearly three decades, without the resources of a single "mother church." In 1992, American Presbyterians established the first virtual Christian congregation, a nondenominational church called "The First Church of Cyberspace"; it hosted services until 2007. Alpha Church, planted in 1999 by the Reverend Patricia Walker, continues to operate as a fully online church. For more on Alpha Church, see chap. 8.

31. "About," Life.Church, https://www.life.church/online.

Still another approach occurs when an established church adopts an existing church that is ready to close its doors. The adopting church contributes financial resources and people to jump-start what becomes in essence a new church. This happened at Munger Place Methodist Church, founded in 1913 in East Dallas. Nearly a century later, in 2009, when the congregation became too small to continue, a large-membership church three miles away, Highland Park United Methodist Church (HPUMC), assumed responsibility of the Munger Place site, renovated the building, and planted a new church. Munger Place Church, resurrected in 2010 as an extension campus of HPUMC, now consists of a sizeable congregation of its own.[32]

Church planting is currently so widespread that an amorphous, global network, called the Church Planting Movement (CPM), has emerged. CPM churches spring up with relative spontaneity; they multiply rapidly by sweeping through a people group.[33] In the CPM network, there are reports of seventeen hundred churches and more than forty-two thousand new believers within one people group in India alone, as well as reports of a new church plant nearly every day in another people group in India.[34] The key strategy of these churches is to encourage the multiplication of new churches quickly and regularly. Once a church is planted, the pressing goal becomes to plant another church. In this respect, CPM is committed largely to only the first stage of McGavran's model: making disciples. The next stage, perfecting those disciples, tends to be supplanted in CPM churches by an all-out effort to keep planting new churches.

Appraisal

The church growth model of evangelism is a paradigm of practicality. With its penchant for statistical analysis, it peels off layers of alibis and excuses

32. "Our History," Munger Place Church, https://www.mungerplace.org/about/our-history. HPUMC continues to replicate this approach to church planting. See also the Grove Church: https://www.grove.org/.

33. David Garrison, *Church Planting Movements: How God Is Redeeming a Lost World* (Arkadelphia, AR: WIGTake Resources, 2004), 21.

34. "A Church a Day," Church Planting Movements, August 24, 2010, http://www.church plantingmovements.com/index.php/vertprofiles/vertcpmprofiles/113-a-church-a-day; "Tribal CMP in Middle India," Church Planting Movements, August 26, 2010, http://www.church plantingmovements.com/index.php/vertprofiles/vertcpmprofiles/114-tribal-cpm-in-middle-india. For best practices regarding the CPM, see www.churchplantingmovements.com.

in order to calculate whether a church is growing, then analyzes why or why not. Its reproducible principles for the stimulation of growth—create new ports of entry, develop homogeneous units, engage in E-1 evangelism, cultivate bridge people for negotiating E-2 and E-3 evangelism, and disciple receptive peoples—have been well researched and well tested for decades in contexts around the globe. Vital to these numbers, statistics, and strategies is that they serve a single vision of bringing the gospel to all unreached peoples by establishing a "living church of Jesus Christ in every segment of society."[35]

What can easily be overlooked in a preoccupation with numbers is the *kind* of growth that takes place. British pastor Ian Stackhouse offers a trenchant critique along these lines: "What is absent in church planting literature, and, more generally, in the whole gamut of methods deployed by churches in their desire to realise growth is an appreciation of the need for ongoing Christian nurture—nurture that is the basis upon which missionary congregations, so-called, can be sustained in the long-term."[36] This statement can be framed in terms of several probing questions: Is church growth figured quantitatively in increasing conversion statistics, bigger budget dollars, and a collection of spin-off churches? Are these the only indicators of growth to measure? When does perfecting, the second stage of church growth (the qualitative measure), enter the equation? Certainly, an emphasis on making disciples and planting churches can overwhelm church leaders and cause them to overlook the need for perfecting disciples by reaching down into the riches of Scripture and tradition.

Is It Valid to Separate Discipling and Perfecting?

The impact of the separation of discipling and perfecting, according to critics, is the following: without an emphasis on the ethical and transformational component of the good news, which McGavran relegates to a later phase of perfecting, evangelism inspires a shallow, unreflective, and impoverished faith. Critics contend that evangelism is more than winning the lost or getting someone saved; it must inculcate—from the start—a conviction that one's lifestyle and actions matter. Anything less, to use Dietrich Bonhoeffer's

---

35. McGavran and Arn, *Ten Steps for Church Growth*, 21.
36. Ian Stackhouse, *The Gospel-Driven Church: Retrieving Classical Ministry for Contemporary Revivalism* (Milton Keynes, UK: Paternoster, 2004), 28.

phrase, is "cheap grace": "Cheap grace is the preaching of forgiveness without requiring repentance, baptism without church discipline, communion without confession. . . . Cheap grace is grace without discipleship, grace without the cross, grace without Jesus Christ, living and incarnate."[37] Perfecting, if left to an indeterminate later phase, may seem ancillary or optional, if it happens at all.

Stackhouse again weighs in on the dichotomy McGavran championed, when he writes, "When growth replaces qualitative Christian nurture as the rationale of the church, traditional notions of initiation into the gospel are sacrificed on the altar of expediency, and pastoral care of the saints, in the somewhat ambiguous and messy business of real life, is set in opposition, unnecessarily and unbiblically, to the call to evangelise."[38]

Equally challenging to this dichotomy is the question of whether Mc-Gavran has read it into rather than out of the Great Commission in Matthew 28:18–20. In other words, Is it biblical? From the standpoint of Greek syntax, it is not. The command to "make disciples" is accompanied by three Greek participles: going, baptizing, and teaching. Though syntax is never quite so simple, we might put Matthew 28:18–20 in this way: Making disciples is the overall command. How are Jesus's followers to fulfill this command? By going, baptizing, and teaching. These are the three elements of making disciples. From this standpoint, making disciples does not precede perfecting them. It entails going to them, baptizing them when they believe, and teaching them about their belief. Going, baptizing, and teaching are part and parcel of making disciples. The syntax of the Great Commission, then, cannot be neatly subdivided into making disciples and perfecting disciples.

Add to this that the resurrected Jesus tells his followers they are to teach people "to obey everything that [he has] commanded [them]" (Matt. 28:20). This is hardly an afterthought. Not, at least, in the Gospel of Matthew, which contains the Sermon on the Mount, in which Jesus demands a better righteousness of his followers, in which Jesus demands complete integrity, in which Jesus claims that "until heaven and earth pass away, not one letter, not one stroke of a letter, will pass from the law until all is accomplished" (5:18). It can hardly be that now, resurrected and vested with all authority on heaven and earth, Jesus would relegate meticulous teaching to the back

37. Dietrich Bonhoeffer, *The Cost of Discipleship* (New York: Macmillan, 1963), 47. See also William J. Abraham, *The Logic of Evangelism* (Grand Rapids: Eerdmans, 1989), 84.

38. Stackhouse, *Gospel-Driven Church*, 28.

burner. Preferable to a sequential two-step, discipling first then perfecting at a later time, is to balance the two, spiritual growth and church growth advancing hand in hand, even including a modicum of perfecting from the start.

What Are the Implications of the Homogeneous Unit Principle?

Church growth advocates and their critics argue vociferously over the homogeneous unit principle. Advocates are quick to point out that they did not manufacture the principle; they *observed* it. In statistic after statistic, they saw that churches grew more rapidly when people found others with whom they felt at home. This observation about a rapid rate of growth—and the impulse to reach unreached people as quickly as possible—aligns with harvest theology. The appeal to enter the harvest is urgent; the compulsion to spread the good news is immediate. Once growth slows, advocates contend, there will be plenty of opportunity for the perfecting stage. At that point, when homogeneous units populate and even saturate a people group, churches will be able to reach across racial and ethnic divides and incorporate the ethical implications of the gospel, which breaks down "the dividing wall [of] hostility" between separated groups (Eph. 2:14).

Critics find the homogeneous unit principle reprehensible; they contend that it reinforces a status quo that rejects, inadvertently or intentionally, diversity. Think of the infamous quip that the eleven o'clock hour on Sunday morning is the most segregated block of time in the United States. Is it a credit to Christianity that people are willing—even eager—to gather in separate groups, divided by social status, race, and theological perspective? Is this not the very status quo that the good news of Jesus Christ is intended to overthrow?

Like advocates of the church growth model do, critics also appeal to the book of Acts, where they discover not just homogeneous units but churches like the one in Antioch, whose leaders come from different classes, ethnicities, and regions. Consider this description of the heterogeneous leadership team at Antioch: "Now in the church at Antioch there were prophets and teachers: Barnabas, Simeon who was called Niger, Lucius of Cyrene, Manaen a member of the court of Herod the ruler, and Saul. While they were worshiping the Lord and fasting, the Holy Spirit said, 'Set apart for me Barnabas and Saul for the work to which I have called them.' Then after fasting and praying they laid their hands on them and sent them off" (13:1–3).

There is so much to be said about this church. They were ethnically and economically diverse. Barnabas no longer owned what he once did, since he sold his property and laid the proceeds at the apostles' feet in Jerusalem (Acts 4:36–37). Acts 13:1 describes the prophets and teachers of the church at Antioch: Simeon was probably from North Africa. Lucius was from Cyrene, on the northern coast of Africa. Manaen was—or had been at one time—wealthy and Herod Antipas's friend from youth. Saul, from Tarsus, a coastal city in Asia Minor, was a trained Pharisee. Jack Levison writes of this group, "This is no homogeneous unit, held together by ethnic or social or economic uniformity. This is not a church with a target demographic, such as twentysomethings or suburbanites or urban dwellers or males between eighteen and forty—the target demographic of many megachurches. We have plenty of churches like this today."[39] The church at Antioch was not a homogeneous unit, yet it is this very church where believers were first called Christians (11:26), and it is this church that launched the first Christian mission (13:3).

The impasse between church growth advocates and critics may, at least in some situations, have begun to dissipate. Skip Bell, founding director of the Christian Leadership Center of Andrews University, offers several case studies that combine diversity with an emphasis on church growth. Sunrise Church, a Caucasian Baptist church launched nearly sixty years ago in Rialto, California, stagnated for years. Rather than continue to plateau as a homogeneous church, Sunrise opted to reflect more closely its community, which was 50 percent Hispanic. As a result, they began to grow. Racial and ethnic diversity are now a key part of Sunrise's DNA. Bell, a champion of churches such as Sunrise, notes, "The witness of the church communities we observed is that the emerging heterogeneity of some churches is the new 'homogeneity.' We are seeking places where diversity is the commonality that draws us together. As we live and work in multi-cultural settings, we wish to experience worship in the same context."[40]

---

39. Jack Levison, *Fresh Air: The Holy Spirit for an Inspired Life* (Brewster, MA: Paraclete, 2012), 162–63. Missiologists Steve Bevans and Roger Schroeder reiterate this same point: "As Acts begins, the community of disciples . . . sees itself as the true Israel . . . upon which the reign of God will dawn imminently. But as Acts progresses, the community slowly and even painfully begins to realize that something else is going on as the Spirit 'drives' or 'leads' it to include 'half-Jews' (Samaritans), individual Gentile proselytes or 'God-fearers' (the Ethiopian official), worthy Gentiles (Cornelius and his household) and, finally, Gentiles *en masse* (in Antioch)." Steve Bevans and Roger Schroeder, *Constants in Context: A Theology of Mission for Today* (Maryknoll, NY: Orbis Books, 2004), 10.

40. Skip Bell, "What Is Wrong with the Homogeneous Unit Principle? The HUP in the 21st Century Church," *Journal of the American Society for Church Growth* (January 2003): 16.

Where Does the Kingdom of God Fit into Church Growth?

An undue emphasis on numbers in the church growth model lends credence to the concern that sociological foundations are stronger than theological ones. The discussion of harvest theology, for instance, remains shallow and disconnected from other theological topics, such as Christology (Jesus Christ) or Pneumatology (the Holy Spirit). It could be argued that what this model lacks in theology it makes up for in practical strategies and statistically grounded principles. But in any model of evangelism, there should be a connection between theology and practice, between Scripture and strategies.

For instance, with such a strong commitment to *church* growth, where does the kingdom of God fit? There is little talk of the kingdom of God in most discussions of church growth, which is puzzling because Jesus himself spoke of the kingdom of God in terms of *growth*: a mustard seed, the smallest of all seeds, grows into a great bush (Mark 4:31–32). Even harvest language in this text is linked to the kingdom of God. Given criticisms leveled against the church growth movement, not least that it produces a shallow faith rooted in cheap grace, it would be wise for its advocates to draw a clearer and closer association between church growth and the growth of God's kingdom.

Some of church growth's most vocal critics are Latin American liberation theologians who contend that in their context of rampant, palpable oppression, evangelism must consist of more than an invitation into a port of entry alongside others from the same people group; it demands engagement on behalf of God's kingdom. To proclaim salvation in Jesus Christ, then, is to announce the coming of God's kingdom, which challenges—even reverses—the present world order. The good news of God's kingdom, rooted as it is in the teaching and actions of a crucified Messiah, is not good news to those who want nothing to do with a crucified life here and now. Mortimer Arias writes, "Part of the task of the Christian messenger is to criticize false gods and false prophets, to unmask the powers and principalities, to confront them, and to denounce anything that is against God's dream, against God's purpose."[41] For these theologians, it is imperative to consider church growth as one aspect of the larger goal, which is to labor toward the fulfillment of Jesus's prayer:

41. Mortimer Arias, "Ministries of Hope in Latin America," *International Review of Mission* 71 (January 1982): 7.

Your kingdom come,
your will be done,
　　on earth as it is in heaven. (Matt. 6:10)

Reflection Questions

- How would you appraise the church growth model of evangelism?
- Is your church experiencing growth of any kind? If so, why? If not, why?
- Which church growth strategy is most needed in your church? How would you implement that strategy? Offer several concrete proposals.
- Use the E-1, E-2, and E-3 rubric to assess the ways in which your church is / is not involved in evangelism.
- Which other model of evangelism best complements church growth? Why?

SIX

PROPHETIC

Spencer Perkins's reflection on the gospel as presented and lived by his father, John Perkins, captures the essence of this next model of evangelism—prophetic evangelism:

I listened as Daddy acknowledged that he had not been preaching the whole gospel, but that now he was determined more than ever to live the rest of his life preaching and living a gospel that would burn through all the racial, social, and economic walls erected to keep people separated—some even in the name of God. He went on to say that a gospel that reconciles people only to God and not to each other cannot be the true gospel of Jesus Christ. . . . It would be an understatement to say that the events of that night in Brandon [when John Perkins was beaten nearly to death in jail by white police officers] had changed our lives. It was more than that. They had changed our Christianity. For my father, there would no longer be a salvation gospel and a social gospel. There would be one gospel—a gospel that reconciled people to God but at the same time reconciled people to each other. To separate the two could allow the state troopers to beat Daddy almost to death and still be Christians. A gospel that taught no responsibility for your neighbor could not be accepted as the true gospel.[1]

This is prophetic evangelism in a nutshell. Easier said than done, of course, but Perkins's story encapsulates this type of evangelism.

1. Spencer Perkins, "How I Learned to Love White People," *Christianity Today*, September 13, 1993, 38.

Before we proceed further, let's take a quick detour to consider the dilemma of terminology with respect to this model of evangelism. To capture the holistic nature of this model, proponents often pair the word *evangelism* with a short phrase that includes the word *social*, such as "evangelism and social responsibility," "evangelism and social service," or "evangelism and social reform."[2] The point of this combination of *social* and *evangelism* is to emphasize that evangelism involves more than saving individual souls, "as if souls existed in isolation from all that makes a person human—relationships, inheritance, social context, bodies, minds, emotions and wills."[3] Other advocates of this model call it *service* evangelism, *holistic* evangelism, *compassionate* evangelism, or *liberation* evangelism.[4]

Still others, as I do in this chapter, call this model *prophetic* evangelism because its foundation in the biblical prophets underscores the integration of word and deed, action and proclamation.[5] Prophets denounce the hypocrisy

2. See, e.g., J. Andrew Kirk, *The Good News of the Kingdom Coming: The Marriage of Evangelism and Social Responsibility* (Downers Grove, IL: InterVarsity, 1983); John Marvin Dean, *Evangelism and Social Service* (Philadelphia: Griffith & Rowland, 1913). As discussed below, under the heading "Historical Foundations," Charles G. Finney used the term *social reform*.

3. Kirk, *Good News of the Kingdom Coming*, 88.

4. Service evangelism combines the social and personal dimensions of the gospel through an amalgamation of visitation and prophetic evangelism (see Richard Stoll Armstrong, *Service Evangelism* [Philadelphia: Westminster, 1979]). On holistic evangelism, see Priscilla Pope-Levison, "Is a Holistic Evangelism Possible?," in *Questions for the Twenty-First-Century Church*, ed. Russell E. Richey, William Benjamin Lawrence, and Dennis M. Campbell (Nashville: Abingdon, 1999), 38–44. Harvie Conn also adopts the term *holistic evangelism* (see Harvie Conn, *Evangelism: Doing Justice and Preaching Grace* [Grand Rapids: Zondervan, 1982], 50). On compassionate evangelism, see Bryan P. Stone, *Compassionate Ministry: Theological Foundations* (Maryknoll, NY: Orbis Books, 1996), 155. On liberation evangelism, see Priscilla Pope-Levison, *Evangelization from a Liberation Perspective*, American University Studies 69 (New York: Peter Lang, 1991).

5. Leonardo Boff and David Lowes Watson adopt the term *prophetic evangelism* to refer to evangelism that addresses society and structures with the gospel. Both also distinguish prophetic evangelism from person-to-person evangelism, what Boff calls *pastoral evangelism* and Watson calls *personal evangelism*. (Leonardo Boff, *Desde el Lugar del Pobre*, 2nd ed. [Bogotá: Ediciones Paulinas, 1986]; David Lowes Watson, "Evangelism: A Disciplinary Approach," *International Bulletin of Missionary Research* 7 (1983): 6–9; David Lowes Watson, "Prophetic Evangelism: The Good News of Global Grace," in *Wesleyan Theology Today: A Bicentennial Theological Consultation*, ed. Theodore Runyon [Nashville: United Methodist Publishing House, 1985], 219–26. For a discussion of Boff's differentiation between prophetic and pastoral evangelism, see Pope-Levison, *Evangelization from a Liberation Perspective*, 22–24. For a discussion of Watson's use of prophetic and personal evangelism, see William J. Abraham, *The Logic of Evangelism* [Grand Rapids: Eerdmans, 1989], 61–68.) The prophetic evangelism model presented here does not follow the two-pronged approach of Boff and Watson. Rather, it strives, as does John Perkins, to hold individual and collective, structural and societal together in a holistic approach. In

of words and pious practices without just deeds—a fast from food without fasting from injustice (Isa. 58:3–9) or Sabbath practices that do nothing to keep people from rushing back to the business of exploiting the poor (Isa. 58:13–14; Amos 8:5–6). Add to this how deftly Israel's prophets fused the political, economic, and religious dimensions of life into one powerful message. These prophets anticipated what Spencer Perkins attests to, how damaging a gospel could be that allows "state troopers to beat Daddy almost to death and still be Christians."

Biblical Foundations

In what must be one of the most monumental instances of taking a seat, Jesus "rolled up the scroll, gave it back to the attendant, and sat down" (Luke 4:20). With the eyes of his audience fixed on him, Jesus spoke in unprecedented terms of the actual fulfillment of the prophetic vision of justice. During his first sermon, in a synagogue in Nazareth, Jesus read the words of Isaiah 61:1–2 and then, with a flourish, announced that his presence fulfilled them: "Today this scripture has been fulfilled in your hearing" (Luke 4:21). The prophetic text from which he read offers a stunning and lavish vision of justice:

> The spirit of the Lord God is upon me,
>   because the Lord has anointed me;
> he has sent me to bring good news to the oppressed,
>   to bind up the brokenhearted,
> to proclaim liberty to the captives,
>   and release to the prisoners;
> to proclaim the year of the Lord's favor. (Isa. 61:1–2)

This is a startling platform that crescendos with a fierce commitment to a year of justice, most likely the Year of Jubilee imagined in Leviticus 25, when all debts were remitted and justice restored to the oppressed. What Jesus proclaims in Luke includes one line that does not actually appear in Isaiah 61. The line "to let the oppressed go free" is one Jesus imports from Isaiah 58:6

---

my continued thinking on this model since my first book on the topic, *Evangelization from a Liberation Perspective*, I have gravitated away from *liberation evangelism* in favor of *prophetic evangelism*. I prefer the term *prophetic evangelism* because it ties evangelism directly to the biblical prophets and their holistic message of salvation, peace, and liberation.

(a magnificent vision of fasting, not from food but from injustice), no doubt to accentuate how liberating the Year of Jubilee will be for the poor, the oppressed, and prisoners in debt.

Most startling of all, perhaps, is that this proclamation of liberation for the oppressed, for captives, for prisoners, is called good news. Jesus's plan to fulfill the prophet's vision is good news:

> The Spirit of the Lord is upon me,
>   because he has anointed me
>   to bring good news to the poor. (Luke 4:18)

The good news Jesus proclaims to the poor in his initial programmatic sermon is the essence of prophetic evangelism.

Jesus also teaches that God's kingdom is a festive banquet table, filled with those plucked unexpectedly from the streets—"the poor, the crippled, the lame, and the blind" (Luke 14:13)—who would become for Jesus the quintessential symbol of God's kingdom. These were the people of the kingdom, the recipients of good news, the beneficiaries of prophetic evangelism.

What unifies Jesus's words and actions is a sustained effort to liberate those in pain, those oppressed, those ostracized. This proves to be the essence of the kingdom of God, which is what Jesus proclaims from the start. His first words, recorded in the first Gospel, make this claim: "The kingdom of God has come near" (Mark 1:15). His model prayer, which he teaches his disciples, sets out its parameters:

> Your kingdom come.
> Your will be done,
>   *on earth* . . . (Matt. 6:10)

Through Jesus's miracles, God comes concretely to the aid of those whom no one else can help. Each healing is a concrete liberation from some type of oppression: lifting the social ostracism of a leper (Matt. 8:1–4; Mark 1:40–45; Luke 5:12–15), relieving the economic constraint of a blind beggar (Mark 10:46–53; Luke 18:35–43), or removing the religious taboos that excluded a hemorrhaging woman (Matt. 9:20–22; Mark 5:25–34; Luke 8:43–48).[6]

6. John R. (Jack) Levison and Priscilla Pope-Levison, *Jesus in Global Contexts* (Louisville: Westminster John Knox, 1992), 36.

Jesus situates himself in a prophetic-liberative stream that commences with the exodus, when God rescues the Hebrew slaves from the powerful Egyptian empire. This stream permeates the Old Testament: in the prophets' demand for justice from kings (e.g., Amos 8:6–8; Mic. 6:8); in the concern of Wisdom literature for the poor (e.g., Prov. 19:17; 23:10–11); and in the literature of the exile, in which prophets promise a new exodus, when God will rescue the exiled Israelites from Babylonian captivity (e.g., Isa. 43:15–17, 19–20; 48:20–21; 51:9–11; Jer. 16:14–15; Ezek. 20:33–39).[7]

All this is good news, particularly to those with nothing left to lose, but it's not good news for those with much to lose. Jesus never wavers from this commitment, and it leads him into an impassioned critique and censure of those with power and authority. Like the prophets before him, Jesus challenges the misuse of authority. He challenges the priests' authority by overturning the temple's tables (Mark 11:15–17). He challenges the Pharisees' authority by disputing what he considers the misuse of their oral tradition (Matt. 5:17–48), the placing of heavy burdens on others (23:4). He even challenges the authority of Caesar by arguing that taxes be paid to Caesar but one's whole self be given to God (Mark 12:13–17).

By simultaneously mobilizing the poor and confronting the rich, by championing the oppressed and censuring the powerful, Jesus threatens to upset the delicate status quo among the religious and political authorities of first-century Palestine. By raising the dignity of the poor while simultaneously undermining the leaders' authority, Jesus brings to light the injustice that is structurally embedded in his society. His apparently *religious* proclamation of the kingdom of God, therefore, takes on an alarming *political* tone.

Jesus knew that standing in this prophetic stream and adopting its critique of the powerful would lead to martyrdom, for that had been the fate of many prophets before him (Matt. 5:11–12). The prophets' view of a God who demands justice as the true form of worship, who requires "mercy, not sacrifice" (Matt. 9:13; cf. Hosea 6:6), who calls rulers to account for their injustice, has been met with rejection. Having challenged the authority of the elite and sided with the powerless, Jesus has little left to do than to side with them in his death on the cross. In keeping with his life and ministry to those on the periphery and margins of society, his crucifixion outside the city

7. Levison and Pope-Levison, *Jesus in Global Contexts*, 141.

walls is not at all surprising; he died in keeping with how he lived.[8] Jesus's death was the culmination of a life's commitment, which began in the early, inauspicious days in Nazareth, where he claimed for himself,

> The Spirit of the Lord is upon me,
>> because he has anointed me
>>> to bring good news to the poor.
> He has sent me to proclaim release to the captives
>> and recovery of sight to the blind,
>>> to let the oppressed go free,
> to proclaim the year of the Lord's favor. (Luke 4:18–19)

Theological Foundations

Christology is a central theological foundation for prophetic evangelism, which is particularly focused in the interpretation of Jesus as Liberator. This portrait, as we have just seen, is rooted in the life of the historical Jesus, as he is portrayed in the Synoptic Gospels, in which the advent of the kingdom of God takes center stage. Theologians who focus on Jesus as Liberator do not simply proof-text verses about the poor, though there are many from which to choose. Instead, they recognize the underlying structure of Jesus's liberating life, death, and resurrection—what many refer to as a "preferential option for the poor,"[9] an option captured in Philippians 2:5–7, according to which Jesus renounces the heavenly glory that is his and spends his earthly energy as a slave. "Let the same mind be in you that was in Christ Jesus," urges Paul, because Jesus,

> though he was in the form of God,
>> did not regard equality with God
>> as something to be exploited,
> but emptied himself,
>> taking the form of a slave,
>> being born in human likeness.

8. See Orlando Costas, *Christ outside the Gate: Mission beyond Christendom* (Maryknoll, NY: Orbis Books, 1982).

9. See the discussion on a "preferential option for the poor" in the Puebla Document. *Puebla: Evangelization at Present and in the Future of Latin America, Conclusions*, Third General Conference of Latin American Bishops (Washington, DC: National Conference of Catholic Bishops, 1980), para. 1134–65.

Paul made this same claim in 2 Corinthians 8:9 as well, according to which Jesus, "though he was rich, yet for your sakes he became poor, so that by his poverty you might become rich."

Another theological foundation for prophetic evangelism is Soteriology, a term based on the Greek word *sōtēria*, which is typically translated as "salvation." The word *salvation*, understood most often in terms of an individual's salvation in a spiritual sense, is a poor substitute for the biblical meaning, which encompasses well being, healing, and restoration. *Sōtēria* is not unlike the Hebrew word *shalom*, which denotes wholeness and peace. Even the English word *salvation* communicates this larger meaning, since it has the word *salve* in it. When I introduced soteriology—the doctrine of salvation—in my Introduction to Theology class at a Christian college where I taught, I teased my students by asking, "Have you been *salved*?" rather than the question they had heard more often, "Have you been *saved*?" The inclusion of *salve* in *salvation* suggests a full gamut of health, healing, peace, and wholeness.[10]

The richness of salvation (understood as more than just spiritual and individualistic) emerges in Isaiah 52:7. In the Septuagint, the verb form of *evangelism* (*euangelizō*) appears twice (italicized):

> like season upon the mountains,
>> like the feet of one *bringing glad tidings* of a report of peace,
>> like one *bringing glad tidings* of good things,
> because I will make your salvation [*sōtērian*] heard,
>> saying to Sion, "Your God shall reign."[11]

The evangelist announces peace (*shalom*), a vision of "social well-being, productivity, creativity, and harmonious relations with the neighbor and the environment. This is made possible by a just ordering of life."[12] The evangelist announces salvation, which in the context of Isaiah 40–52 includes the liberation of exiles from Babylonian captivity. The evangelist proclaims the restoration of that which was destroyed and reconciliation for an exiled people with God, neighbor, and the land.

---

10. Jack Levison, "Settling in without Settling Down: Acts 3–4," *Lectio: Guided Bible Reading* (blog), Seattle Pacific University, Center for Biblical and Theological Education, http://blog.spu.edu/lectio/settling-in-without-settling-down.

11. *A New English Translation of the Septuagint*, trans. and ed. Albert Pietersma and Benjamin G. Wright (Oxford: Oxford University Press, 2007).

12. Orlando Costas, *Liberating News* (Grand Rapids: Eerdmans, 1989), 35.

All this is possible—at least in the future—because God reigns. This was not yet a reality for the Babylonian exiles, and it is not yet a reality for us. The kingdom of God may have been inaugurated in Jesus's life, but it is yet to be fulfilled. This leads to another theological cornerstone of prophetic evangelism: eschatology, the study of the end of human history and the full realization of God's kingdom.

Eschatology is a fundamental tenet of prophetic evangelism because an unshakable hope in the kingdom of God lies at its core. The kingdom of God dawned in Jesus's birth, life, death, and resurrection, prompting the early Christians to experience God's kingdom concretely in their midst. "God had moved decisively to establish his reign," writes theologian Billy Abraham. "The events of the new age were already under way; the kingdom had come already in Jesus Christ; they now experienced the fullness of the Holy Spirit in their personal lives, in their corporate worship, and in their service to the world; and they eagerly looked forward to the full dawning of the consummation of God's final act when at long last his purposes for the cosmos would be realized."[13]

At the heart of God's kingdom lies hope. The good news is good because it instills hope. On the day when the kingdom of God will come, it will triumph decisively over the present order. It will topple the status quo. It will be a reign of justice, community, and salvation—economic, political, and spiritual salvation. It will bring "a world in which the creative plan of God is finally fulfilled; where hunger, poverty, injustice, oppression, pain, even disease and death have been definitively overcome; . . . where the love of God is 'all and in all.'"[14]

This is not only hope for eternal life, though it is that. It is not only hope for a blissful afterlife, though it is that as well. Hope in the advent of the kingdom of God is hope for the growth of God's mission in this world. It is the hope that what Jesus began when he rolled up the scroll, handed it to the attendant, sat down, and said, "Today this scripture has been fulfilled in your hearing," will be fulfilled. So God labors and *co-labors*—collaborates—still within human history through those who commit to a life aligned with the values of God's kingdom.

Prophetic evangelism takes place, therefore, when the followers of Jesus continue to do what Jesus did. When this happens, when Christians "bring

13. Abraham, *Logic of Evangelism*, 19.
14. José Míguez Bonino, *Room to Be People*, trans. Vickie Leach (Philadelphia: Fortress, 1979), 41.

good news to the poor," "proclaim release to the captives and recovery of sight to the blind," "let the oppressed go free," and "proclaim the year of the Lord's favor," then the good news is a vivid and authentic reminder of Jesus as well as a harbinger of the kingdom he inaugurated.

Historical Foundations

We could "people" the following paragraphs with a litany of women and men who have championed a prophetic model of evangelism. Instead, we will look at just three, who each embraced and embodied the good news of the gospel by blending proclamation and action on behalf of the oppressed. They are, in light of Jesus's life, two sides of the same coin—not a coin kept in a pocket but one given generously to those in need.

During the Second Great Awakening, a religious revival in the United States spanning from 1790 to 1830, Charles Finney (1792–1875) merged revival and social reform. In his bestselling book, *Lectures on Revivals of Religion*, he explained that revivals entail much more than notching up conversions; rather, in obedience to Jesus's teachings, revivals must stretch into social reform, especially for the most vulnerable. Two centuries ago, Finney insisted that resistance to reform negates revival: "Revivals are hindered when ministers and churches take wrong ground in regard to any question involving human rights."[15] The human rights issue he tackled vociferously was slavery, and he blamed the dwindling of revivals and "the low state of religion at the present time" on the American church's failure to condemn slavery.[16] The impact of Finney's revivals on social reform is evident in how communities voted after a Finney revival; communities typically increased their support of antislavery political parties.[17]

Finney brought a fusion of revival and social reform to Oberlin College, beginning in 1835, when he accepted a teaching post as the college's first professor of theology; he later served as president from 1851–66. Finney and other like-minded advocates created an unlikely center of social reform in rural northern Ohio. Oberlin was the first coeducational college in the world, and one of its alumna, Antoinette Brown (1825–1921), was the first

15. Charles G. Finney, *Lectures on Revivals of Religion* (New York: Revell, 1888), 272.
16. Finney, *Lectures on Revivals of Religion*, 272.
17. John L. Hammond, "Revivals, Consensus and American Political Culture," *Journal of the American Academy of Religion* 46, no. 3 (September 1978): 294.

woman ordained in the United States. African-American students were integrated into the student body, and the college formed a major station on the Underground Railroad, by which fugitive slaves escaped to freedom in Canada. Historian Mark Noll claims of Finney that "more than any other individual of his day he succeeded in joining evangelical religion to social reform."[18]

Fast-forward more than a century to John Perkins (1930–), whose life's work bridges evangelism and social justice. Born into a Mississippi sharecropping family, Perkins experienced a childhood of economic and educational disadvantage. As a result, he left school before finishing third grade. After a white sheriff shot and killed his brother, a decorated World War II veteran, Perkins left Mississippi, vowing never to return to the South. But his religious conversion changed all this: "I left Mississippi with hate in my heart. God brought me back with a heart that was overflowing with His love. I had been reconciled to Christ, and He prepared me to return to Mississippi to be reconciled to my white brothers and sisters."[19] Back in Mississippi, he preached the gospel and worked for social justice by advocating for voter registration, school desegregation, and economic boycotts of white-owned stores. Then, on February 7, 1970, white police officers arrested Perkins and tortured him nearly to death. Remarkably, he emerged from this horrific experience with an even deeper commitment to the whole gospel—a commitment to which his son gave ample testimony in the opening paragraph of this chapter. This legacy continues in the John & Vera Mae Perkins Foundation, whose mission "is to spread the holistic Gospel of Jesus Christ which transforms lives and communities."[20]

Perkins was one of two African Americans to participate in a Thanksgiving weekend conference in 1973 in which participants sought to strengthen the social concern of American evangelicals. The result of the conference was a groundbreaking document, "The Chicago Declaration of Evangelical Concern," which heralded the need for Christians to repent of their capitulation to injustices, including racism, sexism, materialism, and militarism. These concerns emanate not from a *new* gospel, the authors of this document claimed,

18. Mark Noll, "Glimpses of Finney," *Reformed Journal* 36, no. 5 (May 1986): 22.
19. John Perkins with Karen Waddles, *One Blood: Parting Words to the Church on Race and Love* (Chicago: Moody, 2018), 37–38.
20. "Dr. John M. Perkins Biography," John & Vera Mae Perkins Foundation, https://www.jvmpf.org/dr-john-m-perkins.

but from "the Gospel of our Lord Jesus Christ who, through the power of the Holy Spirit, frees people from sin so that they might praise God through works of righteousness."[21] Evangelicals for Social Action, an organization founded by Ron Sider, also emerged from the conference and continues today to promote "a holistic expression of the Christian faith, motivated by a desire to fully live into the hope of reconciliation, wholeness, and restoration promised by the whole gospel."[22]

While many others could be included in a litany of those who discerned an indispensable link, rather than dissonance, between evangelism and social justice, one other notable person who urged the American church to adopt the model of prophetic evangelism was Orlando Costas (1942–87). Born in Puerto Rico, Costas emigrated to the United States with his family at the age of twelve. He would claim that three subsequent conversions provided the framework for his embrace of prophetic evangelism. During the Billy Graham New York Crusade in 1957, Costas experienced a religious conversion through which he found stability during a turbulent time as a teenager when he was living in an impoverished neighborhood. He later returned to Puerto Rico to pastor a local church, and there he experienced a second conversion in the discovery of his Latin American cultural roots. "In Puerto Rico I was able to understand that the son of God not only had a Jewish identity (Jesus of Nazareth) but a Puerto Rican and Latin American one (the Christ of Brown America). From this point on, my cultural experience gave me a new Christological understanding."[23]

His third conversion, a "conversion to the world," happened through his social and political activism with a Spanish-speaking congregation he pastored in Milwaukee.[24] Out of these three conversions—to Christ, to Christ in his

21. "Chicago Declaration of Evangelical Social Concern (1973)," Evangelicals for Social Action, November 25, 1973, https://www.evangelicalsforsocialaction.org/about-esa-2/history/chicago-declaration-evangelical-social-concern.

22. "Our Vision," Evangelicals for Social Action, https://www.evangelicalsforsocialaction.org/vision-and-mission.

23. Quoted in Elizabeth Conde-Frazier, "Orlando E. Costas," Christian Educators of the 20th Century, Talbot School of Theology, https://www.biola.edu/talbot/ce20/database/orlando-e-costas.

24. In the summer of 1968, when Latin American and African-American protestors picketed the Allen-Bradley Company plant in Milwaukee, charging job discrimination, Costas became involved and organized a Latin American Union for Civil Rights. About this work, he offered this comment: "I came to recognize that the Christian mission has not only the personal, spiritual and cultural dimensions, but also the social, economic and political. This implied that the object of mission was not the community of faith, but the world in its complexity and

roots, and to Christ in the world—and until his untimely death in his forties, Costas raised a relentlessly prophetic voice, calling on North American churches to embrace prophetic evangelism: "It is my sincere conviction that . . . if and when their churches begin to follow in the footsteps of minority churches and apply their model of evangelization to the concrete situation of mainstream society, there will be a transformation in the personal and collective lives of women, men, and children such as the United States has never known."[25]

Practical Foundations

Although every model in this book has practical foundations, none is more demanding and less forgiving than prophetic evangelism, rooted as it is in Jesus's words and deeds announcing and making visible the kingdom of God.

1. Get to Know the Context

Prophetic evangelism begins with getting to know the context. Evangelism of any sort, in any model, entails engaging real people, flesh and blood individuals who live in a particular context. They are not faceless targets in some universal or abstract vacuum; they are people who have a name, a story, who live in a context that indelibly shapes them. Evangelists evangelize best when they know the context, its value systems, predominant ideologies, culture, prevailing problems and issues, and political and economic realities.

For prophetic evangelism, the context to become familiar with is a specific one—the margins and those who live there. Jesus preached good news to the poor, the captives, the prisoners. So, too, do prophetic evangelists. And who are today's poor, captives, and prisoners? Racial minorities. Native peoples. The unemployed. Refugees. Asylum seekers. LGBTQ+ persons. Undocumented immigrants. Inmates. Here at the periphery, the message of God's kingdom as peace, justice, and liberation means something concrete,

---

concreteness, and that one of my principal pastoral responsibilities was to mobilize the church for an integral, liberating praxis." Orlando Costas, "Teólogo en la Encrucijada," in *Hacia una Teología Evangélica Latinoamericana*, ed. C. René Padilla (San José, Costa Rica: Editorial Caribe, 1984), 22. Translation mine.

25. Costas, *Christ outside the Gate*, 185–86.

something literal, something inescapably social and economic and political. It is not for this reason any less spiritual; it is spirituality embedded in real-life contexts, actual oppressive structures, seemingly inescapable cycles of poverty. As Costas writes, "It is when the gospel makes 'somebody' out of the 'no-bodies' of society, when it restores the self-worth of the marginated, when it enables the oppressed to have a reason for hope, when it empowers the poor to struggle and suffer for liberation and peace, that it is truly good news of a new order of life—the saving power of God (Rom. 1:16)."[26]

John Perkins is even more concrete when he calls Christians to evangelize this context by relocating there, among poor or otherwise marginalized people. Perkins champions relocation, which involves precisely what it sounds like: becoming a neighbor to the poor by living in their midst. Perkins points to the incarnation of Jesus, the one who counted equality with God as nothing in order to become a slave (Phil. 2:7), as the paradigm of this relocation. Perkins says, "We relocate our bodies and our hearts with those who enjoy no human rights, because that is what Jesus did."[27] What better way to get to know the context than by living in it.

2. Announce the Good News

The good news is that God's salvation, made available to all through the life, death, and resurrection of Jesus Christ, is holistic, even cosmic in scope. Jesus reconciled to God "all things . . . , things in heaven and things on earth" (Eph. 1:10). *All things* includes individuals, powers and structures, and even nature. According to the vision of Israel's prophets—a vision adopted by Jesus—nothing lies outside the purview of God's reign. Nothing. Not even the world as it is, with its poverty and hopelessness and exclusions and injustices. *All things* includes these, too, which can, in the scope of the good news, be reconciled.

Further, the good news makes known that the saving power of God through Jesus Christ is for *all time*, here and now and in God's age to come. It is an announcement full of hope for today, for tomorrow, and for the future that God's kingdom will fully establish. It imagines for the hopeless the inevitability of a coming reversal of the present evil order. It proclaims the replacement

---

26. Orlando Costas, "Christian Mission from the Periphery," *Faith and Mission* 1 (1983): 8.
27. John Perkins, "What It Means to Be the Church: Reflections on Mission and Human Rights," *International Review of Mission* (July 1, 1977): 246.

of present injustice with justice, present oppression with liberation, present poverty with plenty, present alienation with community, and present death with life. It embraces the biblical vision of a full, rich, real incarnation of the good news.

This is the good news of Jesus Christ: the assurance that one day there will be neither Jew nor Greek, neither slave nor free, neither male nor female (Gal. 3:28); when "the wolf shall live with the lamb," "the leopard shall lie down with the kid," "the lion shall eat straw like the ox," and "the earth will be as full of the knowledge of the LORD as the waters cover the sea" (Isa. 11:6–9); when everyone will know God, "from the least . . . to the greatest" (Jer. 31:34); when justice will "roll down like waters, / and righteousness like an ever-flowing stream" (Amos 5:24); when there will be no more sound of weeping, nor cries of distress; when all children shall live beyond infancy and all older people shall live out their days; when those who build houses shall live in them, and not have others possess them; when those who plant vine-yards shall eat of them, and not have others take them away (Isa. 65:19–25).[28]

3. Denounce the Bad News

This element of prophetic evangelism is an extremely difficult one in which the evangelist calls out sin as the root of all injustice both within an individual and within inequitable societal structures. The traditional focus of denouncing sin as part of the gospel message has been restricted to an individual's engage-ment in activities considered illicit, such as drinking, smoking, gambling, extra-marital sex, and so on. Prophetic evangelists do not shy away from denouncing individual sins, even if those sins make up a different list from the one above. They also underscore that the whole gospel demands a denunciation of struc-tural sin, such as racism, sexism, economic exploitation, and a capitulation to structures that serve the status quo. As evangelists become more involved at the margins, they learn firsthand which institutions and power brokers profit from keeping people in unjust conditions—and they denounce them. Noel Castellanos writes, "This is when you must identify and confront injustice. We might discover this injustice in our government or schools or police forces or even churches—no institution is immune to injustice."[29]

28. David Lowes Watson, "Christ All in All: The Recovery of the Gospel for North American Evangelism," *Missiology* 19, no. 4 (October 1991): 453.

29. Noel Castellanos, "5 Elements of Kingdom Ministry," *Leadership* (Summer 2010): 41.

How could it be otherwise when Jesus preached good news to the poor, to the captives, to the oppressed, to the prisoners—and demanded that those who follow him should give away all their possessions to the poor? He recognized that the drive for prestige and the draw of power and wealth were sins that made it impossible—or nearly so—to follow him. Jesus preached good news to the rich by denouncing the wealth that held them back from discipleship. Consider the many times Jesus called his followers to divest, give away, lend without expecting anything, and, in return, to live without a place to lay their head. Annunciation and denunciation accompany each other in the proclamation of a holistic gospel.

4. Call to Conversion

Like so much in this model of evangelism, conversion is full-orbed; it includes individual transformation in the sense of turning away from self and toward God, *and* turning toward one's neighbor. Conversion is two-directional: it changes both the vertical relationship (with God) and the horizontal relationship (with neighbor). In prophetic evangelism, this two-fold movement happens as a new believer turns simultaneously to God and neighbor. When a person receives God's love and, in turn, acts to make one's neighbor a brother or sister, this is referred to as the "gift of filiation." The more a person exercises the "gift of filiation," the more he or she receives God's love; the more a person receives God's love, the more he or she loves a neighbor.[30]

The quintessential biblical illustration of this dual conversion is Zacchaeus, whose story signals the end to Jesus's long journey through Samaria to Jerusalem (Luke 19:1–10). In this journey, Luke includes many stories of poverty and wealth that occur only in his Gospel, including the troubling parable of the rich man and Lazarus, in which the poor man, Lazarus, died and went to be in Abraham's bosom for no other reason than that he was poor and oppressed and ignored during his earthly life (16:19–31). Zacchaeus altered his entire life and changed all his priorities, including economic ones, because he encountered Jesus. His conversion was full-orbed—personal, social, economic, and religious. It entailed, too, a simultaneous turn to God and to neighbor: he met Jesus and immediately offered to give half his money

---

30. Gustavo Gutiérrez, *The Power of the Poor in History*, trans. Robert Barr (Maryknoll, NY: Orbis Books, 1992), 63.

away and to pay back fourfold those he had defrauded. Small wonder that Jesus responded as magnanimously as he did when he proclaimed, "Today salvation [*sōtēria*] has come to this house, because [Zacchaeus] too is a son of Abraham" (19:9). Zacchaeus straightening out his economic and social relations with neighbors, his change in priorities, and his integration into the people of God were what Jesus called salvation.

I return to John Perkins to conclude this section on the sort of conversion a prophetic evangelist proclaims. In addition to relocation, Perkins also champions reconciliation with God and neighbor—but with a twist. This sort of reconciliation is not just something an evangelist proclaims to the unconverted. This sort of reconciliation must begin in the body of Christ between believers who are different from each other, particularly with regard to race: "To do the work of reconciliation, then, we must begin by being a reconciled fellowship. . . . We must model the kind of relationships into which we want to invite others. Our love for each other gives credibility and power to our witness."[31]

In contrast to the strategy of church growth evangelism's homogeneous unit principle, Perkins encourages planting a *multiracial* church. He adopts the mother-daughter church-planting strategy discussed in the previous chapter; however, in his scenario, the mother church commissions a heterogeneous ministry team to relocate to a poor neighborhood and begin a church there. The daughter church, multiracial from the start, invites seekers to be reconciled to God and neighbor in the midst of a reconciled fellowship. The hope is that, along with the new believers who grasp the fullness of reconciliation, the mother church will learn from its offspring and follow suit, even while she lends her support.

5. Enact the Good News

Acting to make the good news a reality for those who need to see and receive it is essential. Effective actions concretize the proclamation. These actions, even those presented in this chapter, cover a wide swath of concerns. A prophetic evangelist can stand up for human rights (Finney), denounce racism (Perkins), work for economic and educational opportunities for the poor (Perkins), and organize politically (Costas)—to name just the emphases of

---

31. John Perkins, *With Justice for All: A Strategy for Community Development* (Grand Rapids: Baker Books, 2014), 145.

the three prophetic evangelists highlighted in this chapter. Effective actions can also include building a well, teaching adult literacy, or planting trees.[32] Effective actions can include eliminating discrimination through working and worshiping alongside people of other races, exercising a generous sharing of resources, and acting compassionately toward those who suffer.

Some might interpret this step in prophetic evangelism as confirmation of Saint Francis's famous quip (which many scholars think he never uttered): "Preach the Gospel at all times. When necessary, use words."[33] This adage is quoted often by those resistant to verbal evangelism. Still, while it is not difficult to grasp why people bristle at the thought of verbal proclamation, neither the words attributed to Saint Francis nor the proponents of prophetic evangelism suggest using deeds rather than words. This is a false dichotomy. "Words are far more necessary than this quote [attributed to Saint Francis] leads us to believe. The Christian faith would not exist—it cannot exist— without words. They are the way the religion produces progeny."[34] Proclamation speaks the good news, while the deed makes the good news a reality in a tangible way. Think of a parent saying "I love you" to a child while giving them a hug, a kiss, or some loving gesture that accompanies their words; the two in concert, word and gesture, magnify the power of each other.[35] It is, in fact, this rich symbiosis between word and deed that makes prophetic evangelism so compelling—and so challenging.

Appraisal

The heartbeat of prophetic evangelism is an all-out effort to be holistic in scope. While it is easy to introduce misleading dichotomies into our perspective— spiritual versus material, religious versus political, personal versus social, deed versus word—prophetic evangelists repudiate them. A horizontal reach toward neighbor joins with a vertical reach toward God. A spiritual decision to follow Jesus, the Messiah, the Liberator, the inaugurator of the kingdom

32. For a discussion of eco-evangelism, see Elaine Health, *The Mystic Way of Evangelism: A Contemplative Vision for Christian Outreach*, 2nd ed. (Grand Rapids: Baker Academic, 2017), 101–4.

33. Jamie Arpin-Ricci, "Genuine Evangelism: Friday with Francis," Jamiearpinricci.com (blog), May 9, 2008, http://www.jamiearpinricci.com/2008/05/genuine-evangelism-friday-with-francis.

34. Jonathan Merritt, *Learning to Speak God from Scratch: Why Sacred Words Are Vanishing—And How We Can Revive Them* (New York: Convergent Books, 2018), 49.

35. Kirk, *Good News of the Kingdom Coming*, 104.

of God, is also political. And an individual commitment is authenticated by that Christian's effort to eradicate structural sin—sin that transcends and ensnares individuals—and to create a world that reflects the authority and equity of the kingdom of God. "Your kingdom come, your will be done" rises above all dichotomies.

Prophetic evangelists offer no panacea, no hope for heaven that bypasses the hard work of God's kingdom on earth. They allow for no easy entry into faith, with the demands of discipleship set aside until sometime later for the sake of attracting now as many people as possible. The message they proclaim—and attempt to enact and embody—is horizontal, political, and structural from the start because the people to whom they proclaim the good news, and the evangelists themselves, are embedded in broken social relationships, in political structures that serve the status quo, and in structures that are invariably, without the pressure the kingdom of God exerts, tilted in favor of the wealthy and powerful.

Critics of prophetic evangelism often express the concern that evangelism will revert to social action, words will yield to deeds, the appeal to individuals will be supplanted by an appeal to change structures. They worry, in short, that prophetic evangelism will be nothing more than a return to the Social Gospel of the early twentieth century and that the simple message of faith in Jesus Christ will be weighted by too much other baggage that is ancillary, even detrimental, to this straightforward appeal.[36]

36. A significant group within American Protestantism, in the late nineteenth and early twentieth century, championed the social dimensions of Jesus's teachings, known variously as Social Christianity, Christian Socialism, or the Social Gospel. Proponents believed that the Social Gospel held the key, if pursued strategically by the American church, to transforming society and its institutions, as well as individuals. Congregational minister Josiah Strong (1847–1916), for instance, urged churches to broaden their conception of redemption to encompass the whole earth without forsaking the individual: "As fast as the churches regain Christ's point of view and come to believe that the earth is to be redeemed from its evils, they see that it is their duty to labor for the realization of Christ's social ideal, and they adapt their methods accordingly; they no longer look upon duty as a circle described around the individual as the center, but rather as an ellipse described around the individual and society as the two foci." Josiah Strong, *Religious Movements for Social Betterment* (New York: Baker and Taylor, 1900), 21.

The Social Gospel had its critics in Josiah Strong's day, and they continue to point out its flaws today. Mark Labberton, president of Fuller Theological Seminary, explains that for critics of the Social Gospel "an emphasis on justice . . . leads to a human-centered gospel that makes too much of this life and fails to make enough of the life-to-come. It treats the social symptoms but not the spiritual root of human suffering." Thus "matters of justice . . . are a distraction from the most-urgent task of saving souls." Mark Labberton, "A Mighty River or a Slippery Slope? Examining the Cultural and Theological Forces behind the New Interest in Justice," *Leadership* (Summer 2010): 22.

Is Prophetic Evangelism Too Overwhelming and Multifaceted?

Proclaiming the whole gospel and acting to make it a reality may seem impossible, unless one is Richard Stearns, who led World Vision, an international Christian aid organization, for twenty years. Stearns, though he knows the harsh reality of Christian aid, can still speak and act with attention to the whole gospel. "Proclaiming the whole gospel," contends Stearns, "means much more than evangelism in the hopes that people will hear and respond to the good news of salvation by faith in Christ. It also encompasses tangible compassion for the sick and the poor, as well as biblical justice, efforts to right the wrongs that are so prevalent in our world. God is concerned about the spiritual, physical, and social dimensions of our being. This *whole gospel* is truly good news for the poor, and it is the foundation for a social revolution that has the power to change the world."[37] Stearns, along with Finney, Costas, and Perkins, tells the gospel story with words that amplify deeds and deeds that authenticate words.

Most of us, however, do not belong among these heroes of prophetic evangelism. For us it is essential to prioritize; with jobs and families and even churches to preoccupy us, we can focus on only one or two things at a time. Prophetic evangelism is an enormous challenge, and it is easy to respond to the difficulty by embracing a dualistic pattern of evangelism—either proclaiming the gospel *or* working for justice. Even with a desire to balance the two, it is extremely difficult to conceive of what that looks like in practice.

Perhaps the best advice to be given here is not to go it alone. A better alternative is to scout out others in a church or small group who are committed to engaging others with the whole gospel. There are also national and international networks to learn from and become involved in, such as Evangelicals for Social Action (ESA).[38] ESA's vision begins here: "We envision a new generation of the church committed to a holistic expression of the Christian faith, motivated by a desire to fully live into the hope of reconciliation, wholeness, and restoration promised by the whole gospel."[39] A new generation of church leaders have embraced this vision, people like Shane Claiborne, who identifies John Perkins as the catalyst of his own vision. Claiborne, founder of the

---

37. Richard Stearns, *The Hole in Our Gospel: What Does God Expect of Us? The Answer That Changed My Life and Might Just Change the World* (Nashville: Nelson, 2009), 22.

38. Explore ESA here: https://www.evangelicalsforsocialaction.org/.

39. "Our Vision," Evangelicals for Social Action, https://www.evangelicalsforsocialaction .org/vision-and-mission.

intentional community Simple Way (located in Philadelphia), writes, "Papa John has fathered a ragtag and dysfunctional spiritual family as diverse as the kingdom of God."[40]

It is important to realize, too, that this model can be readily combined with other models of evangelism in this book, especially those that focus more on the spoken word—personal, visitation, and small group, for instance—so that words are not lost in deeds. This could be done with a neighborhood survey, which many proponents of visitation evangelism have developed. Harvie Conn asks simply, "What about an evangelistic survey for our neighborhoods that begins by asking, 'What do you believe the church should be doing in this community to help people?'"[41] It is not exactly building a community-life center, but it is a beginning.

How Does One Discern God's Kingdom in the World?

Since the kingdom of God is central to prophetic evangelism, it is essential to ask how to discern signs of the kingdom in the world. From the start, this is a difficult mandate, since it is easy to align God's activity in the world with one's own political, economic, social, or even religious agenda. Some in the United States point to signs of God's reign in care for undocumented immigrants and subsidies for those on the margins—as in the Democratic Party platform. Others point to signs of God's reign in prohibitions against abortion or a robust commitment to marriage between one man and one woman—staples of the Republican Party platform. As Abraham writes, "The modern church in the West has its fair share of ideologues of both the left and the right announcing their political convictions in the name of the rule of God."[42] How does prophetic evangelism not become completely overwhelmed by political or other agendas? This mandate is a tall order, which can be followed only through the exercise of extreme humility and caution. Those engaging in prophetic evangelism must "exercise the kind of intellectual and spiritual modesty that becomes those who as yet see through a glass darkly."[43]

One way to cultivate humility is to gather in Christian community with people who do not naturally or fully align with your perspective on how and where

40. Tim Stafford, "Grandpa John," *Christianity Today*, March 9, 2007, https://www.christianitytoday.com/ct/2007/march/35.48.html.
41. Conn, *Evangelism*, 56.
42. Abraham, *Logic of Evangelism*, 66.
43. Abraham, *Logic of Evangelism*, 67.

God is working in the world. John Wesley recommended such an approach. He commended his followers to read the Bible in conference with others; in other words, he promoted a communal approach to biblical study to complement one's own personal study. Further, he counseled that reading the Bible in conference with others be marked by "a spirit of openness to dialogue." Wesley himself invited any who "believed that he presented mistaken readings of the Bible in his *Sermons* [the written collection of his preached sermons] to be in touch with him, so that they could confer together over Scripture."[44] Imagine what this open-to-dialogue approach to Bible study might initiate for congregations—whole denominations, too—presently divided over a host of issues from homosexuality to abortion, from immigration to gun control. Studying the Bible together provides a platform for discerning God's work in the world and laboring together across differences.

What Is the Holy Spirit's Role in Prophetic Evangelism?

Prophetic evangelism is thoroughly christological. As we have seen, Jesus's teaching and actions on behalf of God's kingdom, his preference for the poor, and his condemnation of corrupt authorities and institutions are thoroughly entrenched in this model. Yet it has been argued that this emphasis on Christology has eclipsed an interest in the Holy Spirit. Orlando Costas raised this concern as early as the 1970s; he lamented that evangelism suffers when the Holy Spirit is overlooked. He insisted instead that the Holy Spirit must be understood as active in evangelism from the first dawning of faith in a person to empowering the work of transformation in the world. He pinpointed four areas where the Spirit's presence can effectively empower prophetic evangelism:

- The Spirit is the fundamental witness to Jesus's significance.
- The Spirit convicts persons of their sin and injustice and need for reconciliation in God's kingdom.
- The Spirit anticipates the future of new life in God's kingdom.
- The Spirit converts new life into signs of hope for the world.[45]

44. Randy L. Maddox, "The Rule of Christian Faith, Practice, and Hope: John Wesley on the Bible," *Methodist Review* 3 (2011): 1–35, https://divinity.duke.edu/sites/divinity.duke.edu /files/documents/faculty-maddox/31a_Rule_of_Christian_Faith.pdf.
45. Costas, *Liberating News*, 78–79.

Prophetic evangelists are involved in daunting work that demands a reorientation of individuals and a transformation of structures in a liberative way that aligns with the kingdom of God. This work will undoubtedly encounter resistance not only from individuals but also from the intractability of the principalities and powers of this world, which do not easily give up their stranglehold. To sustain the necessary prophetic stance for this work, evangelists must rely constantly, daily, on the power, assurance, creativity, and giftedness of the Holy Spirit. They will need the Holy Spirit to lead, guide, and empower their words and actions, as much as those who receive the message require the prompting and filling of the Holy Spirit.

Reflection Questions

- How would you appraise prophetic evangelism?
- What does the phrase "the whole gospel" mean to you?
- I have cited several examples of prophetic evangelists. Who would you add to the list?
- "Preach the Gospel at all times. When necessary, use words." What is your reaction to this frequently cited quotation?
- Which other model best complements prophetic evangelism? Why?

SEVEN

REVIVAL

Y ou're a part of America's evangelistic history!" the young man shouted, mouth wide open, white teeth gleaming. The man in black—leather jacket and skinny jeans, with the hint of a tattoo peeking out of his T-shirt—welcomed the one hundred thousand people gathered in AT&T Stadium outside Dallas, the livestream participants gathered at six thousand host sites in all fifty states, a television audience, and a radio audience listening on six hundred stations nationwide. On a Texas-hot August night, the stadium's center stage did not feature the Dallas Cowboys. This night it sported a spirited rally of another sort—a revival. Harvest America, the revival's name that night, rolled out one top-notch Christian entertainer after another—Chris Tomlin, Mercy Me, Lecrae, Switchfoot, and revivalist Greg Laurie. Harvest America was an answer to the prayers of 750 churches across the Dallas–Ft. Worth metroplex, whose faithful attendees offered enough money, prayer, and volunteer support to pull off this spectacular example of the revival model of evangelism. And the legacy of nights such as this would continue well beyond this one. Thanks to the internet, Harvest America revivals remain accessible on YouTube, where they continue to propel to conversion the people who watch them online.[1]

That great author of Americana, Mark Twain, is thought to have said, "The reports of my death are greatly exaggerated." The same can be said

1. Access Laurie's YouTube page here: https://www.youtube.com/user/HarvestTV. See also Andrew Careaga, *eMinistry: Connecting with the Net Generation* (Grand Rapids: Kregel, 2001), 149.

of the revival. After the death of revivalist Dwight L. Moody in 1899 on the eve of the millennium, one minister quipped, "The old-fashioned revival is a thing of the past. The people of this country who are still young will have none of it."[2] Several decades later, William Warren Sweet (known as "the dean of church historians"), a professor at Ohio Wesleyan University, DePauw University, and the University of Chicago, wrote in the preface to his book on revivalism, "Of one thing we can be reasonably sure, and that is that old type of revivalism will never again meet the religious needs of America, as it once did."[3] Harvest America puts the lie to this prediction. It may be wearing T-shirts and skinny jeans, but the revival is not dead. William Warren Sweet is, however; he died on January 3, 1959, in Dallas, where Harvest America, nearly sixty years later, would gather hundreds of thousands physically and virtually for a revival of epic proportions.

The revival has confounded its critics and continues strong to this day as a phenomenon especially of American religion, not only because it has been repackaged (though not repurposed) but also because it is the beneficiary of an icon of revival. For more than a generation, Billy Graham, revivalist par excellence, held sway, expressing his integrity with an impeccable private morality and flawless financial accountability, while at the same time exerting his considerable influence in the religious and public spheres. While the revival still has its defenders and detractors, no one can doubt that it endures as a model of evangelism.

Biblical Foundations

The Hebrew verb *ḥayah* translates easily into English as "to revive" and appears in Psalm 85:6 in the plaintive cry for God to revive God's people. "Will you not revive us again, / so that your people may rejoice in you?" the poet begs.[4] In the previous verses, the psalmist begins by recalling God's favor toward God's people, which abruptly turns to fury, anger, and displeasure (vv.

2. William G. McLoughlin Jr., *Modern Revivalism: Charles Grandison Finney to Billy Graham* (New York: Ronald Press, 1959), 279–80; citing David C. Utter, "The Passing of the Revivalist," *Arena* 21 (1900): 107.

3. William Warren Sweet, *Revivalism in America: Its Origin, Growth, and Decline* (New York: Scribner's Sons, 1944), xiii–xiv.

4. In this verse, *ḥayah* is in the piel (or intensive) Hebrew stem. *Ḥayah* is a common verb in the Hebrew Bible. It can also be translated into English as "to restore," "to bring back to life," or "to repair (a city)." For further information on the Hebrew, consult *The Hebrew and*

3–5). The psalmist then asks God, "Will you not revive us again, / so that your people may rejoice in you?" God is the subject of the verb *revive*, which can mean "to reinvigorate with fresh life."[5] The recipients, should God decide to revive them, are collectively the people of Israel. Israel, the psalmist knows, is in need of fresh life, of reinvigoration.

Proponents of the revival model of evangelism often turn to the book of Acts for precedent. In this narrative of the early church, the outpouring of the Holy Spirit coincides with evangelistic preaching and a massive number of conversions. During the Jewish festival of Pentecost, the outpouring of the Spirit arrives with theophanies—divine manifestations—of sound and sight (Acts 2:1–4). A miraculous fluency powered by the Spirit inpires the earliest followers of Jesus to communicate the praiseworthy acts of God to a host of different ethnic groups. Those who hear and understand the message are "Parthians, Medes, Elamites, and residents of Mesopotamia, Judea and Cappadocia, Pontus, and Asia, Phrygia and Pamphylia, Egypt and the parts of Libya belonging to Cyrene, and visitors from Rome . . . , Cretans and Arabs" (vv. 9–11). They marvel, "Are not all these who are speaking Galileans? And how is it that we hear, each of us, in our own native language?" (vv. 7–8). For proponents, this is the birth of the revival: a Spirit-driven spectacle of outsized proportions, choreographed to preach the good news of Jesus Christ to a collection of hearers—multicultural, multiethnic, multilingual—who marvel at both what they hear and how they hear it. Then Peter stands up and preaches to this crowd (vv. 14–36) and quotes Joel 2:28–29, a prophetic text announcing that God will "pour out [his] spirit on all flesh"—sons and daughters, old men and young men, male and female slaves. Here, the Holy Spirit ensures that the message of God's deeds of power is available to all.

This pattern carries on through the first half of the book of Acts. Later in Jerusalem, Peter, on trial, is "filled with the Holy Spirit" and led to preach a compelling speech, which includes a quotation from Psalm 118 and the climactic conclusion, "There is salvation in no one else, for there is no other name under heaven given among mortals by which we must be saved" (Acts 4:12). This elicits a response of wonder: "Now when they saw the boldness of Peter and John and realized that they were uneducated and ordinary men,

Aramaic Lexicon of the Old Testament, ed. Ludwig Koehler and Walter Baumgartner (Leiden: Brill, 1994), 1:309.

5. Raymond C. Ortlund Jr., *Revival Sent from God: What the Bible Teaches for the Church Today* (Leicester, UK: Inter-Varsity, 2000), 7.

they were amazed and recognized them as companions of Jesus" (v. 13). Peter is not alone in this boldness. Later, but still in Jerusalem, the entire community of Jesus's followers is "filled with the Holy Spirit and [speaks] the word of God with boldness" (v. 31).

Another great harvest occurs, not in Jerusalem but about seventy miles away in a seaside city called Caesarea, in the home of a gentile who is sympathetic to Judaism. Invited to Cornelius's house after receiving a vision and being instructed not to distinguish between clean and unclean foods, Peter travels to Caesarea. While he is still speaking with Cornelius's friends and family, "the Holy Spirit [falls] upon all who heard the word" (Acts 10:44). The word *all* in this line is significant, since it includes, for the first time, gentiles who do not share the taboos and practices of the Jews.

This event changes everything for the early church. When it comes time for the church in Jerusalem to decide whether or not to circumcise male gentile followers of Jesus, Peter appeals to this experience to say that the church should not require circumcision. Peter stands up in the council and recalls, "And God, who knows the human heart, testified to them by giving them the Holy Spirit, just as he did to us; and in cleansing their hearts by faith he has made no distinction between them and us. Now therefore why are you putting God to the test by placing on the neck of the disciples a yoke that neither our ancestors nor we have been able to bear? On the contrary, we believe that we will be saved through the grace of the Lord Jesus, just as they will" (Acts 15:8–11). The phrase "just as he did to us" is telling because it connects the outpouring of the Spirit upon the gentiles with the initial outpouring of the Spirit at Pentecost. It might even be possible to call this the second great harvest in the book of Acts; even Peter's language seems unabashedly revivalistic, with phrases such as "cleansing their hearts by faith" and "saved through the grace of the Lord Jesus."

Theological Foundations

The biblical attribution of revival to the Holy Spirit gives this model its primary theological underpinning in Pneumatology. The Holy Spirit, it is believed, breaks down the resistance of those with hardened hearts and the skepticism of those with unconvinced minds. The Holy Spirit wings the message to the hearer so that it permeates and convicts (John 16:7–11). The Holy Spirit communicates the message through human vessels and is, in the eyes of Billy Graham, "the great Communicator." Graham notes that "it is this

Third Person of the Trinity who takes the message and communicates with power to the hearts and minds of men and women." Graham continues on, explaining that the Holy Spirit breaks down barriers, convicts of sin, and applies the truth of the gospel that revivalists proclaim.[6]

At this point in our study together, you may discern similarities among various models. This perspective on the Holy Spirit, for example, mirrors the view that we discovered in our discussion of personal evangelism. Though revival evangelism addresses a large crowd, it is still the individual, under the unseen but inevitable influence of the Spirit, who makes his or her own response to the message.

Another theological foundation is far more disputed. Since the mid-nineteenth century, revivalists in North America have debated this question: What is God's role in a revival, and what is the revivalist's role? To frame the question another way, Is a revival fully dependent on God's sovereign action, or is it generated, orchestrated even, by the revivalist?

Revivalists tend to fall on one end of the spectrum or another, either emphasizing God's sovereignty (in an embrace of Calvinism) or lifting up human activity (in an adherence to Arminianism).[7] On the one hand, Solomon Stoddard (1643–1729), a Congregational pastor in Northampton, Massachusetts, for forty-seven years, articulated his unwavering belief in God's sovereign creation of the seasons of revival. "There are some special Seasons wherein God doth in a remarkable Manner revive Religion among his People," declared Stoddard. "God doth not always carry on his Work in the Church in the same Proportion. As it is in Nature, there be great Vicissitudes . . . , so there be times wherein there is a plentiful Effusion of the Spirit of God, and Religion is in a more flourishing Condition." Stoddard bolstered his argument for God's

6. Billy Graham, *A Biblical Standard for Evangelists* (Minneapolis: World Wide Publications, 1984), 66–67.

7. Arminianism promotes the belief that "salvation is available to anyone who exercises faith." Faith comes by the individual exercising his or her will, sovereignty, and self-determination. Particularly after the Revolutionary War, Arminianism emerged in a context where Americans were exercising their own political agency. They responded enthusiastically "to a message that assured them that they controlled their religious destinies as well." Arminianism is reflected in Billy Graham's message to "make a decision for Christ" (Randall Balmer, *Encyclopedia of Evangelicalism*, 2nd ed. [Waco: Baylor University Press, 2004], 32). Calvinism takes the opposite position, contending that God is sovereign and acts not according to humanity's bidding, intervention, or prayers but solely as God wills. Calvinism embraces the doctrine of predestination in which God's sovereign determinations, even before the beginning of time, establish who will be saved and who will not. Balmer, *Encyclopedia of Evangelicalism*, 122–23.

sovereignty with two biblical texts: Habakkuk 3:2 ("O LORD, I have heard of your renown, / and I stand in awe, O LORD, of your work. / In our own time revive it; / in our own time make it known; / in wrath, may you remember mercy") and Psalm 85:6, which we discussed earlier.[8]

Jonathan Edwards (1703–58) took up—literally, in the same pulpit—where Stoddard, his grandfather, left off, and he continued with the same sentiment. Edwards saw the Great Awakening as "a surprising work of God."[9] This theological understanding of God's sovereignty in revivals continues today. Revivalist Greg Laurie, introduced earlier, claims that God makes revival happen. "Revival is a work of the Holy Spirit; it's not something we can make happen. Revival is God's responsibility. It's what God does for us."[10]

On the other hand, Charles Finney (1792–1875), lawyer turned revivalist, championed unapologetically the conviction that revivals arise as the result of "man's work." Finney claimed in a section heading in his famed *Lectures on Revival*, "A Revival of Religion Is Not a Miracle." A revival, rather, proceeds from "the *right* use of the appropriate means." God established these means precisely because they "have a natural tendency to produce a revival. Otherwise God would not have enjoined them."[11] If these divinely ordained means and strategies were utilized appropriately by the revivalist, wrote Finney, then revival would necessarily happen.

This theological debate is hardly a relic of bygone eras; it does not languish on a dusty shelf in a forgotten corner of American history. The debate continues to influence our understanding of revivals today. In his book, *Global Awakening: How 20th-Century Revivals Triggered a Christian Revolution*, Mark Shaw encapsulates this debate between a Calvinist and an Arminian perspective in a set of questions he poses: "Are global revivals acts of God or inventions of humans? Can I plan a global revival and pull it off through a combination of careful preparation and talented performers? Or are revivals hands off propositions? Are they so much an act of God, like creation,

---

8. Keith Hardman, *Issues in American Christianity: Primary Sources with Introductions* (Grand Rapids: Baker, 1993), 47.

9. Balmer, *Encyclopedia of Evangelicalism*, 32.

10. Greg Laurie, "Does America Need a Revival?," ChurchLeaders.com, June 30, 2014, https://churchleaders.com/outreach-missions/outreach-missions-articles/175195-greg-laurie-does-america-need-a-revival.html.

11. Charles G. Finney, *Lectures on Revivals of Religion* (New York: Revell, 1888), 12–13. William J. Abraham sets out the radical difference between Edwards and Finney. See William J. Abraham, *The Art of Evangelism: Evangelism Carefully Crafted into the Life of the Local Church* (Sheffield, UK: Cliff College Publishing, 1993), 12–14.

that to suggest a human role is almost heretical?"[12] Shaw himself occupies a middle ground by characterizing revivals as "theoanthropic (divine-human) events."[13] He reasons that under the umbrella of God's sovereignty, God can enlist human activity in revivals, what he refers to as "secondary causes."[14]

Similarly, Michael McClymond, an historian of revivalism, cautions against overemphasizing the disjuncture between spontaneity spawned by divine sovereignty (as in Calvinism) and the claim that revival is the product of human planning (rooted in Arminianism). McClymond's findings are not wholly theological; he roots them in the pragmatic as well. "Yet my analysis suggests," he notes, "that the hard and fast theological distinction between the two positions breaks down on a practical level. In *theory*, Calvinists do nothing but wait on God for revivals and Arminians exert themselves to cause revivals. In *reality*, Calvinists exert themselves for revivals while they are waiting and Arminians wait for revivals while they exert themselves."[15]

This debate may be a moot point if we take into serious consideration a phenomenon such as Harvest America. Greg Laurie—and a host of Christians from Dallas to Ft. Worth and beyond—surely prayed for God to bring a season of revival, but it is difficult to conceive of an event at a professional football stadium happening without enormous vision, meticulous preparation, the invitation of marquee singers and speakers, and coordination among local churches. That is to say, revival—this revival, at least—is hardly possible without painstaking planning alongside belief in God's sovereignty to engender a season of revival.

Historical Foundations

The history of the revival is nothing if not fascinating, and it is nothing if not quintessentially American: entrepreneurial, with a charismatic preacher

---

12. Mark Shaw, *Global Awakening: How 20th-Century Revivals Triggered a Christian Revolution* (Downers Grove, IL: IVP Academic, 2010), 207.

13. Shaw, *Global Awakening*, 207.

14. Shaw, *Global Awakening*, 207.

15. Michael J. McClymond, "Issues and Explanations in the Study of North American Revivalism," in *Embodying the Spirit: New Perspectives on North American Revivalism*, ed. Michael J. McClymond (Baltimore: Johns Hopkins University Press, 2004), 45 (italics added). Delos Miles agrees: "Revival is both a surprising work of God and the hard work of fervent Christians. All of our local church revivals should seek to preserve this delicate balance between the sovereignty of God and the responsibility of the people." Delos Miles, *Introduction to Evangelism* (Nashville: Broadman, 1983), 297.

or performer at the helm appealing to each and every individual to make a personal decision for Jesus Christ. The noteworthy role that the revival has played throughout American Christianity can be illustrated by a litany of revivalists:

- Solomon Stoddard (1643–1729), in the century before the Revolutionary War, pioneered a homiletical strategy that became the model of revival preaching, adopting such novel techniques as speaking without notes, using plain speech and familiar illustrations, integrating graphic imagery (with vivid descriptions of hell and its horrors), presenting the possibility of hope for a new life in Christ, and pressing for an immediate response to his message.[16]
- Jonathan Edwards (1703–58) is credited with generating the First Great Awakening from his grandfather's pulpit. His preaching, like Stoddard's, evoked strong responses with garish images, as in the opening line in his famous sermon "Sinners in the Hands of an Angry God." He declared, "The God that holds you over the pit of hell, much as one holds a spider or some loathsome insect over the fire . . ."[17]
- Barton W. Stone (1772–1844), whose Kentucky church (along with an ecumenical group of churches) hosted the famous Cane Ridge Revival in 1801, drawing crowds estimated from ten thousand to twenty thousand. This revival cemented the camp meeting as a genre of revivalism that flourished around the country throughout the nineteenth century.[18]
- Charles Finney (1792–1875) introduced controversial "new measures," such as encouraging women to pray and testify in public meetings, setting up an "anxious bench" where those under conviction could be prayed over, holding multinight protracted meetings, and forming an

16. Historian Perry Miller described Stoddard's sermons in this way: "His sermons were outstanding in his day for the decision with which he swept away the paraphernalia of theology and logic, to arouse men to becoming partakers of the divine nature, and he was the first minister in New England openly to advocate the preaching of Hell-fire and brimstone in order to frighten men into conversion." Perry Miller, "Solomon Stoddard, 1643–1729," *Harvard Theological Review* 34, no. 4 (1941): 316–17.

17. Jonathan Edwards, "Sinners in the Hands of an Angry God," sermon preached in Enfield, CT, July 8, 1741, https://digitalcommons.unl.edu/cgi/viewcontent.cgi?article=1053&context=etas.

18. George C. Bedell, Leo Sandon Jr., and Charles T. Wellborn, *Religion in America* (New York: Macmillan, 1975), 160–61.

evangelistic association with "like-minded associates," who spread a Finney-style revival farther afield than he could on his own.[19]

- Phoebe Palmer (1807–74) preached the "shorter way" to sanctification in her revivals, which were held on several continents. She declared that instantaneous sanctification was possible for those who consecrated themselves entirely on the altar and believed God's promise to sanctify then and there whatever rested on the altar.[20]

- Isaac Hecker (1819–88), an adult convert to Catholicism, founded the Paulist order in 1858 as an apostolate to non-Catholics in the United States. The Paulists held parish missions that featured, like their Protestant counterparts, itinerant revivalists, music, publicity, and how-to handbooks.[21]

- Dwight L. Moody (1837–99) brought to revivals a conspicuous business savvy. Planning a year ahead of the revival, he recruited leading business executives and ministers of the largest churches in the host city. From these churches and businesses came the voluminous number of volunteers who were the worker bees for these committees: finance, executive, prayer, home visitation, charitable work, temperance, ticket arrangement, choir members, ushers, and publicity.[22]

- Maria Woodworth-Etter (1844–1924), known as "the trance evangelist," set the barns of Indiana ablaze, metaphorically speaking, with

19. Keith Hardman, *Seasons of Refreshing: Evangelism and Revivals in America* (Eugene, OR: Wipf & Stock, 1994), 153.

20. For more on Palmer, see Priscilla Pope-Levison, *Turn the Pulpit Loose: Two Centuries of American Women Evangelists* (New York: Macmillan, 2004), 61–71. For more on Palmer's altar metaphor, see Susie C. Stanley, *Holy Boldness: Women Preachers' Autobiographies and the Sanctified Self* (Knoxville: University of Tennessee Press, 2002), 69–79; and Diane Leclerc, *Singleness of Heart: Gender, Sin, and Holiness in Historical Perspective* (Lanham, MD: Scarecrow, 2002), 116–21.

21. Jay Dolan, *Catholic Revivalism: The American Experience, 1830–1900* (Notre Dame, IN: University of Notre Dame Press, 1978), 189–92. At the same time, Dolan points out two significant differences between Catholic and Protestant revivals. For Protestants, integrating the local church tended to be a hit or miss affair. Sometimes meetings began in a church and then outgrew it, requiring the crowd to move to a tent or a temporary tabernacle. In that case, there might remain only a tangential link to a local church. Also, literally anyone, even children converted at a camp meeting, and certainly laypeople, including women, could preach. In contrast, Catholic revivals were sponsored by a Catholic parish so that both its location and its objective related to the local church, and only priests conducted parish missions because of the central role of the sacraments. Dolan, *Catholic Revivalism*, 196–97.

22. For more on Moody's revivals, see Priscilla Pope-Levison, *Building the Old Time Religion: Women Evangelists in the Progressive Era* (New York: New York University Press, 2015), 42–43.

miracles and protracted sermons that caught the attention even of a *New York Times* reporter, who made the trip to witness firsthand her revivals.[23]

- Martha Moore Avery (1851–1929) was a Roman Catholic laywoman who traveled around New England and Canada, along with her colleague David Goldstein, in a highly decorated, customized Model-T nicknamed "Rome's Chariot." The Model-T was modified to hold revivals from its very doors: a portable platform folded out at a 45 degree angle from the front of the car, and its four seats could be stacked on top of one another to form a table.[24]

- Billy Sunday (1862–1935), a professional baseball player turned revivalist, made famous the phrase "hitting the sawdust trail" to describe when people came forward at the altar call on floors covered with sawdust to muffle the sound. At the height of his popularity, he preached in a colossal tabernacle, built in 1917 exclusively for his New York City revival, with a seating capacity of sixteen thousand and standing room for an additional four thousand.[25]

- Mary Lee Cagle (1864–1955) preached revivals in rural Texas, Alabama, and Arkansas. She and a cadre of women revivalists were ordained ministers in the New Testament Church of Christ, which merged with the Church of the Nazarene in 1917.[26]

- Helen "Ma" Sunday (1868–1957) directed the business side of the Billy Sunday Organization that reached the heights of an elite group of early twentieth-century businesses, like the Standard Oil Company, United States Steel, and National Cash Register.[27] After Billy's death, Ma Sunday began preaching revivals and shared the platform with the next

23. For more on Woodworth-Etter, see Pope-Levison, *Turn the Pulpit Loose*, 97–109, and Pope-Levison, *Building the Old Time Religion*, 36–42, 56–59.

24. For more on the Catholic Truth Guild, see Pope-Levison, *Building the Old Time Religion*, 27–36, 41–47, 55–56. For more on Avery, see Pope-Levison, *Turn the Pulpit Loose*, 111–21.

25. William G. McLoughlin Jr., *Billy Sunday Was His Real Name* (Chicago: University of Chicago Press, 1955), xvii.

26. For more on Cagle, see Pope-Levison, *Turn the Pulpit Loose*, 147–55; Pope-Levison, *Building the Old Time Religion*, 80–81; Priscilla Pope-Levison, "Mary Lee Cagle (1864–1955): Autobiography of an Evangelist Preacher," *Southern Women in the Progressive Era: A Reader*, ed. Giselle Roberts and Melissa Walker (Columbia: University of South Carolina Press, 2019), 59–91.

27. Homer Rodeheaver, *Twenty Years with Billy Sunday* (Winona Lake, IN: Rodeheaver Hall-Mack, 1936), 119.

generation of revivalists, including Billy Graham, who had been converted during a Billy Sunday revival.[28]

- William Seymour (1870–1922), born to former slaves, helped to fan into flame the initial spark of the Azusa Street Revival, which broke out in 1906 in Los Angeles and served as a catalyst to the worldwide Pentecostal movement.[29]

- Aimee Semple McPherson (1890–1944) was a faith-healing revivalist whose star quality rivaled the leading movie stars of the day. Despite the negative press garnered from her so-called abduction to a Mexican desert, the faithful unswervingly stood by her and tuned in to hear her early morning radio broadcast, *The Sunshine Hour*, and thronged to her revivals.[30]

- Bishop Ida Robinson (1891–1946) was an energetic revivalist whose several-hours-long sermons alternated between the spoken word and the sung word. She, along with a caravan of black-robed female preachers, held revivals along the Eastern Seaboard from New York to Florida and planted churches for the denomination she founded, the Mount Sinai Holy Church of America.[31]

- Kathryn Kuhlman (1907–76) was a faith-healing revivalist who, in her customary flowing, long white dress, preached in venues like the fourteen-thousand-seat Civic Center in Providence, Rhode Island, while ten thousand people gathered outside. Her radio program *Heart-to-Heart* was regularly broadcast for over forty years, and her long-running television program on CBS, *I Believe in Miracles*, catapulted her into America's living rooms.[32]

- Uldine Utley (1912–95), famed child revivalist, filled Madison Square Garden in 1926 for four weeks of twice-daily sermons. Dressed in her standard all-white uniform (white shoes; white hose; and a white, collared dress), she held revivals from east to west in Canada and the United States.[33]

28. For more on "Ma" Sunday, see Pope-Levison, *Turn the Pulpit Loose*, 169–77, and Pope-Levison, *Building the Old Time Religion*, 43–45, 62–64.

29. Priscilla Pope-Levison, "William J. Seymour (1870–1922)," BlackPast.org, January 26, 2007, https://www.blackpast.org/vignette_aahw/seymour-william-j-1870-1922.

30. For more on McPherson, see Pope-Levison, *Turn the Pulpit Loose*, 187–203, and Pope-Levison, *Building the Old Time Religion*, 173–82.

31. For more on Robinson, see Pope-Levison, *Turn the Pulpit Loose*, 205–11.

32. For more on Kuhlman, see Pope-Levison, *Turn the Pulpit Loose*, 213–21.

33. For more on Utley, see Pope-Levison, *Turn the Pulpit Loose*, 223–33.

- Billy Graham (1918–2018) became a national figure in revivalism beginning in 1949 with the enormous success of his Greater Los Angeles Crusade. In 1950, he launched his popular radio show, *Hour of Decision*, and formed the Billy Graham Evangelistic Association (BGEA). Through the BGEA, he continued to develop ever-expanding media expressions of his revival message in a daily syndicated newspaper column, film, television, a monthly magazine, books, simulcasts, and social media.[34]

This litany of revivalists could be expanded into the thousands, so pervasive have revivals been to American Christianity. At the same time, this list is sufficient to impress upon us the diversity in denomination, gender, race, theology, and region of those who have contributed to the revival model of evangelism.

Practical Foundations

While it is neither Northern nor Southern, neither Protestant nor Catholic, the revival model of evangelism in America does enlist common features. Dress may differ—music, too—but some basic elements unite this model and provide the practical foundations for undertaking it.

1. Organize and Pray

Orchestrating a revival requires more than a modicum of advanced planning and diligent organization. Securing a venue suitable for the anticipated crowd size, booking marquee speakers, advertising across neighborhoods or cities, cultivating online communities through social media—every part of a revival demands careful attention.

Moody's organizational strategies from the nineteenth century still dictate the general flow of revivals to this day: "music, sermons, counsellors at mass rallies, media campaigns, and training in the fine art of personal evangelism."[35] Several weeks out, trainers in personal evangelism worked with would-be counselors to equip them "to help inquirers clarify their decisions and direct

---

34. "History," Billy Graham Evangelistic Association, https://billygraham.org/news/media-resources/electronic-press-kit/bgea-history.

35. William J. Leonard, "Evangelism and Contemporary Life," *Review and Expositor* 77, no. 4 (Fall 1980): 495.

them into Bible-believing churches."[36] Their training groomed them to be especially effective in leading those who came forward to faith in Christ. Visitors were also sent to neighborhoods to engage in visitation evangelism so that the opportunity to respond to the gospel would be offered even before the revival began. This well-managed approach to a revival underscores the revivalist's involvement in and impact on logistical matters.

Another essential aspect of the revival is prayer—before, during, and after. In advance of the Harvest America revival, 750 churches from different backgrounds joined forces in prayer. On a smaller (and more manageable for most of us) scale, John Kilpatrick, former pastor of Brownsville Assembly of God, attributed the outbreak of the 1995 revival in Pensacola, Florida, to the congregation's prayers over several years.[37] This aspect highlights the divine outpouring on a revival.

The two aspects come together when prayers for the revival are organized by pairing partners who covenant to pray together daily for several weeks beforehand. During these prayer sessions, each person prays specifically for seekers they know. The next step is to visit the seekers for whom the pair prayed. The visit might involve an invitation to the revival, or it may simply be an instance of practicing friendship and establishing trust.

2. Lead with Music

Following a long-established pattern, a revival begins with music, often with celebrity musicians as Harvest America does. Upbeat music, in particular, energizes the audience, prompting them to listen in an engaged way to the spoken message; this is a key strategy of a revival. While some revivalists perform the music themselves, like gospel singer and preacher Juanita Bynum, most depend on expert musicians for the "one-two punch of message and music"—musicians like Ira Sankey (who worked with Dwight L. Moody), Homer Rodeheaver (who worked with Billy Sunday), and Cliff Barrows (who worked with Billy Graham).[38] During Moody's large-scale meetings, a sizeable choir performed several songs, then the congregation, led by his intrepid musician, Ira Sankey, sang hymns and gospel songs, especially the perennial

---

36. William Martin, *A Prophet with Honor: The Billy Graham Story* (New York: Morrow, 1991), 113.

37. Steve Rabey, *Revival in Brownsville: Pensacola, Pentecostalism, and the Power of American Revivalism* (Nashville: Nelson, 1998), 71.

38. Rabey, *Revival in Brownsville*, 110–11.

favorites "Rescue the Perishing," "Pass Me Not, O Gentle Savior," and "Jesus, Keep Me Near the Cross," all penned by the famed and treasured hymnwriter Fanny Crosby.

Billy Graham ranked music as "the star attraction" alongside his preaching.[39] In addition to congregational and choral singing, including the trademark hymn "Just As I Am" ("The buses will wait," urged Graham, to the background strains of the hymn), Graham's revivals hosted an astonishingly wide range of musical styles "from Gaither Family toe-tappers, to Johnny Cash and Ricky Skaggs country, Ethel Waters and Mahalia Jackson spiritual, Robert Goulet and Cliff Richard pop, Jerome Hines and Kathleen Battle classical, DC Talk rap, Take 6 jazz, Paul Stookey folk, Marine Corps Band patriotic, Norma Zimmer easy listening, Michael W. Smith and Jars of Clay contemporary Christian, Blackwood Brothers and Statler Brothers Southern gospel, and Brooklyn Tabernacle Choir black gospel."[40]

3. Preach an Evangelistic Message

With the crowd primed by music, the revivalist's message doubles down on one goal: to present the gospel in a simple, accessible way. To emphasize this point, Billy Graham repeated a quip originally spoken by Dr. James S. Stewart, of Edinburgh, who said, "If you shoot over the heads of your hearers, you don't prove anything except you have a poor aim."[41] Echoes of Solomon Stoddard reverberate down the centuries: use straightforward language, vivid images, and direct address. (There is even more on the framework of an evangelistic message in chap. 4, where we discuss liturgical evangelism.)

This is what most of us know about a revival: its message-bearers, who are known today in church circles as the "attractional" figure.[42] The success of a revival often rises or falls on the charisma of the revivalist. It rises or falls as well on the *integrity* of the revivalist. Immorality—shady finances, lives of excess, and extramarital sexual affairs—have led time and again to the

---

39. Grant Wacker, *America's Pastor: Billy Graham and the Shaping of a Nation* (Cambridge, MA: Harvard University Press, 2014), 146.

40. Wacker, *America's Pastor*, 147.

41. Billy Graham, "The Evangelist and His Preaching," in *The Calling of an Evangelist: The Second International Congress for Itinerant Evangelists, Amsterdam, The Netherlands*, ed. J. D. Douglas (Minneapolis: World Wide Publications, 1987), 98.

42. See Elaine A. Heath and Larry Duggins, *Missional, Monastic, Mainline: A Guide to Starting Missional Micro-Communities in Historically Mainline Traditions* (Eugene, OR: Cascade Books, 2014), 40–45.

downfall of a revivalist, as well as to the sadly justified caricature of evangelism as manipulation of the masses for the personal gain of the revivalist. What distinguished Billy Graham, apart from personal charisma and endless energy, was his personal integrity, which gave ballast and effectiveness to his message. Graham also repeatedly emphasized teamwork, downplaying his own contribution, even though he was the internationally renowned evangelist. As discussed in chapter 1, the lifestyle of an evangelist (in this case, a revivalist) is inescapably connected, as it should be, to the message he or she communicates.

4. Invite a Response

After the evangelistic message comes the invitation, the clear call to repent and believe the gospel that has just been preached. This is an essential ingredient in a revival: the call for decision. The BGEA's long-running magazine was titled simply *Decision*. Calling for a decision, in the words of evangelist Leighton Ford, emulates God: "God calls people to decision. From Moses ('Who is on the Lord's side?') through Elijah ('How long will you waver between two opinions?') to Peter ('Repent and be baptized, every one of you') and Paul ('I preached that they should repent and turn to God and prove their repentance by their deeds')—the scriptural tradition is *crisis preaching* that calls for a decision."[43]

Music again comes to the fore because it often signals the transition from preaching to the invitation by slowing down the tempo and playing softer background melodies. While this use of music can galvanize the moment of decision, some revivalists contend that the invitation should begin much earlier in the spoken message. It can happen first during the introduction, when the speaker reveals her intention to ask for a response later. The expression might go like this: "Tonight at the end of my talk I am going to ask you to do something about it, to make your decision." The preacher may even outline up front how the public response to an invitation will be handled at this particular venue.[44]

Another form of inviting a response follows Charles Finney's protocol for the after-service. After his preaching, Finney asked those "anxious about the state of their souls" to come forward and sit in a designated area termed "the

43. Leighton Ford, "How to Give an Honest Invitation," *Leadership* 5, no. 2 (1984): 106.
44. Ford, "How to Give an Honest Invitation," 106.

anxious seat," which could even be in a separate room or building from the gathered congregation. He would conclude the regular service, pronounce the benediction, then move to the "anxious seat" area to begin the after-service, in which he instructed those who had come forward in the basic tenets of Christianity.[45] This approach blends, even in an abbreviated format, catechesis and evangelism.

5. Connect with Churches

The most successful revivalists, from Moody to Graham, took great care to establish close relationships with leading churches long before they arrived in a city. One of Graham's biographers explained that his preached theology was communal: "Though it aimed to encourage the conversion of individuals, it also sought to define and invigorate local congregations, families of believers, and ultimately the nation. Conversion might have started as a private transaction between the person and God, but if it remained that way, it was a stunted experience that did not fulfill its intended purpose."[46] Graham repeatedly underscored the revivalist's responsibility to help those who responded favorably to the invitation to find a local worshiping community. He believed that many revivalists, by giving too little attention to the aftermath of the revival, neglected their responsibility to those who responded affirmatively to the invitation to commit their lives to Christ. He said, "They recognize their role as spiritual harvesters, but do little, if anything, to preserve the results of their ministries. They may accept that new Christians need to be nurtured, but are quite content to leave this to others."[47]

Local churches should be prepared ahead of time to assist in the catechesis and integration of new believers. This can happen, quite simply, through the creation of small groups ready and waiting to welcome those who respond during the revival.[48] Such groups serve, in church growth terms, as new ports of entry open specifically to persons new to the Christian faith and the church community.

---

45. Charles Bradley Templeton, *Evangelism for Tomorrow* (New York: Harper & Brothers, 1957), 169. Templeton suggested that the minister or another leader be prepared to explain in simple yet clear terms what a Christian commitment entails. Literature providing additional information was to be distributed as well. Templeton, *Evangelism for Tomorrow*, 172.

46. Wacker, *America's Pastor*, 51.

47. Graham, *Biblical Standard for Evangelists*, 27.

48. Graham, *Biblical Standard for Evangelists*, 109.

Appraisal

With a long and sometimes torturous history in North America, complete with the sharp rise and precipitous fall of famous revivalists, revival evangelism is—justifiably—both beloved and belittled, both disdained and adored. Marked by what it means to be American—entrepreneurial, adaptable, spectacular, and geared to the faith of every individual—revival is welcomed by some and shunned by others. Nevertheless, holding fast to long-held patterns but adapted to contemporary culture in terms of pace, music, and technology, revivals continue to thrive in America. Whether you appreciate or denigrate this model of evangelism, it is difficult to deny its appeal when audiences of thousands—and tens of thousands more worldwide—attend a Harvest America revival.

Still, critics find revivals to be harmful because of their reliance on emotions, which critics consider to be simply mass hysteria. Emotions are more easily heightened, even manufactured, in the context of a crowd, with moving music and powerful preaching and throngs responding. An emotional decision, rather than an intellectual one, can lead to an authentic experience, but it can just as easily lead to a shallow religious commitment that fades quickly after the glow of revival subsides.

Revival critics also resist the notion that conversion can be equated with a precise moment in time. They dismiss the veracity of this conviction: "You can date it. You can mark it. You can know when you were saved, because you know the exact moment when you prayed what is typically called 'the sinner's prayer.'"[49] This emphasis on instantaneous conversion prompted by an individual decision lays far too much emphasis, critics contend, on the individual and his or her personal experience.

What Are the Implications of a Crowd-Centered Model of Evangelism?

A revival takes place in the midst of a crowd, whether in the 100,000-seat AT&T Stadium or in a small church sanctuary. This can be a strength because it gives many people, particularly when a well-known speaker draws a large crowd, the opportunity to hear the gospel message in clear terms. Crowd-based delivery of the gospel can expedite evangelism. Add to this the

49. Gordon T. Smith, *Transforming Conversion: Rethinking the Language and Contours of Christian Initiation* (Grand Rapids: Baker Academic, 2010), 5.

advantage of being able to witness people's active responses to the invitation, such as walking down the aisle, which in turn encourages others to follow suit. When thousands streamed peacefully but purposefully down the aisles of a baseball stadium to the strains of "Just As I Am" at a Billy Graham crusade, many in the crowd experienced something real, something authentic, about what was taking place. At that moment, however ephemeral, there was a sense of community in the crowd.

Another benefit of a crowd-centered model of evangelism is to provide a setting of anonymity, which enables people to enter the venue surreptitiously, away from the gaze of people they know. This can be safer than walking into a church sanctuary on a Sunday morning, where everyone knows each other and newcomers stick out like sore thumbs—or, worse yet, where visitors watch people greet each other but they leave ungreeted.

An obvious challenge of a revival is how difficult it is, in a crowd, to assess the strength of conversion for those who make a decision. George MacLeod, founder of the Iona Community on an isolated Scottish island, predicted in 1954 in advance of Billy Graham's revival in Glasgow, "If Billy Graham comes, I believe there will be a harvest of a sort, and I am sure it will feel like summer for a while. What I am afraid of is that when the harvest is past and the summer is over we will still not be saved."[50] Billy Graham himself worried about such a response: "That's leading them astray, and leaving them in a worse situation than before. Also, we may build great resentment against the Gospel."[51] Still, many of those converted during Graham's revivals stayed true to their decision and went on to evangelize others—people like Tom Phillips, who led Chuck Colson to Christ.

While the crowd-centered aspect of a revival presents clear challenges that must be anticipated and addressed, it also creates the opportunity for seekers to hear—or overhear in relative security—a clear and accessible interpretation of the good news of Jesus Christ. Following Graham's strategy about the necessity of follow-up, consider linking revival evangelism with other models of evangelism that provide catechesis (such as small group and liturgical evangelism) or an avenue for service (such as prophetic evangelism). Revival evangelism should always be accompanied by worshiping Christian communities, which we will consider next.

50. Frank D. Bardgett, "The Tell Scotland Movement: Failure and Success," *Records of the Scottish Church History Society* 38 (2008): 124.
51. Graham, *Biblical Standard for Evangelists*, 61.

How Can the Church Be Better Integrated into a Revival?

There is a longstanding tradition of itinerant revivalists blowing into town, setting up a tent or renting a stadium, preaching for a bit, and then leaving for the next town. In this all-too-familiar scenario, the revival risks becoming a self-contained entity, void of significant preparation or, especially, follow-up. Revivalism, in other words, has often been disconnected from the church and, therefore, had little impact on it. Michael Riddell poignantly paints such a portrait of revivalism in his New Zealand homeland: "I have lost count of the number of revivalist movements which have swept through my homeland promising a massive influx to the church in their wake," he writes. "A year after they have faded, the plight of the Christian community seems largely unchanged, apart from a few more who have grown cynical through the abuse of the goodwill, energy and money."[52]

Still, there is the possibility that a revival, when partnered with local churches as Moody, Graham, and other revivalists championed, has the potential to engender a renewed focus on evangelism, to cultivate a catechumenate of instruction for initiating newcomers into the Christian faith, and to spark a fresh commitment to ecumenical outreach in the community, as churches of various stripes band together to reach neighborhoods, towns, and cities for Christ.

One such occasion for churches to accomplish this is in a *shalom* revival, which combines the best of the prophetic and revival models of evangelism. As a revival, it will follow the same template discussed above, including a call or invitation to conversion. The unique element of a shalom revival is that it will "feature a vigorous call to Christians to share with the poor and seek justice for the oppressed."[53] The invitation for seekers to accept Christ will be accompanied by an invitation for already committed Christians "to come forward if they sensed God calling them to make new concrete commitments for Christian service—whether in new evangelistic efforts or a new engagement to solve the tragedies of world hunger, broken inner cities, and a devastated environment; whether in new programs of Christian renewal, or concrete political engagement."[54]

52. Michael Riddell, *Threshold of the Future: Reforming the Church in the Post-Christian West* (London: SPCK, 1998), 4.
53. Ronald J. Sider, *One-Sided Christianity? Uniting the Church to Heal a Lost and Broken World* (Grand Rapids: Zondervan, 1993), 193.
54. Sider, *One-Sided Christianity?*, 194.

Other models of evangelism can come into play here as well. Preparation for a shalom revival can be bolstered by visitation evangelism as Christians come to know, doorbell by doorbell, the needs of their neighborhoods and as they extend invitations to their neighbors to come to the revival. After the revival, those who responded to the invitation will be linked to churches and organizations engaged in prophetic evangelism, perhaps through new ports of entry. It would be ideal as well for churches to tailor their liturgies to outsiders during this season of revival, especially through the strategies proposed by liturgical evangelism. A shalom revival, then, can be the occasion for implementing strategies from several models of evangelism.

Are Revivals Still Relevant Today or Too Much a Relic of the Past?

A revival, on the whole, is carefully scripted, and that script is centuries old. We might even call a revival *liturgical*, as historian Russ Richey does, since it has such a familiar, enduring format.[55] Although updated in revivals like Harvest America through contemporary music, state-of-the-art sound systems, skinny jeans, and dramatic lighting, the liturgy of the revival remains remarkably consistent over the centuries. This predictability, this revivalistic liturgy, provided consolation as North American settlers left their home churches to travel west in the nineteenth century. This liturgy also offered comfort to rural folk coming to urban enclaves in the early twentieth century. The question critics raise is whether these same techniques smack of an outdated religion modified to look modern. In other words, Is revivalism too outmoded and cheesy, appealing primarily to Christian insiders longing for a conservative theology dressed up in trendy clothes?

Precisely this timelessness appeals to some who feel that a Christian America is rapidly fading and needs to be recaptured by blending patriotism with Christianity. This blend is hardly new. The customized Model-T that revivalist Martha Moore Avery drove sported a quotation from a Roman Catholic archbishop on one side and a quotation from George Washington on the other, a miniature star-spangled banner on the hood, a large crucifix topped by an electric light on the roof, and the yellow and white chassis colors of the papal flag. Evangeline Booth, commander of the Salvation Army in the United States from 1904–34, had her portrait taken holding the American

---

55. Russell E. Richey, "Revivalism: In Search of a Definition," *Wesleyan Theological Journal* 28, nos. 1–2 (Spring/Fall 1993): 170.

flag. Billy Sunday's revival message combining patriotism and Christianity helped propel him to the height of popularity when the United States entered World War I. "When flushed with patriotism, [Sunday] would end his sermon by jumping on top of the pulpit and waving the American flag." Interspersed with such antics was his oft-repeated phrase, "Christianity and Patriotism are synonymous terms, and hell and traitors are synonymous."[56]

Some revivalists continue to back this connection between American patriotism and Christianity by claiming that it is America's obedience or disobedience to God that will promote or diminish revivals. The most popular biblical text adopted to make this point, which was even plastered on a billboard I passed on I-20 in east Texas, is 2 Chronicles 7:14: "If my people who are called by my name humble themselves, pray, seek my face, and turn from their wicked ways, then I will hear from heaven, and will forgive their sin and heal their land." While the historical context of 2 Chronicles 7:14 is the temple dedication during King Solomon's reign, Greg Laurie uses it to point out America's need for revival: "I think the United States of America is standing at a crossroads," wrote Laurie in a 2016 blog post. "We have never been in worse shape morally. Crime continues to explode. Families continue to splinter. The fabric of society continues to unravel. What we need in America today, and for that matter, around the globe, is a far-reaching, heaven-sent revival." Then, he glosses 2 Chronicles 7:14, "God has given us his prescription for the healing of a nation, and it includes repentance."[57]

The association of revival and the nation often represents a certain brand of politics in which the United States is the heir of Israel's place as God's chosen nation. Greg Laurie's events are not called Harvest *the World* or Harvest *the Kingdom*. They are purposefully called Harvest *America*. The result of this perspective, perfectly scripted and meticulously planned, is that "revivalism often becomes a plea for national greatness. Applied to a nation state, such rhetoric distorts its primary application to the people of God, equated in the Old Testament with the combined nation church of Israel but in the New Testament identified with the international church of God."[58]

56. George Marsden, *Understanding Fundamentalism and Evangelicalism* (Grand Rapids: Eerdmans, 1991), 51.

57. Greg Laurie, "The '3 Rs' of Personal Revival," Harvest.org, July 2, 2016, https://harvest.org/resources/gregs-blog/post/the-3-rs-of-personal-revival.

58. Steve Latham, "'God Came from Teman': Revival and Contemporary Revivalism," in *On Revival: A Critical Examination*, ed. Andrew Walker and Kristin Aune (Carlisle, UK: Paternoster, 2003), 179.

Yet the genius of the revival model of evangelism is that its content is not constrained by strategy or liturgy. Revivals can champion American exceptionalism. But they may also be fostered by churches more keyed to a shalom revival. Such a revival can be the means by which the whole gospel can be communicated through song, message, and invitation—and all in coordination with local churches readied to serve their neighborhoods.

Reflection Questions

- How do you appraise the revival model of evangelism?
- Have you attended a revival? If so, what was your reaction to it? If you haven't attended a revival, why not?
- Can a conversion to Christ be authentic when it happens in a crowd? Why or why not?
- Do you consider acceptable or unfair the concerns many people, even Christians, have about a revival in the twenty-first century?
- Which other model of evangelism best complements a revival? Why?

EIGHT

MEDIA

H ere . . . is a great new art which has laid hold of all classes of people. . . . Wisdom would seem to direct that the Church cooperate in its development and utilize it in every possible way . . . in reaching the unchurched masses."[1] What is this great new art? The computer? The internet? Social media? Or maybe, ages ago, Gutenberg's printing press? Telegraph? Radio? Actually, the great new art in this 1916 quotation is film. A century ago, moving pictures represented the cutting edge of media, and the question before the church was whether to utilize them for evangelistic purposes. For those who did, a whole new world emerged.

The word *media* means simply "tools of communication."[2] Media featured in this chapter include radio and television, the printed word, and the internet, whose influence grows more widespread every day. Most media ministries currently engage those who already claim to be Christian. Christian radio and television programs broadcast to the faithful, providing them with resources

1. Orrin G. Cocks, "Urging an Alliance of Church and Motion Picture," *Literary Digest* (1916), quoted in John P. Jewell, *Wired for Ministry: How the Internet, Visual Media, and Other New Technologies Can Serve Your Church* (Grand Rapids: Brazos, 2004), 147.

2. Peter Horsfield, *From Jesus to the Internet: A History of Christianity and Media* (Hoboken, NJ: Wiley-Blackwell, 2015), 5. Angela Williams Gorrell, *Always On: Practicing Faith in a New Media Landscape* (Grand Rapids: Baker Academic, 2019), 40. Also related to definitions, terms such as *cyberspace*, *digital space*, and *digital worlds* will be used interchangeably as shorthand for "any form of digital technology that involves user engagement with software via a screen interface." Rachel Wagner, *Godwired: Religion, Ritual and Virtual Reality* (New York: Routledge, 2012), 1.

for daily Christian living. In the digital world, the same is true; most media meet the needs of the Christian tribe.[3]

Media *evangelism* focuses instead on seekers and surfers in an effort to engage them in gospel conversations and presentations. Before reading further, take a moment to click on several media evangelism sites, like SearchforJesus .net, an online evangelism platform sponsored by the Billy Graham Evangelistic Association. This site alone reveals media evangelism's global reach; the top ten countries reached compose a surprising global kaleidoscope: the United States, Brazil, Algeria, Thailand, Egypt, Syria, Nepal, Colombia, Morocco, and Myanmar. Or peruse the Facebook page for Internet Evangelism Day—one day a year focused on increasing awareness of evangelism in the digital world.[4]

Consider still one more scenario for media evangelism: avatars. An avatar is a representation of the self in a virtual world. Often an avatar approximates its human creator as she really is; for others, an avatar offers the chance to adopt or try on a new identity, role play, and even explore a belief system radically different from one's offline life. Through an avatar, people may ask harder questions than they would pose in their ordinary lives, and they may be, from the perspective of evangelism, more receptive to the good news of Jesus Christ. Douglas Estes, in his book *SimChurch*, even wonders whether "in a very real sense, this loosening of inhibition could allow a person a starting point for becoming a fully devoted disciple of Christ in the virtual world better than in the real one."[5]

A century after the emergence of cinema as the cutting edge of evangelistic possibilities, the church confronts another media revolution with the rise of the internet. On the one hand, proponents of media evangelism have responded with alacrity to the internet, running full speed into its technological capabilities and the opportunities it presents to extend the gospel across the globe. On the other hand, keen observers of media raise the point that media of any kind indelibly shape the gospel even while facilitating its

3. According to a Hartford Seminary study, "For the most part, the technologies are being used by congregations to communicate to membership rather than take full advantage of the interactivity of the technologies." "New Study Examines Technology and Internet Use in American Congregations," Hartford Seminary, March 7, 2012, https://www.hartsem.edu/2012 /03/new-study-examines-technology-and-internet-use-american-congregations.

4. "Internet Evangelism Day," Facebook, https://www.facebook.com/internetevangelismday.

5. Douglas Estes, *SimChurch: Being the Church in the Virtual World* (Grand Rapids: Zondervan, 2009), 80, 93.

communication and circulation. This two-way interaction between media and gospel is not neutral or inconsequential, which leaves churches in the same quagmire as they were in a century ago with the new media of the cinema—how to utilize the prospects of media for evangelism while minimizing its pitfalls and perils.[6]

Biblical Foundations

The biblical text that saturates the discussion of media evangelism is the Great Commission in Matthew 28:16–20, particularly Jesus's command to "go therefore and make disciples of all nations [*panta ta ethnē*]." Emphasis invariably falls on media's global reach, particularly in light of the technological development and sophistication of the internet. There is a heady, almost doe-eyed, sanction of the internet as a God-given media tool to evangelize all nations. A blogger on the site for the Christian Broadcasting Network, arguably the leader in Christian media, relishes the possibilities when she writes, "The Internet is just one more tool that many ministries are using to reach the world for Christ. When Jesus gave the commandment, 'Go ye into all the world and preach the Gospel,' the disciples were on foot. There was no television, no radio, no airplanes, and certainly no Internet. What a difference 2,000 years can make! Or for that matter, 10 years. Today, more and more people are coming to faith in Christ by logging onto the World Wide Web."[7] Others, even less restrained, suggest that, with his reference to *the whole world* in the Great Commission, Jesus actually foresaw the future development of the internet. Even more extreme—and questionable—is the notion that Jesus specifically envisaged the inter*net* in Matthew 13:47, when he used the word *net* in the proclamation, "Again, the kingdom of heaven is like a *net* that was thrown into the sea and caught fish of every kind."[8]

6. I am grateful to Angela Williams Gorrell for pointing me to this insight in Peter Horsfield's book, *From Jesus to the Internet*. Horsfield frames the conundrum in this way: "Christianity is a mediated phenomenon in itself: a phenomenon that has developed and been constructed in the process of being communicated. . . . How Christianity communicates itself becomes an indistinguishable part of what Christianity is," no matter the media through which it is expressed. Horsfield, *From Jesus to the Internet*, 7.

7. Wendy Griffith, "Internet Evangelism: Casting a New Kind of Net," Christian Broadcasting Network, http://www1.cbn.com/churchandministry/internet-evangelism-casting-a-new-kind-of-net.

8. Andrew Careaga, *E-vangelism: Sharing the Gospel in Cyberspace* (Lafayette, LA: Vital Issues, 1999), 9. Another internet evangelist proponent repeats the sentiment: "Jesus knew, when

Proponents also find ballast for media evangelism in the communication strategies of two highly successful communicators—Jesus and Paul. In his public speaking, Jesus integrated images and illustrations from the first-century Palestinian context of his hearers; he spoke of farming, fishing, shepherding, kneading dough, and even sweeping the floor. He also employed all sorts of rhetorical strategies to communicate his message, such as telling stories, asking questions, launching debates, initiating dialogues, commanding evil spirits to depart, and uttering prophetic predictions. In order to extend his message, champions of media evangelism note that he set up a social network with his disciples and then sent them out two by two with a clear message.[9] Leonard Sweet concurs and observes that "it's no accident that Jesus serves as the world's leading storyteller. He excelled at connecting people to one another, to himself, to creation, and to God."[10] In short—to return to the definition of media we adopted at the start of this chapter—Jesus was an able communicator, who utilized "tools of communication" at his disposal. Had he been born today, claim proponents, Jesus undoubtedly would have exploited the internet to develop a robust, worldwide social network.

The apostle Paul, another able communicator, preached and debated in public places throughout Asia Minor, particularly synagogues and marketplaces, in order to engage with all sorts of people, Jew and gentile alike. When people came to believe, he planted churches—social networks—throughout the Mediterranean world. He communicated with them in letters carried by couriers, such as Timothy; this method of communication utilized the best technology, not least the Roman roads, to spread the gospel. Such an energetic effort to employ a swath of communication strategies—from intense travel to open debate to letters—has earned Paul the moniker "the first cyber apostle." By capitalizing on the available technology of his day, from ships

---

He spoke the words recorded in Matthew 28, what we would be doing with silicon in the year 2000. . . . When He said that He would be with us until the end of the age . . . , He most certainly saw the information age." Walter P. Wilson, *The Internet Church* (Nashville: Word, 1999), 14.

9. "He definitely understood the power of word of mouth, and he valued the viral—or infectious—nature of friends and family sharing the good news and bringing others to a life-transforming faith in God. If you remember Luke 10, Jesus even sent people out in pairs to spread the gospel. They told two friends, and so on . . . and so on. You get the picture" ("Social Networking Overview," ResourceUMC, http://www.umcom.org/learn/social-networking -overview). See also Meredith Gould, *The Social Media Gospel: Sharing the Good News in New Ways*, 2nd ed. (Collegeville, MN: Liturgical Press, 2015), chap. 2.

10. Leonard Sweet, *Viral: How Social Networking Is Poised to Ignite Revival* (Colorado Springs: WaterBrook, 2012), 6.

to roads to letters, he was able "to be virtually present in different churches as well as different eras."[11]

Paul communicated the gospel to the cultures he encountered by integrating their beliefs and practices into his message. On the Areopagus in Athens, which stands in the shadow of the Parthenon, he quoted some of their poets (Acts 17:28). More boldly, he connected the good news of Jesus Christ to their religious culture by directly referencing an altar they had made to an unknown God. "You Athenians," preached Paul, "I see that in every respect you are very religious. For as I walked around looking carefully at your shrines, I even discovered an altar inscribed, 'To an Unknown God.' What therefore you unknowingly worship, I proclaim to you" (17:22–23 NABRE).[12]

Pope John Paul II, in *Redemptoris Missio* (*The Mission of the Redeemer*), highlighted Paul's example as one for Christians to emulate in our vastly different age of media and technology. "The first Areopagus of the modern age is the *world of communications*. . . . It is not enough to use the media simply to spread the Christian message. . . . It is also necessary to integrate that message into the 'new culture' created by modern communications."[13] Pope John Paul II made this statement before the rise of the internet; certainly now there is even more existence of a "new culture" to consider when communicating the gospel.

Proponents of e-vangelism, as it is often called, use the internet as a means of gaining access to a global mission field. It is the online equivalent of ancient and apostolic preaching and church planting. The rationale for evangelistic engagement through the internet is simple, as simple and straightforward as the compulsion of early Christians to plant churches throughout the Mediterranean world: "Christians should establish a presence" on the internet, "just as missionaries had always traveled to proclaim the gospel in new lands."[14]

---

11. Patrick Dixon, *Cyberchurch, Christianity and the Internet* (Eastborne, UK: Kingsway, 1997), 17, quoted in Heidi Campbell, "Evangelicals and the Internet," in *Evangelical Christians and Popular Culture: Pop Goes the Gospel*, ed. Robert Woods (Santa Barbara, CA: Praeger, 2013), 2:285.

12. Fr. Eugene LaVerdiere, "What Is 'Inculturation' Really All About?," Catholic News Singapore, February 10, 2009, https://catholicnews.sg/2009/02/10/what-is-inculturation-really -all-about.

13. John Paul II, *Redemptoris Missio*, Vatican Publishing House, December 7, 1990, http:// w2.vatican.va/content/john-paul-ii/en/encyclicals/documents/hf_jp-ii_enc_07121990_redemp toris-missio.html, paragraph 37.

14. Pam Smith, *Online Mission and Ministry: A Theological and Practical Guide* (London: SPCK, 2015), 3, cited in Tim Hutchings, *Creating Church Online: Ritual, Community and New Media* (New York: Routledge, 2017), 28. Smith is the priest at i-church. Visit their website

Theological Foundations

The incarnation is the primary foundation for media evangelism. This, we just saw, is practical: Jesus adopted modes of communication that are relevant through various media. Yet there is more to this theological foundation. This same Jesus—who communicated with peasants and priests, with disciples and the demon possessed—is the Word who was with God, who *was* God, in the beginning (John 1:1). He is more than a communicator; he, in his flesh and bones, is also the divine means—the divine *medium*—of communication. Jesus, the living and speaking and healing Word, through whom "all things came into being" (v. 3), took on flesh and engaged the world for the purpose of communicating God in an intimate, inhabited way (v. 14). Such incarnate communication was necessary so that God could be communicated through the words of Jesus the Word. "No one has ever seen God. It is God the only Son, who is close to the Father's heart, who has made him known" (v. 18). Such incarnate communication was necessary so that God could bring light—unquenchable light—to a dark world (vv. 9–14).

The incarnation pops up in discussions about media evangelism, especially those related to the internet. "There's something deeply incarnational about the digital age," say three researchers and writers who are speaking about digital communication and the church. They support this statement with a paraphrase of Hebrews 1:1–3, with bits of John 1:1–4 mixed in:

> In the past God spoke to our ancestors through papyrus and paper in many different and various ways, but in these last days, his Word is shown through the digital realm. God is all about communication. John's Gospel opens with the Word being present with God and communicating with God. Immediately, that Word is associated with light and life and creativity, the very hallmarks of the digital age, and is transmitted to the world, enfleshed amongst us and we have seen his glory. That communicated Word, that enfleshed Word, makes known God, exegetes God to all of us.[15]

---

at https://www.i-church.org/gatehouse/index.php/home/information/4-community. For more about i-church, see Hutchings, *Creating Church Online*, 90–112.

15. Peter Phillips, Bex Lewis, and Kate Bruce, "Digital Communication, the Church and Mission," *Church Growth: Resourcing Mission Bulletin*, June 2013, http://www.churchgrowthrd.org.uk/UserFiles/File/Resourcing_Mission_Bulletin/June_2013/Digital_Communication_the_Church_and_Mission.pdf, 3.

Another theological foundation we have encountered in other chapters—ecclesiology—surfaces again in this final chapter. Dulles's model of the church as herald offers one lens for understanding media evangelism, particularly when it comes to online churches. Most online churches are missional in nature, striving to reach seekers and surfers. One example we discussed in chapter 5 is Church Online. Life.Church, which is based in Edmond, Oklahoma, set up Church Online, complete with a building seating avatars that attend church.[16] This online church makes the Christian message accessible around the world. There is a peculiar salience to this strategy, which allows Church Online to reach people even in countries where Christianity is presently illegal—and where missionaries are physically prohibited from entering. Estimates of several hundred thousand people a week around the globe access Church Online, with the highest number currently joining from India and Pakistan. The Church Online service always offers an invitation to follow Jesus Christ, as well as to participate in an online Christian community.

Dulles also identified another model, which we have encountered previously, called the church as servant. Here the church is not just the carrier of a message to the world; it is the bearer of the world's needs. This model of the church as recipient, as bearer, as servant, opens up a vista for viewing the internet as an opportunity *to listen* rather than to speak. Pope Francis has tapped into this essential ecclesial vocation by insisting that the church utilize social media to listen to people and hear them express their needs and hopes. In his 2014 message on World Communications Day he stated, "The Church needs to be concerned for, and present in, the world of communication, in order to dialogue with people today and to help them encounter Christ. She needs to be a Church at the side of others, capable of accompanying everyone along the way. The revolution taking place in communications media and in information technologies represents a great and thrilling challenge; may we respond to that challenge with fresh energy and imagination as we seek to share with others the beauty of God."[17] In this poignant call, Pope Francis places others at the center of the church's vocation. The church accompanies them; the church is at their side.

16. Estes, *SimChurch*, 21.
17. Pope Francis, "Message of Pope Francis for the 48th World Communications Day," Vatican Publishing House, June 1, 2014, http://www.vatican.va/content/francesco/en/messages/communications/documents/papa-francesco_20140124_messaggio-comunicazioni-sociali.html.

During a recent visit to Rome, I heard a similar refrain in an illuminating conversation with Dr. Natasha Govekar, who oversees the pope's Twitter and Instagram accounts. Five years after Pope Francis's call to accompany others through communication media, Dr. Govekar expressed this same conviction to me. She said, "How do we best connect social media networks to human communities? Look out the window. What are these people looking for? With social media, there's an immediate response. You hear back. If you don't listen to people, [to] their profound desires, then you're at risk of asking questions nobody asks. With social media, you have numbers, feedback. You can see answers. We use that feedback to put out a better message." Dr. Govekar understands, as does Pope Francis, the energizing connection between a rich ecclesiology and a robust view of evangelism. In fact, twice in the course of that single conversation, the overseer of the pope's Twitter and Instagram account posed the essential question, "How do we best connect social media networks to human communities?"[18]

Historical Foundations

Thanks to Johannes Gutenberg's revolutionary invention of movable type for the printing press in the mid-fifteenth century, which virtually replaced hand-copying texts, the publishing and distribution of Christian literature has been a staple of media evangelism. Take, for example, Florence Crawford (1872–1936), founder of the Apostolic Faith Mission (AFM), in Portland, Oregon. In 1908, the first issue of her denomination's newsletter, *Apostolic Faith*, came hot off the press; the print run quickly increased to 150,000 bi-monthly issues and expanded into German and Norwegian editions.[19] By 1920, the AFM published religious material in ten languages and mailed it to destinations across the globe, from Panama to China. To disseminate the literature even more broadly, Crawford capitalized on two vehicles: a twenty-eight-foot motorboat, the *Morning Star*, and a three-passenger Curtiss Oriole airplane, the *Sky Pilot*. Merchant ships with sailors from many countries docked in Portland's harbor, located about one hundred miles from the Pacific Ocean on the Willamette River. AFM workers steered the *Morning Star* alongside docked ships and used an extension ladder to climb aboard, when given permission,

18. Natasha Govekar, personal conversation, Rome, Italy, February 25, 2019.
19. Estrelda Alexander, *Limited Liberty: The Legacy of Four Pentecostal Women Pioneers* (Cleveland: Pilgrim, 2008), 41.

to distribute gospel literature. When captains prohibited their access, AFM workers launched "gospel grenades" or "waterproof packets of papers and tracts in the language of the men on that ship."[20] Factoring in the height differential between the *Morning Star* and a seagoing freighter, the grenades had to be thrown as high as fifty feet in the air to land on deck. With such ingenuity—and persistence—the AFM spread the gospel message across the globe, as sailors from other countries took the packets back home.

The *Sky Pilot*, purchased in 1919 and piloted by Raymond Crawford (1891–1965), Florence's son, was used for the aerial distribution of literature. Once the plane was airborne, Crawford let loose thousands of pieces of gospel literature or copies of John's Gospel over targeted areas that included Oregon's state penitentiary, reform schools, poor farms in Multnomah and Clackamas counties, and public parks throughout greater Portland on a Saturday afternoon. This practice only lasted for a few years because in 1922 a court order prohibited the practice of letting loose leaflets from the air, and the *Sky Pilot* was sold. But that did not stop the AFM. Media evangelism through religious literature continues today in their Portland headquarters, where the publishing department churns out over two million pieces of literature annually in three main languages—English, Spanish, and Portuguese.[21]

When radio technology arrived, religious broadcasting instantly became a new venue for media evangelism. The first religious broadcast took place during a Sunday evening service from Calvary Episcopal Church on January 2, 1921, over KDKA Pittsburgh. The next year, John Roach Straton (1875–1929), pastor of Calvary Baptist Church in New York City, spent $1,000 installing a transmitter to broadcast sermons and music. Within five months, WQAQ's 250-watt signal could be heard along the Atlantic coast from Maine to Georgia. "I shall try to continue to do my part," promised Straton, "tearing down the strongholds of Satan, and I hope that our radio system will prove so efficient that when I twist the Devil's tail in New York, his squawk will be heard across the continent."[22] Radio evangelism hit its summit in the 1940s, with Charles Fuller's highly successful *Old-Fashioned Revival Hour*, which played to an estimated audience

20. *The Apostolic Faith: History, Doctrine, and Purpose* (Portland: Apostolic Faith Mission, 2005), 153.

21. The AFM also stocks literature in Chinese, French, Burmese, Russian, and Kiswahili, while their international contacts in Africa and India print their own literature in other dialects. Rick Olson (Distribution Supervisor, Apostolic Faith Church), e-mail correspondence with the author.

22. John Roach Straton, quoted in "Twisting the Devil's Tail," *Time*, March 16, 1953, 83.

of twenty million people over 456 stations—roughly 60 percent of all radio stations in the United States.[23] In many letters to Fuller, people testified that the radio became an altar, as they knelt before it to commit their lives to Christ.[24]

Next came commercial television, and leading evangelists from the second half of the twentieth century made their way into this media. Kathryn Kuhlman (1907–76) started by hosting the popular radio program *Heart-to-Heart*, which opened with her folksy, conversational question, "Hello there, and have you been waiting for me?" She later branched out into television broadcasting. Her long-running television series *I Believe in Miracles* included her own short inspirational talk followed by an interview with someone healed at one of her services. On the heels of Kuhlman, Pat Robertson launched *The 700 Club* and became the "first televangelist to broadcast via satellite television, allowing his Christian Broadcasting Network to reach millions of people twenty-four hours a day."[25]

Then, of course, the internet emerged in the early 1980s. Less than two decades later, when *Time* magazine's special issue "Jesus Online" appeared in 1996, dozens of religious websites already populated the internet, and the first virtual Christian congregation, "The First Church of Cyberspace," had been up and running for four years.[26] That same year, a Barna Group study recommended that church organizations should quickly establish their presence in cyberspace or they would lose touch with many members of their own churches.[27] By 2004, *Church of Fools*, sponsored by the British Methodist Church, held weekly services online for several months, allowing participants to be present through avatars that worshiped and interacted with each other synchronously in a 3D multiuser environment. Within its first twenty-four hours online, the church had forty-one thousand visitors.[28]

23. Quentin J. Schultze, "Evangelical Radio and the Rise of the Electronic Church, 1921–1948," *Journal of Broadcasting and Electronic Media* 32, no. 3 (Summer 1988): 301.

24. "Right by my radio, at long last, I have accepted the Lord as my Saviour. I have listened to you for a long time and you have convinced me that I am a sinner in need of a Saviour." Michael E. Pohlman, "Broadcasting the Faith: Protestant Religious Radio and Theology in America, 1920–1950" (PhD diss., Southern Baptist Theological Seminary, 2011), 167.

25. Stewart Hoover, *Mass Media Religion: The Social Sources of the Electronic Church* (Newbury Park, CA: Sage, 1988), 73.

26. Heidi Campbell, *When Religion Meets New Media* (New York: Routledge, 2010), 23.

27. Christopher Helland, "Popular Religion and the World Wide Web: A Match Made in (Cyber) Heaven," in *Religion Online: Finding Faith on the Internet*, ed. Lorne L. Dawson and Douglas E. Cowan (New York: Routledge, 2004), 26.

28. Campbell, *When Religion Meets New Media*, 24.

Among the first "full-service" online churches, Alpha Church began in 1999 and continues today under the pastoral leadership of its founder, Reverend Patricia Walker. She explains the evangelistic impulse that spurred her to plant Alpha Church: "Yes, the Lord called me out of UM (United Methodist) ministry 20 years ago to offer Christ on the Internet when no one was doing anything to evangelize globally on the Internet. . . . It was amazing to see folks hack out of the closed China portal to find Christ awaited them at Alpha Church."[29] Alpha Church offers "communion, baptisms, offerings, sermons, [and] singing" via the internet, and roughly seven thousand people participate in this online church on a weekly basis.[30]

Christian groups host almost 78 percent of all online religious websites, and within Christianity, Roman Catholicism is the largest church represented.[31] This is not surprising in light of the Catholic Church's longtime support for media evangelism. In 1930, Archbishop Fulton Sheen (1895–1979) launched a radio show program, *The Catholic Hour*, which reached an estimated four million listeners at the height of its popularity. He then moved to network television (ABC) where he hosted a weekly series, *Life Is Worth Living*, that attracted about thirty million viewers weekly.[32] The Catholic Church welcomed the internet in the early 1990s as a tool to accomplish its mission. Pope John Paul II saw the potential in "opportunities offered by computer telecommunications to fulfill the Church's mission, which he called the 'new evangelization.'"[33] In 1995 the Vatican launched a website and years later created its own YouTube channel. With the addition of up-to-date social media, millions have now signed up to follow Pope Francis on Twitter at @Pontifex (18.1 million) and on Instagram at @franciscus (6.5 million).

Practical Foundations

Media choices in the twenty-first century are legion—the printed word, telephone, radio, television, film, and, of course, social media. Given the rapid

29. Patricia Walker, e-mail correspondence with the author, March 18, 2019.

30. Bill Easum and Bill Tenny-Brittian, *Under the Radar: Learning from Risk-Taking Churches* (Nashville: Abingdon, 2005), viii.

31. Dawson and Cowan, *Religion Online*, 27.

32. Sheen's program is "unique in the history of American broadcasting. It was, and is, the only religious program ever to have competed on a commercial basis on network television." Hoover, *Mass Media Religion*, 53.

33. Joshua Ramo, "Finding God on the Web," *Time*, December 16, 1996, 55.

revolution taking place in social media, by the time this book is in print, there is no doubt that some of this chapter will be obsolete. For this reason, the strategies recommended below are basic enough to allow for their application to a wide variety of media. At the same time, the focus in this section will be on e-vangelism—evangelism via the internet—for the following reasons: it is relatively affordable for individuals, small groups, and local churches of every size; it is popular among every age demographic; it is interactive; it is global; and it can readily increase the number and scope of Christians sharing their faith.[34] "With a comparatively small financial investment, internet users can make their religious views known, at least potentially, to millions throughout the world."[35]

1. Establish a Media Team

The first step is to identify an intergenerational group interested in being a part of a media evangelism team. Even if, at some future point, hiring a technology professional may make sense, in the meantime, volunteers provide the core because most media evangelism options require regular tending to keep an audience engaged. Consider tapping those who inhabit what Leonard Sweet calls a TGIF (Twitter, Google, iPhone, Facebook) world,[36] or to borrow other terms from him, they are *Googlers* rather than *Gutenbergers*.[37] E-vangelism

34. According to a recent Barna Group study, 53 percent of self-identified Christians believe technology has made sharing their faith easier. (Barna Group, *Spiritual Conversations in the Digital Age: How Christians' Approach to Sharing Their Faith Has Changed in 25 Years* [Ventura, CA: Barna Group, 2018], 38). In a recent study about how people come to faith, Bryan P. Stone claims that "television and radio are far less important for the communication of faith than newer online media. . . . Within a given week, almost half of all adults in the US are exposed to someone else sharing their religious faith online." Bryan P. Stone, *Finding Faith Today* (Eugene, OR: Wipf & Stock, 2018), 78.

35. Dawson and Cowan, *Religion Online*, 10.

36. L. Sweet, *Viral*, 15.

37. Sweet writes,

> The Gutenberg tribe is unapologetically grounded in text, and I use *text* here as a noun. Long ago they accepted as a primary mission the task of getting the printed Word of God into the hands of members of every language group on the planet. . . . In Gutenberg Christianity, the text that backs up belief (the Bible) tends to receive as much emphasis (if not more) as the daily life of faith. . . . Googlers have rewritten the rules of forming networks, connections, and relationships. . . . A primary way these things happen in Googler Culture is through the use of metaphors for storytelling, story catching, and story sharing. . . . Googlers harken back to the era of Jesus. And it's no accident that Jesus serves as the world's leading storyteller. He excelled at connecting people to one another, to himself, to creation, and to God. (L. Sweet, *Viral*, 6)

If you're still not sure which camp you belong to, Sweet offers a set of questions along with a scoring rubric to provide the answer. L. Sweet, *Viral*, 4–5.

necessitates particular familiarity with social media culture and language and the ability to handle nearly daily changes and technological updates.

Certainly include young people on the team, perhaps a confirmation class whose members are fluent in the requisite language and technological skills. Older people should also be brought onto the team. Their social media usage is increasing exponentially as they use the internet to keep in contact with family and friends who live elsewhere. Also, as people age out of the workforce, they have more time to devote to media on a daily basis. Here the potential for an intergenerational team, in which old mentor young and young mentor old, is enormous. In this way, outreach—evangelism—becomes a powerful means of reaching into the church, transforming it through the development of lifelong relationships among age groups that might not otherwise interact.

The media evangelism team should engage regularly in substantive conversations about the possibilities and pitfalls, the ethics and eccentricities, of media evangelism. Media expert and theologian Angela Williams Gorrell encourages conversations that are "meaningful, imaginative, critically and theologically reflective, Spirit-guided, and fruitful . . . , *interested* in asking and answering the essential questions that motivate faithful living in a new media landscape." She underscores the necessity of the team's praying together regularly for God's guidance as they utilize media for evangelism: "Pray that God will teach your community what God is up to in this landscape. With each movement of interested conversation, invite the Spirit to lead and teach your community and to help you listen to and care for one another as you discern what it means to be a Christian community traversing the new media terrain."[38]

2. Focus on a Receptive Audience

The next step in media evangelism is to ascertain carefully what audience to connect with over social media. This question requires careful deliberation because a megaphone approach—plastering the digital world with a disembodied gospel message—is not nearly as effective as purposefully developing contacts through media and engaging relationally toward a deeper connection with Jesus Christ. It is most advantageous for the audience to be connected to someone on the media evangelism team and ideally to the church community that supports the team as well. So, the question to ask is, For what audience

38. Gorrell, *Always On*, 33–34.

can the media evangelism team best be a bridge?[39] To answer this question, look for shared interests, shared demographics, or shared geographical location, which will make it easier, in step 4, for an offline conversation to take place face to face.

Once the audience is selected, find out as much about them as you can, especially their media preferences. Do they read newspapers or magazines? Do they prefer books, and if so, what genre? Do they watch certain TV channels or Netflix shows? Do they listen to certain radio programs or podcasts? Which social media platforms do they use? The goal of these research questions is to develop an actual persona for the audience and then to keep this persona always in mind as the team creates and disseminates media content.[40]

3. Choose the Media

The information garnered from step 2 will help to prioritize the media to which the team devotes time and funds. Some media are more expensive than others. A radio or television presence, for example, is beyond the reach of most churches. Sherwood Baptist Church in Albany, Georgia, is a notable exception. Sherwood Baptist launched a movie ministry in 2009 with $20,000 in donations, and it remains viable financially because the films they produce earn income beyond expenses.[41] Since various social media, in contrast to television and radio, are relatively affordable and highly utilized, we will focus our attention on them in particular.

Each of the social media options below requires a delicate balance between e-vangelism and other types of content, because if the extent of what is offered on social media (or any kind of media) is 100 percent evangelistic, audience engagement will tend to decline. Human interest stories, music, art, drama, short reflections on theological topics, book reviews, and FAQs about Christianity all contribute to media that is interesting, informative, and seeker friendly. These need not be invented by the media evangelism team; they can be included via hyperlinks to blogs, articles, videos, or photos. The reverse is true as well. Demonstrate interest in your audience by engaging their posts through comments, likes, and reposting or retweeting. Social media is *social*:

39. For more on what being a bridge entails, see chap. 5, "Church Growth."
40. *Social Media for Missions: An Introductory Guide*, version 1.2, Mobile Ministry Forum, February 2018, https://drive.google.com/file/d/1di5zYLh4O20oN7cvVW-aPzDwob__mqHa /view, 17–18.
41. For more on Sherwood Pictures, see http://sherwoodpictures.com.

"Social media is called that because it is meant to be about interaction. Our efforts on social media must involve a lot more than simply broadcasting our message. Tune in to the lives and feeds of others you are connecting with. . . . Strive for an 80/20 ratio of four interaction communications for every one promotional message."[42]

With this in mind, I will briefly catalog some social media options that can be beneficial in media evangelism.

Website

A website, "the front window of the Internet," is an indispensable place to begin media evangelism.[43] If a website for your church already exists, take time to work through it slowly and critically, adopting the persona established in step 2. In other words, engage the church website from the perspective of an outsider. Most likely, this exercise will point out that information available on the website appeals to insiders, not visitors to the site. Many church websites function like an old-fashioned bulletin board, occasionally posting announcements about church programs and photos of members at worship and play. Even basic information guiding visitors to the church's location, noting service times, and listing staff names and numbers is sometimes unavailable or difficult to find. If this is the case, then an intentional, inviting connection with seekers and surfers is missing altogether.

The aim is to develop a website that is a "sticky site, one that draws people back for more."[44] A must-have starting point is a "Contact Us" button (in bold typeface) and someone on the media team to check it regularly, even daily. After that is taken care of, the possibilities are vast. Include interactive forums that will be conducive to a variety of folk sharing ideas, experiences, and insights. Insert hyperlinks to service opportunities and to blogs and videos that take people deeper into the life of faith. Post a provocative biblical reflection or a personal testimony aimed specifically at introducing an internet surfer to God. One person came to faith by googling this straightforward question: Is there a God? She found her way to a Campus Crusade for Christ (Cru)

---

42. *Social Media for Missions*, https://drive.google.com/file/d/1di5zYLh4O20oN7cvVW-aPzDwob__mqHa/view, 28–29. See also M. Gould, *Social Media Gospel*, chap. 10.

43. Keith Knight, "The E-vangelist: Taking the Gospel into Cyberspace," *Presbyterian Record* 127, no. 5 (May 2003): 41.

44. Wilson, *Internet Church*, 132.

website and eventually prayed what Cru calls the sinner's prayer. A Cru staff person responded to her e-mail by connecting her with a local Cru chapter at her college.[45]

A Pew study recommends a variety of methods to grab seekers' attention: general information about Christianity, discussions about social issues, guided meditations, devotionals, or other material for personal prayer.[46] There is no end to interactive possibilities; the limitations will be determined by time and personnel who post and participate and respond.

FACEBOOK

As the number one social networking tool currently available, Facebook offers a prolific outreach opportunity. A Barna Group study found that most online faith sharing now involves posting on Facebook, so this is a commonsense place to begin reaching out to a target audience with the gospel. Currently, over two billion people are active users on Facebook.[47] Five new Facebook profiles come online every second, which "adds up to a rate of 18,000 new users per hour."[48] In addition, "Fully 74% of Facebook users say they visit the site daily, with around half (51%) saying they do several times a day."[49] Overwhelming statistics to say the least, but with careful attention to step 2, the media team should know what their persona does with Facebook—which pages, groups, friends, and stories they value. Use these to connect with your audience. Considering that the average Facebook user has 155 friends, a media evangelism team already has a terrific opportunity to create a friends list with whom to share meaningful posts about the gospel.[50]

45. Campbell, "Evangelicals and the Internet," 277.

46. Aubrey Malphurs and Michael Malphurs, *Church Next: Using the Internet to Maximize Your Ministry* (Grand Rapids: Kregel, 2003), 138.

47. Andrew Hutchinson, "Facebook Reaches 2.38 Billion Users, Beats Revenue Estimates in Latest Update," Social Media Today, April 24, 2019, https://www.socialmediatoday.com/news /facebook-reaches-238-billion-users-beats-revenue-estimates-in-latest-upda/553403.

48. Bernadette Coleman, "6 Important Facts about Facebook and Local Presence Management," Social Media Today, May 9, 2017, https://www.socialmediatoday.com/social-networks /6-important-facts-about-facebook-and-local-presence-management.

49. Aaron Smith and Monica Anderson, "Social Media Use in 2018," Pew Research Center, March 1, 2018, https://www.pewinternet.org/2018/03/01/social-media-use-in-2018.

50. Sarah Knapton, "Facebook Users Have 155 Friends but Would Trust Just Four in a Crisis," *The Telegraph*, January 20, 2016, https://www.telegraph.co.uk/news/science/science -news/12108412/Facebook-users-have-155-friends-but-would-trust-just-four-in-a-crisis .html.

TWITTER

More than five hundred million tweets, often with a photo, video, or hyperlink added to each 280-character tweet, are sent daily.[51] A tweet's brevity allows for real-time responses to and engagement with events as they happen. If you make your Twitter profile public, anyone can follow you, view your tweets, and retweet them. By creating group lists that engage your audience persona, interacting with your audience can prove to be surprisingly quick and direct.

YOUTUBE

Among eighteen- to thirty-four-year-olds, YouTube is "the second most-preferred platform for watching video on TV screens," and two billion users access it monthly. YouTube appeals to both young and old. Just over 80 percent of fifteen- to twenty-five-year-olds in the United States use it, as do 58 percent of internet users age fifty-six and older.[52] Again, with the audience persona in mind, create and post a video on YouTube. It sounds elaborate, but it can be as simple as telling the story of how someone from the media team or church community came to faith or sharing an insight from a Bible study or your prayer time that you think is relevant for others and recording it on a smartphone. Or, with permission, capture aspects of events you attend—elements of a worship service, a conversation during a Bible study—and post it on YouTube. Then share this and other relevant content on other social media sites, like Facebook and Twitter, or via e-mail.

INSTAGRAM AND SNAPCHAT

Launched in 2010 and 2011 respectively, both Instagram and Snapchat offer millions of users the opportunity to post images, words, and brief videos. With visual media at the center of these sites, their popularity continues to grow exponentially: "Images are particularly conducive to engagement and rank 180% higher in terms of interactivity than text only posts."[53] These sites can also fuse online and offline presence, as happens when Instagrammers meet

51. Paige Cooper, "25 Twitter Stats All Marketers Need to Know in 2020," Hootsuite Inc., October 30, 2019, https://blog.hootsuite.com/twitter-statistics.

52. Paige Cooper, "23 YouTube Statistics that Matter to Marketers in 2020," Hootsuite Inc., December 17, 2019, https://blog.hootsuite.com/youtube-stats-marketers.

53. *Social Media for Missions*, https://drive.google.com/file/d/1di5zYLh4O20oN7cvVW-aPzDwob__mqHa/view, 29.

face to face in InstaMeets. This capacity for online communities to become offline communities leads to the next step in media evangelism.

4. Cultivate Relationships Online and Offline

Social media provides an excellent way to initiate connections with seekers and surfers in relatively casual "porch time dialogue."[54] In this step, the aspiration is to transform these connections into deeper relationships. For this to happen, proceed as you would with a new acquaintance face to face; here, the same approach that strengthens a connection offline applies online as well. When communicating via social media with someone you do not know, take time to learn about them. As in person, ask questions about what they do, who is in their family, where they grew up, whether they follow sports, what podcasts they listen to, what experience they have had of religion. Always bear in mind the importance of a personal association as we discovered in chapter 1.

When possible, an online conversation should continue offline, face to face or over the phone. The majority of spiritual conversations—92 percent— still take place in person, according to the Barna Group, while only half as many happen via social media. More telling is their report that 73 percent of conversations that led to a major life change happened in person. Barna also found that many internet users simultaneously use various media platforms (such as Facebook) *and* in-person conversations.[55] This fusion of offline and online, what is referred to as *hybridity*, has become the norm for most Americans. "Interactions online shape offline experiences," Gorrell explains, "and offline communication and practices shape people's online engagement."[56] The takeaway of this observation is that media evangelism should not be approached as a surrogate or substitute for face-to-face relationships; instead, it can be utilized to initiate and develop them.

Appraisal

When tracing media evangelism's historical roots to Gutenberg's invention of the printing press or even further back to the apostle Paul's letter writing,

---

54. Brandon Dollarhite, "Evangelism in the Digital Age: Using Social Media to Spread the Gospel" (DMin thesis, Perkins School of Theology, 2013), 98.

55. Barna Group, *Spiritual Conversations in the Digital Age*, 47, 75.

56. Gorrell, *Always On*, 47.

proponents stake their claim: media evangelism is here to stay. And as new media options become available, evangelists will find ways to share the gospel through them. With each improved media development comes a new opportunity. Media evangelism, particularly through the internet, can connect Christians with those disengaged from the church or completely unaware of Christianity. It is almost unfathomable that people from India and Pakistan would access Life.Church's Church Online at the highest rates. Certainly part of the appeal of this evangelism model comes from the reality that religious conversations via media can feel less threatening for the seeker. The initial contact is not so direct, not so in your face, which leaves time to reflect and to respond.

Yet media evangelism comes with significant challenges. It can be time consuming; it is not seasonal, like liturgical or visitation evangelism, and neither is it an annual event, such as a revival. Once you launch a website or Twitter account, it is essential to "feed the beast." Creating and maintaining a church website or Facebook page does not automatically increase conversions, attendance, financial giving, or even receive notice from anyone new. Add to this how much money professionals put into attracting followers to their product or organization, and the modest efforts of a small or medium-sized church may not be able to offer content that draws the attention of seekers and surfers. Then there is the added reality that sites dedicated to online religions of all sorts rank among the fastest growing on the internet, more numerous even than those dedicated to sex. Given this numerical reality, people can as easily surf their way to Wiccan practices as to Christianity.[57] Finally, and most important, there is a very real safety concern when surfing the internet; it is rife with scams, pornography, gambling, and disinformation—all of these created and posted by lucrative and predatory industries. To meet these and other challenges, the media *team* is key. There is greater safety in numbers as well as in partners with whom you can pray and discern before proceeding.

Should Any Restraints Be Applied to Media Evangelism?

Evangelists from the apostle Paul to Florence Crawford readily adopted the technological developments of their day to broadcast the good news of Jesus Christ. Today, champions of media evangelism set themselves on a similar

57. Teresa Berger, @ *Worship: Liturgical Practices in Digital Worlds* (New York: Routledge, 2017), 2.

trajectory, an evolution, a revolution, in which they are able to spread the gospel more widely, more quickly, and in a more unfettered way than ever before. The global outreach of the internet is certainly stunning in an age when more people around the world own a mobile phone than a toothbrush.[58] E-vangelists view the internet as a present-day means for fulfilling the Great Commission of Matthew 28: "God is doing something big, and we best be clearheaded about what is going on around us. . . . We should not be surprised that God has raised up information technology to communicate His Word to the entire world."[59] The ability of some even to hint at the possibility that Jesus referred to the internet two thousand years ago when he compared the kingdom of God "to a *net* that was thrown into the sea and caught fish of every kind" (Matt. 13:47) demonstrates that, for some at least, the pitfalls of the internet pale in comparison with its promise. Discernment about technology is superfluous; it is all good when used to implement Jesus's Great Commission.

Those with more caution remind us that social media is not neutral; it shapes us in ways that often go unnoticed, especially when we are immersed in it. "Although we use communication technologies extensively, we do not easily perceive how value laden they really are."[60] The selective application of advertisements, the targeted offer of information and disinformation in elections—these dangers of technology apply equally to media evangelism.

Add to this the liabilities that recent studies of social media have identified. It raises stress levels, including cortisol, which is the body's central stress hormone. It presents the danger of anonymity: people responding with hostility and virulence in ways they might never do face to face. (This is the dark side of the internet. Earlier we considered the other side, the promise of such

58. Chris Raines, "More Mobile Phones Than Toothbrushes? Fact or Fiction," Pi Dental Implant Center, August 3, 2016, https://blog.dentalimplants-usa.com/more-mobile-phones-than-toothbrushes-fact-or-fiction.

59. Wilson, *Internet Church*, xiii–xiv. This unbridled embrace of media evangelism fits into one of Gorrell's "four types of fruitless conversations about new media," one which she refers to as utilitarian rather than Christian:

> The basic idea in utilitarian conversations is that if the institution can become more skilled (or find the right staff) or spend more money on better forms of new media, it can use new media to do God's work in the world. People who are excited by technology often neglect to critically assess the malformed visions it is shaped by and its damaging values and practices. The malformed conviction that informs this type of conversation is that new media is just a tool, and if used with good intentions, it contributes to God's purposes. This is too simplistic. (Gorrell, *Always On*, 28–29)

60. Quentin J. Schultze, *Christianity and the Mass Media in America: Toward a Democratic Accommodation* (East Lansing: Michigan State University Press, 2003), 341.

anonymity, for probing more deeply into the claims of Christianity.) It grants easy access to industries such as pornography and gambling. The message cannot readily be divorced from the medium, and the medium, in the hands of the powerful and well funded, can be dark and dangerous.

Some also say that technology sets the dial toward escape, in the direction of amusement and away from substantive thinking and interaction. What Neil Postman said in his bestseller, *Amusing Ourselves to Death* (first published in 1985), continues to be relevant today, in a world where social media is keyed to distract, aimed to please, available twenty-four hours a day, seven days a week—and at our fingertips in public and in private. An escape from the ubiquity of social media can take place only with serious side effects, as one professor demonstrated by using Postman's book in conjunction with an assigned "e-media fast"—that is, refraining from all electronic media for twenty-four hours. Postman's son includes a reflection on this assignment in a twentieth-anniversary edition of the book:

> When she announces the assignment, she told me, 90 percent of the students shrug, thinking it's no big deal. Then when they realize all the things they must give up for a whole day—cell phone, computer, Internet, TV, car radio, etc.— "they start to moan and groan." She tells them they can still read books. She acknowledges it will be a tough day, though for roughly eight of the twenty-four hours they'll be asleep. . . .
>
> "The papers I get back are amazing," says the professor. They have titles like "The Worst Day of My Life," or "The Best Experience I Ever Had," always extreme.[61]

Postman predicted that the mix of religion and television would not end well for religion. "I believe I am not mistaken in saying that Christianity is a demanding and serious religion. When it is delivered as easy and amusing, it is another kind of religion altogether."[62] Now fast-forward two decades: watching network television, as Postman knew it, is nearly a relic, replaced by binge-watching Netflix. How much more might his prediction be coming true?

The takeaway of this tension between the promise and the pitfalls of social media is the need to proceed with caution in the use of media evangelism.

61. Andrew Postman, "Introduction to the Twentieth Anniversary Edition," in Neil Postman, *Amusing Ourselves to Death: Public Discourse in the Age of Show Business* (New York: Penguin, 2005), xii.
62. Postman, *Amusing Ourselves to Death*, 121.

Pope Francis reminds us that "the internet is a gift of God, but it is also a great responsibility."[63] Media evangelism, like all endeavors in the Christian life, is best approached in community, with a strong tether to real people—in a team that provides accountability.

As Paul prayed in Philippians 1:9–11, Christ's followers must practice discernment: "And this is my prayer, that your love may overflow more and more with knowledge and full insight to help you to determine what is best, so that in the day of Christ you may be pure and blameless, having produced the harvest of righteousness that comes through Jesus Christ for the glory and praise of God." This is a communal endeavor. In fact, Paul's prayer is addressed to a community. When he says *your*, the Greek pronoun is plural. When he uses verbs, such as *you may be*, these are plural in Greek. Discernment is a plural process, a community matter. This realization is a fundamental ingredient of media evangelism.

How Can Media Evangelism Intersect More Effectively with the Church?

The hope of media evangelism, as with every evangelism model in this book, is for people to experience life transformation through becoming a disciple of Jesus Christ. What then? Where do new Christians, who came to faith via media evangelism, go for further teaching, mentoring, and support? The concern is that they will live in relative isolation instead of joining a Christian community where they could learn and practice the virtues of cultivating a deeper faith in the rough-and-tumble of the church and the world. We encountered similar questions in our study of the revival model of evangelism. Historically and statistically, once the morning light rises on altar-call decisions after the heat of the evening's revival, more often than not nothing has changed for the person or the church. What, then, can a new convert do so as not to go it alone?

As with revivals, the church must be invested in media evangelism from the start. The support of the church in prayer is crucial to both the launch and the sustained progress of media evangelism. A sincere welcome and port of entry—offline or online—by the church for new followers of Jesus is absolutely necessary. Here is where a longtime online church like Alpha Church—in

---

63. Kathleen N. Hattrup, "The Internet Is a Gift of God, Says Pope; It's Also a Responsibility," Aleteia, June 6, 2018, https://aleteia.org/2018/06/06/the-internet-is-a-gift-of-god-says-pope-its-also-a-responsibility.

which converts can be baptized and participate in the community's meal, the Lord's Supper, and regular worship and discussion—can be highly beneficial for new Christians who want to remain online or who cannot easily access a church in person. Perhaps a new portal is necessary, too, in the form of an online small group. Or service opportunities to engage in justice work through the church—offline or online—can be identified in order to involve the new convert in the whole gospel.

With this list of suggestions, we revisit an insight we have garnered time and again in our study of the eight models of evangelism. These models are not distant islands in a sea of evangelism. They compose, rather, an archipelago. Effective media evangelism requires the relationships of *personal evangelism*. It can be well served by the portals of *small group evangelism*, by the regular worship and education provided by *liturgical evangelism*, and by the opportunity to live out concretely the whole gospel for the whole world through *prophetic evangelism*. In other words, the church is once again the crucible of Christian faith, online and offline. Jesus's mandate to "make disciples of all nations, baptizing them in the name of the Father and of the Son and of the Holy Spirit, and teaching them to obey everything that I have commanded you" (Matt. 28:19–20) is not disembodied. The Word became flesh—not paper, not sound waves, not code. The Word became flesh and lived among us. And now, it is our privilege to live like that Word in our world.

Reflection Questions

- How do you appraise media evangelism?
- Are new media being utilized for evangelism too quickly, too enthusiastically?
- Can a small church or one without plentiful financial resources engage in media evangelism?
- Do you agree with Pope Francis that "the internet is a gift of God, but it is also a great responsibility"? Why or why not?
- Which other model of evangelism best complements media evangelism? Why?

CONCLUSION

When Brian McLaren poses the question, "What if evangelism is one of the things that our world needs most?" he shows himself to be out of step with many Christians—especially mainline Protestants—who wring their hands and apologize for what they call "the e-word," as if evangelism were a curse, a blight, an embarrassment. McLaren admits that some infamous evangelists sell God like vinyl siding, but he recognizes and highlights for our consideration the treasure of good evangelism engaged in by good evangelists, who come alongside people to help them encounter Jesus in a life-changing way. "What if," McLaren probes again, "[there are] people who are literally sent by God to intervene, to help those of us who have mucked up our lives, to give us a taste of grace, a 'rumor of glory,' as songwriter Bruce Cockburn says?" *Good* evangelism and *good* evangelists, McLaren knows, can make all the difference in our frantic, frazzled, and fraying world.[1]

But what makes evangelism *good*? The good news is that you have already discovered the answer to this question in the sections labeled "practical foundations." In the practical section of every chapter, five key qualities of good evangelism recur: hospitality, relationship, integrity, message bearing, and church rootedness. When we consider the dramatic differences that divide the various models we have traversed in this book—think church growth versus prophetic evangelism, revival versus small group evangelism—the recurrence of these five qualities is arresting. They glisten in every model in this book,

---

1. Brian McLaren, *More Ready Than You Realize: Evangelism as Dance in the Postmodern Matrix* (Grand Rapids: Zondervan, 2002), 13–14.

like valuable ore in a deep mine. No matter which model you prefer, no matter which model you choose to implement, no matter whether you pick and choose an element here or there to create your own unique model of evangelism or merge several models together, these five qualities—hospitality, relationship, integrity, message bearing, and church rootedness—are the essential ingredients that gauge your evangelistic effort.

If, as you proceed, you want to assess whether you are on the right track, ask this question: *Are these five qualities essential to the model of evangelism I have developed?* Plans, programs, and personnel will vary, but these five qualities remain the gold standard of an evangelistic endeavor. If you are hesitant to embrace a wholesale evangelistic venture, then adopt these five qualities before you even start. Try them on for size—something you have probably already done, though now you can do so purposefully.

- Practice hospitality.
- Form relationships.
- Live with integrity.
- Bear the Christian message.
- Root yourself in a Christian church.

As you become more conscious of these five qualities, as you practice them day by day, you will, perhaps even without realizing it, be preparing for good evangelism. Good evangelists do not sprout overnight; they mature as they cultivate these qualities. This sort of maturation and mellowing is necessary, especially for a practice that receives more than its share of bad press. To ensure that we engage in good evangelism, we can take a few moments to explore, one last time and in one fell swoop, these five essential qualities.

Hospitality

Remember Iva Dardanet's unassuming invitation, "How about a nice cold Coca-Cola?" Should you remember this? Is this an example of superficial, shallow evangelism—a far cry from what hospitality once was? "At first the word 'hospitality' might evoke the image of soft sweet kindness, tea parties, bland conversations and a general atmosphere of coziness," commented Henri

Nouwen. "Probably this has its good reasons since in our culture the concept of hospitality has lost much of its power and is often used in circles where we are more prone to expect a watered down piety than a serious search for an authentic Christian spirituality."[2]

Nouwen preferred instead to live into the ancient meaning of hospitality as the offer of a space where "change can take place," a space where "the stranger can enter and become a friend instead of an enemy."[3] The Greek word *philoxenia*, translated into English as "hospitality," is a combination of two Greek words: *philia*, the Greek word for love and friendship, and *xenos*, the Greek word for stranger. Connect the dots, and hospitality suggests *love for the stranger*.

This is the gist of the command in the New Testament letter to the Hebrews: "Do not neglect to show hospitality to strangers [*tēs philoxenias*], for by doing that some have entertained angels without knowing it" (13:2). This charge reflects Genesis 18:1–15, which distills the essence of hospitality: Abraham and Sarah welcomed three strangers, who appeared uninvited at the entrance to their tent. Despite their being complete strangers who strangely materialized, Abraham and Sarah lavished splendid hospitality upon them. There, in that hospitable space, their unexpected guests told the old, unsuspecting couple that they would, finally, have a child. Hospitality had turned the tables, surprisingly, as the givers of profligate hospitality—the evangelists—became the evangelized, the recipients of good news.

Nouwen was right. Hospitality is anything but sappy and shallow. It is no small feat to make strangers feel welcome in an evangelistic small group, in a convivial atmosphere with plenty of food and drinks. It is no small feat to plan a revival to which strangers feel genuinely invited. It is no small feat to develop what church growth strategists call new ports of entry designed to extend the warmest of welcomes to strangers. It is no small feat, media evangelists know well, to invite, rather than to inform or intimidate, a stranger to the church through a website. It is certainly no small feat to transform a Sunday morning worship service into a service of hospitality, where members are hosts to strangers rather than just friends to one another.

Hospitality is deep and deliberate. It is strategic. It is well planned and, just as essential, implemented by hosts whose eyes are trained on strangers,

---

2. Henri Nouwen, *Reaching Out: The Three Movements of the Spiritual Life* (Garden City, NY: Doubleday, 1975), 46–47.

3. Nouwen, *Reaching Out*, 51.

whose postures are outward facing, whose relationships lie in the future and not just the past.

So was Iva Dardanet's invitation, "How about a nice cold Coca-Cola?" sappy and superficial, a betrayal of ancient norms of hospitality? It might have been—had Iva not invited her neighbor into her home, into a Bible study, into a Christian community. And when Iva died of cancer as a young woman, she and her neighbor, my mother-in-law, were the best of friends. Iva's own husband, Luis, an immigrant from Peru, had also found a network of friends in the small church that he and Iva had been welcomed into who carried him through this devastating loss. Hospitality. The first essential quality of good evangelism.

Relationship

According to a recent study, a relationship with a Christian is the number one reason why people gravitate toward Christianity; evangelism is practiced most effectively through a personal relationship. The study found that nearly three-quarters of respondents identified a spouse or partner, a congregation, a minister, a family member, or a friend as the central influence on their decision. If children are counted as an influence, then the number increases to 86 percent; nearly nine out of ten people, young and old, trace their faith to another person they know.[4] Even specialists in media evangelism concur. The authors of a one-hundred-page document on using social media in evangelism underscore the centrality of relationships: "Human relationships are precious, whether face-to-face or virtual ones that take place on social media platforms. They require time, prayer, and personal investment." They continue with a word of caution and encouragement that focuses on the centrality of relationships: "While we applaud your interest in pursuing social media as a ministry platform," they write, "we want to impress upon you that the creation and building of relationships . . . is both a magnificent opportunity as well as a heavy responsibility that should not be taken lightly."[5]

Evangelism is not mechanical; evangelism is relational. Strangers to the faith are not targets; they are full-fledged human beings, with whom Christians are called to be in relationship.

4. Bryan P. Stone, *Finding Faith Today* (Eugene, OR: Wipf & Stock, 2018), 48–49.
5. *Social Media for Missions: An Introductory Guide*, version 1.2, Mobile Ministry Forum, February 2018, https://drive.google.com/file/d/1di5zYLh4O20oN7cvVW-aPzDwob__mqHa/view, 23.

The practice of developing and preserving relationships is even more significant in evangelism today because most Christians now come to faith gradually rather than instantaneously. Revivals in America once flourished, full of urgency to decide immediately—"The buses will wait," Billy Graham famously said to calm the masses attending his crusades—yet now their impact has waned dramatically. The study discussed above also claims that "the stereotype of the average person becoming a Christian in a moment of sudden awakening or conversion is for the most part false. It happens, of course, but not for most adults in the US. The preoccupation with getting quick results, moreover, may even be unhealthy considering the kinds of changes in life patterns, practices, commitments, beliefs, and purpose that often end up accompanying conversion."[6]

These statistics and analyses from recent studies demonstrate that evangelism requires time and attention, especially time and attention to relationships. Evangelism is for the long haul. Stone writes, "Those who want to aid others in coming to faith need to take seriously how they might come alongside those who are on a journey of faith, nourishing and nurturing them by understanding faith as a process of cultivating habits, practices, convictions, and dispositions of character over time."[7] Coming to faith in the twenty-first century, in other words, is a journey—not a jog.

Relationships for the long haul are essential in a surprising array of models. An emphasis on relationship naturally suits personal evangelism, which is, obviously, *personal*—an experience catalyzed by a relationship between persons. More surprising, personal relationship is indispensable to media evangelism as well, as it requires keeping up with your contacts through Facebook, e-mail, Instagram, or other social media sites. Liturgical evangelism, too, which spans the church year, relies on relationships built over a multimonth, even multiyear, period of time. Even prophetic evangelism, with its commitment to the connection between word and deed, communication and action, invites relationships to form around the durable communal labor of changing structures and dismantling injustice in every realm.

If hospitality is one essential quality of good evangelism, relationship is another. These two qualities, of course, are joined at the hip. It is challenging to be hospitable while eschewing the possibility of personal relationships,

6. Stone, *Finding Faith Today*, 17.
7. Stone, *Finding Faith Today*, 17–18.

and it is certainly difficult to be in relationship absent a willingness to extend authentic hospitality.

Integrity

In 1927, famed social critic and author Sinclair Lewis trained his sights on American evangelism. Lewis's novel *Elmer Gantry* exposed the hypocrisy and immorality of a barely fictional evangelist. His characterization of the archetypal American evangelist grew into a caricature of a sweaty-browed, striped-tied preacher, selling the gospel like snake oil, with a white-toothed and a sleazy, heavy-handed appeal for money.

The female evangelist in *Elmer Gantry* is a thinly veiled portrayal of Aimee Semple McPherson, whose infamous kidnapping saga in 1926—whether fact or malevolent fiction—captured the American imagination just a year before the book's publication. Since 1927, evangelists, both women and men, have abetted this caricature. In the 1980s, for instance, Jimmy Swaggart, having succumbed to sexual exploits, wept on television. Jim and Tammy Bakker fell as well, forfeiting their vast financial empire, which even included a theme park. Their financial and sexual shenanigans justifiably prompted many people, Christians among them, to recoil at the mere mention of evangelism. If evangelists can be caricatured as self-absorbed, greedy, and untrustworthy, it is not solely the product of Sinclair Lewis's pen; for decades, real-life figures have acted in kind.

Such a troubling legacy demands that good evangelism be done with extraordinary integrity and with impeccable consistency. Some renowned Christian leaders stand as exemplars of integrity, like Oscar Romero, Mother Teresa, and Billy Graham. While they occupied dramatically different vocations, they strove tirelessly to match their words and their deeds.

Integrity is the baseline for good evangelism. This comes to the fore in a 2016 poll of two thousand unchurched Americans who concede that they find the positive impact of Christians to be attractive. When asked the question, "Which, if any, of the following would make you more interested in listening to what Christians had to say?" the responses most often selected from the seven options given highlight the importance of integrity between word and deed:

- I saw them treat others better because of their faith.
- I saw them caring for people's needs because of their faith.

- I saw them standing up against injustice because of their faith.
- I saw them use their faith to solve problems in our community.[8]

These responses are hopeful in terms of good evangelism because they demonstrate that when Christians sync their words and deeds to the good news of the gospel, they chip away, bit by bit, at the negative attitudes and opinions held by non-Christians. In other words, if Christians want non-Christians to dialogue with them, they must be the sort of people to whom others are drawn by seeing integrity in every facet of their lives.

Message Bearing

Over the years, as I have taught courses on evangelism in several theological seminaries, many students have invariably tripped over this next quality of evangelism. Hospitality? Yes. Relationships? Of course. Integrity? Absolutely. But message bearing? Probably not. One student suggested that a T-shirt with a church's name on it served as a presentation of the gospel. Her rationale was that people would read the T-shirt and understand that this service project was done in Jesus's name. Then, of course, there is the inevitable reference to Saint Francis's phrase, "Preach the Gospel at all times. When necessary, use words," even though evidence that Saint Francis actually said this is contested.[9]

Good news, expressed verbally in the context of good evangelism—hospitality, relationship, and integrity—is deeply rooted in the Jewish and Christian traditions. Israel's prophets, time and again, imagined a good day full of healing and hope for their communities. Consider again Isaiah 52:7, which featured in the introduction to this book:

> How beautiful upon the mountains
>   are the feet of the messenger who announces peace,
> who brings good news,
>   who announces salvation,
>   who says to Zion, "Your God reigns."

8. "Unchurched Report," LifeWay Research, http://lifewayresearch.com/wp-content/uploads/2017/01/BGCE-Unchurched-Study-Final-Report-1_5_17.pdf, 20.

9. Jamie Arpin-Ricci, "Genuine Evangelism: Friday with Francis," Jamiearpinricci.com (blog), May 9, 2008, http://www.jamiearpinricci.com/2008/05/genuine-evangelism-friday-with-francis.

Beauty. Peace. Good news. Salvation or wholeness (*yeshu'ah*). There is beauty in the message. There is peace. Goodness, too. And restoration. And all of them—three times, in fact—are proclaimed verbally. The question this prophetic vision raises is not, "Why should we use words to express the good news?" but "How can we *not* use words to express this exquisite good news?"

The Gospels, too, are replete with instances of Jesus preaching the good news of God's impending reign. The earliest Gospel in Christian history begins, "Now after John [the Baptist] was arrested, Jesus came to Galilee, proclaiming the good news of God [*kērysson to euangelion tou Theou*], and saying, 'The time is fulfilled, and the kingdom of God has come near; repent, and believe in the good news [*pisteuete en tō euangeliō*]'" (Mark 1:14–15). This is just the first of countless instances of Jesus's verbal testimony to the good news he brings.

The book of Acts, which narrates the expansion of the church from Jerusalem, through Samaria, into the Mediterranean basin, and finally to Rome, is peppered with sermons, speeches, and conversations. Peter's sermon at Pentecost is just the first of them (Acts 2:14–39). There is Stephen's in Jerusalem (chap. 7), Peter's in Caesarea (chap. 10), and Paul's throughout the Roman Empire, including his renowned speech to Greeks on the Areopagus, in the shadow of the Parthenon (chap. 17). Paul spoke in synagogues as well. At one point, "he entered the synagogue and for three months spoke out boldly, and argued persuasively about the kingdom of God" (19:8). Add to these more public sermons and activities the many private conversations early Christians had—in chariots on desert roads (8:26–39), in prisons (16:25–34), and in upstairs rooms (20:7–8).

Paul's letters, too, are rich with references to the power of words, like his letter to the church in Rome, a church he hopes will be a launching pad for a mission to Spain—the ends of the earth: "But how are they to call on one in whom they have not believed? And how are they to hear without someone to proclaim him? And how are they to proclaim him unless they are sent? As it is written, 'How beautiful are the feet of those who bring good news!'" (Rom. 10:14–15). In these few lines, Paul draws his readers back to Isaiah 52:7, to a world of beauty and goodness—hallmarks of the good news Christians proclaim to the world.

It is essential to remember that a sermon or speech is not the sole or singular medium of the message. This is obvious in personal, visitation, and media evangelism, but it is part and parcel of other models as well. Though in a revival the preacher is the most visible message bearer, so too are those who invite acquaintances and coworkers to sit beside them. In church growth, bridge people—those who are connectors within a social network—are message bearers for the gospel. If the preacher and celebrant in liturgical evangelism are message bearers, so are the laity who sing and declare the words of the liturgy, who teach and mentor catechumens, and who reaffirm their faith in the celebration rites of baptism and communion. The more—and the more diverse—message bearers there are, the richer and wider the impact of the Christian message.

Perhaps Christians, therefore, should modify their memory of the aphorism attributed to Saint Francis. Perhaps it should read, "Preach the gospel, and since they are indispensable, use words." Jonathan Merritt, in fact, when he reflects on Saint Francis's words, concedes that

> words are far more necessary than this quote leads us to believe. The Christian faith would not exist—it cannot exist—without words. They are the way the religion produces progeny.
>
> > Someone spoke and an interest was piqued.
> > Someone spoke and a heart fluttered.
> > Someone spoke and a spirit stirred.
> > Someone spoke and a new convert was born.[10]

Christians inevitably are message bearers, and that message is full of beauty, peace, goodness, and salvation.

Church Rooted

The pervasiveness of this quality across models of evangelism may seem detrimental to the evangelistic impulse, given an overwhelmingly negative perception of the church among the unchurched. In a survey of unchurched Americans, the vast majority of respondents identified their sticking point as the church itself—not Jesus. LifeWay Research director Ed Stetzer notes that 72 percent agree that the church "is full of hypocrites"—people who criticize others for doing the same things they do themselves. In addition, "86 percent believe they can have a good relationship with God without being involved in church."[11]

10. Jonathan Merritt, *Learning to Speak God from Scratch: Why Sacred Words Are Vanishing—And How We Can Revive Them* (New York: Convergent, 2018), 49.

11. Audrey Barrick, "How Do Unchurched Americans View Christianity?," *Christian Post*, January 9, 2008, https://www.christianpost.com/news/how-do-unchurched-americans-view-christianity.html.

On the other hand, those who did come to faith in Jesus Christ, according to a recent study, named the church as the key inspiration. Whether they became Christians gradually (so-called gradualists) or in a moment's resolution (so-called conversionists), these respondents note how a church influenced their decision and provided a place where they found relationships, hospitality, accompaniment, and faith formation.[12]

The reality is that the church *is* an evangelist, whether members and clergy are aware of it or not. Especially in a world of untrammeled media accessibility, the public watches what the church does and listens to what it says or does not say. Imagine the positive Facebook posts or tweets trending on social media about a church committed to hospitality, relationship, and integrity, with a clear message of beauty, goodness, peace, and salvation. It is absolutely essential, therefore, that the modern church embody the qualities that lie at the base of good evangelism.

For this commission, the church does not need to reinvent the wheel, though it may need to reinvent itself along the lines of the earliest church in Jerusalem, which, in the wake of Peter's sermon, ate together, prayed together, learned together, and pooled financial resources (Acts 2:42–47). Like the earliest church in Jerusalem, the contemporary church has the opportunity to cultivate a baseline of integrity that makes no distinction between piety and possessions, economics and euphoria, evangelism and justice. And, like the earliest church, the contemporary church has the opportunity to arouse "the goodwill of all the people," though a better translation of this Greek phrase—one that is entirely apt for our grasp of evangelism—may be "grace [*charin*] in the presence of all the people" (v. 47, author's translation).

Evangelism, then, is not the besetting problem of the church. The *church* is the besetting problem of the church. But the church is also a point of promise, a touchstone for the unchurched. And the church can become a compass for a disoriented world if it embraces the qualities that exemplify *good* evangelism—hospitality, relationship, integrity, a message of the good news of the gospel, and church rootedness. This sort of community embodies the good news; it *is* the good news. With the relentless pursuit of these five qualities, the church can be a distinctive community of disciples centered on Jesus that the world notices, perhaps even admires, and wants to "come and see" (John 1:46).

---

12. Stone, *Finding Faith Today*, 28–29, 34–35.

SCRIPTURE INDEX

Old Testament

Genesis
1:26–27 35
18:1 36
18:2 36
18:1–15 36, 183
18:2 36

Leviticus
25 115

2 Chronicles
7:14 155

Psalms
85:6 136, 140

Proverbs
19:17 117
23:10–11 117

Isaiah
11:6–9 126
40–52 119
43:15–17 117
43:19–20 117
43:21 52
48:20–21 117
51:9–11 117
52:7 119, 188
57:19 72n2
58:3–9 115
58:6 115
58:13–14 115

61 115
61:1–2 71, 115
65:19–25 126
152:7 187

Jeremiah
16:14–15 117
31:34 126

Ezekiel
20:33–39 117

Hosea
6:6 117

Joel
2:28–29 137
2:32 72n2

Amos
5:24 126
8:5–6 115
8:6–8 117

Micah
6:8 117

Habakkuk
3:2 140

New Testament

Matthew
4:18–22 32
5–7 83

5:11–12 117
5:13–16 85
5:17–48 117
5:18 107
6:10 111, 116
8:1–4 116
9:13 117
9:20–22 116
9:35–10:23 52
9:37–38 52, 96
10:7 32
10:14 97
12:28 73
13:47 159, 176
18:12–14 96
18:20 35n9
23:4 117
25:36 51
25:43–46 51
27:55–56 33
27:61 33
28 160n8
28:1–10 33
28:16–20 97, 159, 176
28:18–20 92, 93, 107
28:19 93
28:19–20 179
28:20 107

Mark
1:12–13 84
1:14–15 5, 6, 188
1:15 116

1:16–20 32
1:34 84n31
1:39 84n31
1:40–45 116
4:31–32 110
5:1–20 13n4
5:19–20 26
5:25–34 116
5:40 84n31
6:7 52
9:47 20, 84n31
10:46–53 116
11:15 84n31
11:15–17 117
12:8 84n31
12:13–17 117
15:40–41 33
16:1–8 33

Luke
2:22–24 70
2:25–38 70
2:41–50 70
4:18 116
4:18–19 71, 118
4:20 115
4:21 115
5:12–15 116
8:1 52
8:1–3 33
8:43–48 116
10 160n9
10:1–24 52

10:2   52, 96
10:38–42   33
14:13   116
14:15–24   97
15:3–7   96
15:8–10   96
15:11–32   96
16:19–31   127
18:35–43   116
19:1–10   13n4, 127
19:9   127
23:49   33
24:1–11   33

John

1:1   162
1:1–4   162
1:9–14   162
1:12   18n15
1:14   15
1:18   162
1:39   12, 162
1:40–42   12
1:43   12
1:46   190
2:11–18   33
2:13–25   42
3:1   13
3:1–8   18n15
3:1–21   13
3:16   18n15
3:30   89
4:1–42   13
4:7   13
10:10   18n15
14:6   18n15
14:9   15
14:26   66
16:7–11   138
16:14   66
17:18   15
19:25b–27   33
19:38–42   13
20:1–2   33
20:11–18   33

Acts

1:8   16, 92, 94, 97
1:14   33

2:1–4   137
2:7–8   137
2:9–11   137
2:14–36   72, 137
2:14–39   188
2:38   81
2:38–39   72
2:41   93
2:42   72
2:42–47   190
2:47   190
3–4   119n10
4:12   137
4:13   137, 138
4:31   138
4:36–37   109
6:5–6   29
6:9–7:60   71
7   188
7:23   51
8:5–12   93
8:24–25   29
8:26–39   188
8:26–40   14
8:29–30   14, 16
8:30   14
8:31   14
8:34   14
9:35   93
10   188
10:44   138
11:19–20   95
11:25–26   72
11:26   73, 109
12:12   33
13:1   109
13:1–3   72, 108
13:2   72
13:3   109
13:5   71
13:14–43   71
13:50–51   97
14:1   71
15:8–11   138
15:36   25, 51
16:13   33
16:25–34   188
17   188

17:2   71
17:22–23   161
17:28   161
18:1–3   33
18:20   94
18:26   34
18:27   34
18:28   34
19:8   188
20:7–8   188
21:9   14
27:33   34, 34n8
27:36   34, 34n8
28:2   34

Romans

1:16   95, 125
3:23   18n15, 24n32, 80
5:8   18n15
6:23   18n15, 24n32
8:1   24n32
10:13   24n32
10:14–15   188
10:9–10   24n32
12:1–2   24n32
16:3–5   33

1 Corinthians

1:17–25   95n8
1:18   81
2:2   80
15:3–6   18n15
16:19   33

2 Corinthians

5:17   26
8:9   119

Galatians

3:28   126

Ephesians

1:10   125
2:8–9   18n15
2:14   108
6:11–12   73

Philippians

1:9–11   178
2:5–7   118

2:7   125
2:12   37n18
3:5–6   95

Colossians

4:15   33

Philemon

2   33

Hebrews

1:1–3   162
13:2   183

James

1:27   51

1 Peter

2:9   52

Revelation

3:20   18n15

Septuagint

Genesis

13:12   15n6

Exodus

4:31   51
32:34   51
40:34–38   15n7

Psalms

8:4   51
106:4   51

Isaiah

52:7   6

Jeremiah

15:15   51

Ezekiel

34:11   51

Joel

3:5   72n2

SUBJECT AND NAME INDEX

Abraham and Sarah, 36, 127–28, 183
Abraham, Billy, 82, 120, 132
Adams, John Quincy, 1
African Methodist Episcopal Church, 57
Aldrich, Joseph, 20
Alpha Church, 104n30, 167, 178–79
Alpha course, 42–43, 45
American Baptist Church, 57
American exceptionalism, 154–56
Andrew (disciple), 12, 52
Antioch, church at, 71–73, 95, 108–9
Apollos, 33–34
Apostles' Creed, 25, 83
Apostolic Faith Mission (AFM), 164–65
Apostolic Tradition, The, 75–76, 78
Arias, Mortimer, 110
Arminianism, 139–41
Armstrong, Richard, 3, 4, 51, 59
Asbury Theological Seminary, 99
Athens, 161, 188
Atlanta, 31–32, 39
Augustine, 74n8, 83
avatars, 158, 163, 166
Avery, Martha Moore, 144, 154
Azusa Street Revival, 145

Bakker, Jim and Tammy, 186
baptism, 14, 72, 73, 76–78, 84, 93–94, 107, 167
Barnabas, 71, 72–73, 97, 108–9

Barna Group studies, 3–4, 12, 21, 27, 44, 166, 168, 172, 174
Barrows, Cliff, 147
Bell, Skip, 109
Bevans, Steve, 109n39
Bible studies, 2, 3, 25, 29, 41–42, 83, 133, 173
biblical illiteracy, 82
Billy Graham Evangelistic Association (BGEA), 146, 149, 158. *See also* Graham, Billy
blogs, 59, 159, 170, 171
Boff, Leonard, 114n5
Bonhoeffer, Dietrich, 83, 83n27, 106–7
Booth, Evangeline, 154–55
Boston, 2
bridge people, 99–100, 104, 106, 188–89
Bright, Bill, 18. *See also* Four Spiritual Laws
Brown, Antoinette, 121–22
Brownsville Assembly of God, 147
Bynum, Juanita, 147

Caesarea, 138, 188
Cagle, Mary Lee, 144
Calvary Baptist Church (NY), 165
Calvary Episcopal Church (PA), 165
Calvinism, 139–41
Canada, 1, 122, 145
Cane Ridge Revival, 142
care/concern, 50–51, 60, 114
Castellanos, Noel, 126
catechism, 29, 72, 75–78, 82–84, 86, 88, 150, 153

Catholicism/Catholics, 1, 2, 5, 57, 76, 82, 146, 167. *See also* Roman Catholic Church
    revivals, 143–44
    Rite of Christian Initiation of Adults (RCIA), 76–77, 78
cheap grace, 106–7, 110
Chicago, 17, 55
"Chicago Declaration of Evangelical Concern, The," 122–23
China, 3–4, 164, 167
Cho, David Yonggi, 39–40, 45
Christ. *See* Jesus Christ
Christendom, 75–76, 87
Christian Broadcasting Network, 159, 166
Christology. *See* Jesus Christ
Christus Victor, 73, 84–85
church, the, 29, 189–90
    catechism, 75–78, 82–84, 86, 150, 153
    ecclesiology, 53–54, 73–74, 97, 163–64
    ekklēsia, 53–54, 78, 92
    as herald, 54–55, 74–75, 78, 97, 163–64
    hospitality, 62–63, 178
    house churches, 33–35
    liturgical evangelism, 7, 73–78, 81–85, 88–89
    as Mother, 74
    media evangelism, 178–79
    megachurches, 31, 39, 109
    multiracial/multicultural/diversity, 3–4, 104, 108–9, 128
    newcomers, 45, 62–63, 79, 81–82, 102–3, 150, 152–53
    online, 104, 163, 166–67
    revivals, 150–51, 153–54, 156
    as sacrament, 74–75, 78
    as servant, 54–55, 63–64, 88, 163–64
    visitation evangelism, 52–54, 59–61, 62–64, 65
    worship, 7, 33, 72–75, 78–79, 86, 88, 117
    See also early church
church growth evangelism, 8, 150, 181, 188–89
Church Online/Life.Church, 104, 163, 175
Church of the Nazarene, 57, 144
church planting, 103–5, 128, 161
Church Planting Movement (CPM), 105
Claiborne, Shane, 131–32
Cockburn, Bruce, 181
Colson, Chuck, 18–19, 25, 152
communion. *See* Lord's Supper, the
community, 35–36, 45–46, 72–73, 87–88, 178
compassionate evangelism, 114

Congress, US, 1, 4
Conn, Harvie, 132
Constantine, 76, 82
context/contextualizing, 124–25, 160–61
conversion, 69–70, 81, 124–25, 127–28, 149–50, 151–53, 190
Coral Ridge Presbyterian Church (FL), 57–58
Corinth, 33
Cornelius, 138
Costas, Orlando, 123–24, 125, 128, 131, 133
Crawford, Florence, 164–65, 175
Crawford, Raymond, 165
creation, 35, 140
Crosby, Fanny, 148
Cru (Campus Crusade for Christ), 18, 171–72
    Four Spiritual Laws, 18, 24
Cyprus, 71, 95

Dallas, 2, 5, 64, 67, 135, 136, 141, 151
Dardanet, Iva, 3, 4, 182, 184
Democratic Party, 132
DePauw University, 136
Detroit, 2–3
discernment, 176
discipleship, 7n9, 91–92, 105, 106–8
Disciples of Christ, 98
Dolan, Jay, 143n21
Dulles, Avery, 9, 54, 55, 74, 97, 163

early church, 33–34, 50, 74, 82, 138, 190
    Antioch, church at, 72–73, 108–9
    liturgical evangelism, 70–72, 75–76, 87
Easter, 84–85
ecclesiology, 9, 53–54, 73–74, 97, 163–64
Edinburgh, 148
Edwards, Jonathan, 1, 140, 142
Egypt, 51
ekballō, 84
ekklēsia, 53–54, 78, 92
Elhanan Training Institute, 2
Elijah, 149
Engel scale, 40
Ephesus, 33–34
Epiclesis church (CA), 78, 79n20
eschatology, 120–21, 125–26. *See also* kingdom of God
Estes, Douglas, 158
Ethiopian eunuch, 14, 15–16, 23

Evangelicals for Social Action (ESA), 123, 131
evangelism, 7–9
    definition of, 5–7, 9, 91–92, 98
    essential qualities, 181, 190
    as extreme, 3–4
    motivation for, 27–28
    temperature, 21–22
Evangelism Explosion, 8, 54, 57–58, 65–66
exile, 7, 117, 120
exodus, 117

Facebook, 31, 40, 158, 172, 173–75, 185, 190
faith, talking about, 11–12, 21
Fawcett, John, 37
Federal Council of Churches/National Council
    of Churches, 57
film, 42, 157, 170
Finney, Charles, 121–22, 128, 140, 142–43,
    149–50
First Baptist Church (NY), 104
First Great Awakening, 142
follow-up, 25–27, 62–63, 150
Ford, Leighton, 149
Fort Worth, 141
Four Spiritual Laws, The, 18, 24
Fowler Willing, Jennie, 2
Francis of Assisi (Saint), 129, 187, 189
Francis (Pope), 6, 163–64, 167, 178
Free Methodist, 55
Fuller, Charles, 165–66
Fuller Theological Seminary, 98–99

Galilee, 5, 188
Gallup survey, 38
Gateway of Grace, 3
Gerasene demoniac, 13n4, 26
Goldstein, David, 2, 144
Gorrell, Angela Williams, 169, 174
gospel
    action and, 128–29, 131, 186–87
    sharing/proclaiming, 23–25, 45, 59, 125–26,
        187–89
Govekar, Natasha, 164
Graham, Billy, 17, 80, 138–39, 153
    Billy Graham Evangelistic Association
        (BGEA), 146, 149, 158
    crusades, 123, 145, 146–48, 150, 152, 185
    integrity, 136, 149, 186

Grant, Ulysses S., 56
Great Awakening, 140. *See also* First Great
    Awakening; Second Great Awakening
Great Commission, 92–95, 97, 107–8, 159–60,
    176
group conversion, 93–94, 151–52
Gutenberg, Johannes, 157, 164, 168, 174

Harney, Kevin, 11
Harvest America revivals, 135–36, 141, 147,
    151, 154, 155
harvest theology, 96–97, 100
Heath, Elaine, 64, 129n32
Hecker, Isaac, 1, 143
herald, church as, 54–55, 74–75, 78, 97, 163–64
Highland Park United Methodist Church, 105
Hippolytus, 75, 78
holistic evangelism, 114, 122, 125–26, 127, 129,
    131
Holy Spirit, 6, 15–16, 66, 84n31, 120, 179
    church growth evangelism, 93, 108, 110
    liturgical evangelism, 72, 80, 82–83
    personal evangelism, 14, 15–17, 22, 23, 28, 139
    prophetic evangelism, 120, 133–34
    revival evangelism, 137–39
    visitation evangelism, 65–66
homogeneous units principle, 101–6, 108–9, 128
hope, 120, 125–26
Horsfield, Peter, 159n6
hospitality, 182–84, 185–86
    in church, 62–63
    in personal evangelism, 6, 22–23
    in small groups, 33–34, 36–37, 40–41, 43–44,
        48
house churches, 33–35
Houston, 2
humility, 132–33
Hunter, George, 94n7, 98
hymns, 147–48, 151
hypocrisy, 20–21, 186, 189

Icenogle, Gareth, 35
icons, 36–37
image of God, 35
incarnation, 15, 125, 162
Instagram, 164, 167, 173–74, 185
integrity, 20–21, 41, 74, 107, 182, 186–87, 190
    revivalists, 136, 148–49

internet, 157–60, 161–63, 175–79
Internet Evangelism Day, 158
InterVarsity, 18
Iona, 152

Jackson, Jack, 66–67
Jerusalem, 4, 29, 70, 94, 95, 102, 127, 137–38,
    188, 190
Jesus Christ, 66, 84, 118–19
    ascension, 32, 33, 89, 94
    baptism, 84
    Beatitudes, 83
    birth, 120
    Christus Victor, 73, 84–85
    crucifixion, 32, 71, 80, 84, 89, 110, 117–18, 120
    disciples of, 12–13, 32–33, 52–53, 92–93, 96,
        97, 116
    evangelism, 8, 12–14, 96–97, 160, 188
    Great Commission, 92–95, 97, 107–8, 159–60,
        176, 179
    incarnation, 15, 125, 162, 179
    as Liberator, 115–18, 129, 133
    liturgical evangelism, 70–72
    as Messiah, 13, 129
    miracles, 116
    parables, 96–97, 127, 160
    and religious authorities, 117–18
    resurrection, 32, 33, 71, 89, 94, 120
    Sermon on the Mount, 83, 85, 107
    small groups, 32–33, 41
    social justice, 115–18
    temptation, 84
    visitation evangelism, 52, 53–54, 68
    and women, 33
Jews/Judaism, 2, 57, 71, 75, 93, 95, 102, 187
John (apostle), 137
John the Baptist, 5, 12, 88–89, 188
John Paul II (Pope), 161, 167
Joseph of Arimathea, 13
Jubilee, Year of, 115–16, 118
Judea, 16, 94
justice. *See* social justice

Kavanagh, Aidan, 76n15
Kennedy, D. James, 24, 57–58, 65–66
Kernahan, A. Earl, 52, 57, 61
Kilpatrick, John, 147
Kimball, Edward, 17, 29

kingdom of God, 32, 84, 88–89, 110–11, 116–
    18, 124, 134, 155, 159, 176
    eschatology, 120–21, 125–26
    in the world, 130, 132–33
Kingsley, Bathsheba, 1, 4
Kuhlman, Kathryn, 145, 166

Labberton, Mark, 130n36
laity, 52–53, 57, 189
Latin American liberation theologians, 110
Laurie, Greg, 135, 140, 141, 155
Lazarus, 127
Lee, Jarena, 1
Lent, 83
Leong, Raymond, 2–3
Levison, Jack, 84, 109
Lewis, C. S., 19, 25
Lewis, Sinclair, 186
liberation evangelism, 114
Life.Church/Church Online, 104, 163, 175
lifestyle evangelism, 7n9, 20–21
literature, Christian, 164–65
liturgical evangelism, 7, 27, 69–89, 152, 154,
    179, 185, 189
    church and, 7, 73–78, 81–85, 88–89, 154
    early church, 70–72, 75–76, 87
    seekers, 74, 77, 79, 80–81
Livermore, Harriet, 1, 4
Lord's Prayer, the, 111, 116, 130
Lord's Supper, the, 79, 167, 179
Los Angeles, 145
Lucius of Cyrene, 108–9
Lutheran Church–Missouri Synod, 57

MacLeod, George, 152
Manaen, 108–9
Mary and Martha, 33
Master Plan of Evangelism, 26
McClymond, Michael, 141
McGavran, Donald, 91–92, 93–95, 96–99, 100,
    102, 106–7
McIntosh, Duncan, 24
McIntosh, Gary, 99
McLaren, Brian, 181
McPherson, Aimee Semple, 145, 186
media evangelism, 7, 8, 183–85
    church and, 178–79
    Holy Spirit and, 169

media evangelism teams, 168–70, 145, 146, 172, 175, 188
megachurches, 31, 39, 109
mentoring, 25–26, 28, 33–34, 93, 169
    catechism, 83–84, 86, 87–88
Merritt, Jonathan, 189
message bearing, 181–82, 187–89, 190
Methodism/Methodists, 37–38, 55, 57, 67, 73, 98, 105, 166–67
Miles, Delos, 5–6, 24, 141n15
Milwaukee, 123
Missionaries of Charity sisters, 64
missions, 94–96
Monday Night Callers, 54–55
Moody, Dwight L., 17–18, 29, 55, 136, 143, 146, 147, 150
Moody Bible Institute, 17–18, 55
Moses, 51, 149
Mother Teresa, 186
Mott, John R., 18
Mount Sinai Holy Church of America, 145
multiplication, 26–27, 45
Munger Place Methodist Church (TX), 105
music, 147–49, 167

Nathanael (disciple), 12–13
Navigators, 18
Nazareth, 71, 115–16, 118, 120
newcomers, 45, 62–63, 79, 81–82, 102–3, 150, 152–53
New York City, 56, 68, 165
    revivals, 123, 144, 145
New Zealand, 153
Nicodemus, 13
Niles, D. T., 5
Nixon, Richard, 18
Noll, Mark, 122
non-religious/nones, 3–4
    unchurched people, 38, 186–87, 189
North Point Community Church (GA), 31–32, 39
Nouwen, Henri, 75, 79, 182–83
Nympha, 33

Oak Lane Presbyterian Church (PA), 3, 4, 64, 68
Oberlin College, 121–22
O'Connell, William (Archbishop), 2, 154
Ohio, 1, 91, 122

Ohio Wesleyan University, 136
online churches, 104, 163, 166–67
    Alpha Church, 104n30, 167, 178–79
    Church of Fools, 166
    Life.Church/Church Online, 104, 163, 175
Operation Doorbell, 54–55
Orthodox, Eastern, 36
Osborn, Sarah, 1, 4

Page, Samira Izadi, 3, 5
Pakistan, 163, 175
Palmer, Phoebe, 143
Panama, 164
Passover, 70
patriotism/American exceptionalism, 154–56
Paul (apostle), 25, 51, 53, 71, 72–73, 80, 95, 96, 118–19, 174, 175, 178, 188
    contextualizing, 160–61
    on Jesus, 118–19
Paulists, 1
Peace, Richard, 22
Pentecost, 71–72, 93, 137–38, 188
people movements/group conversion, 93–94, 151–52
perfecting, 87, 94, 101, 105, 106–8
Perkins, John, 113, 114n5, 122–23, 125, 128, 131–32
Perkins, Spencer, 113
Perkins School of Theology, 64
Perry, Mattie, 2, 4–5
personal evangelism, 7, 34, 74, 80, 81, 86–87, 94–95, 114n5, 146–47, 179, 185, 188
    bridge people, 99–100, 104, 188–89
    Holy Spirit, 14, 15–17, 22, 23, 28, 139
    hospitality, 6, 22–23
    prayer, 22, 23, 28
    relationships, 184–85
Peter (apostle), 12, 52, 71–72, 137–38, 149, 188, 190
Peterson, Eugene, 88
Philemon, 33
Philip (apostle), 12, 14, 15–16, 23, 28, 29
Phillips, Tom, 18–19, 25, 152
photos, 171, 172
Pickett, J. Waskom, 98
Pippert, Rebecca Manley, 15
Pneumatology. See *Holy Spirit*
podcasts, 170, 174

poor, the, 124–27, 128, 133
Portland, 164, 165
ports of entry, 8, 42, 102–4, 110, 150, 154,
    178–79, 183
Postman, Neil, 177
prayer, 38, 72, 169, 172, 173, 178
    personal evangelism, 22, 23, 28, 29
    revivals, 146–47
    visitation evangelism, 59, 61, 64, 66
preaching, evangelistic, 80–81, 87, 148–49, 151,
    188–89
Presbyterian Church (USA), 57
Princeton Theological Seminary, 64
Priscilla and Aquila, 33–34
prophetic evangelism, 8, 152, 153, 179, 181,
    185. See also kingdom of God
    and the Holy Spirit, 133–34
prophets of Israel, 114–16, 117, 125, 187–88
Prosser, Anna, 2, 5
Protestants, 5, 57, 146, 181
Puerto Rico, 123
Putman, Robert, 67

radio, 145, 146, 157, 159, 165–66, 167, 170
Ray, Emma, 2, 55–56, 68, 85
Republican Party, 132
receptive people, 100–101, 169–71, 173
reconciliation, 108, 113, 128
Reese, Martha Grace, 6, 94n7
relationships, 22–23, 43–46, 48, 87–88, 174,
    182, 184–86
    community, 35–36, 45–46, 72–73, 87–88, 178
    gift of filiation, 127–28
    mentoring, 25–26, 28, 33–34, 83–84, 86,
        87–88, 93, 169
repentance, 80–81, 149, 155
response, 127–28, 149–50
revival evangelism, 7, 8, 17, 27, 39, 178, 181, 185
    Azusa Street Revival, 145
    Cane Ridge Revival, 142
    Catholic Church, 143–44
    church, 150–51, 153–54, 156
    Harvest America, 135–36, 141, 147, 151, 154,
        155
    Holy Spirit, 137–39
    prayer, 146–47
    shalom revival, 153–54, 156
    social reform, 121–22

revivalists, 17, 136, 139–40, 142–46, 147, 150,
    153
    preaching, 148–49, 155–57
    stereotype, 86, 148–49, 151
revive/ḥayah, 136–37
Richey, Russ, 154
Riddell, Michael, 153
Rite of Christian Initiation of Adults (RCIA),
    76–77, 78
Robertson, Pat, 166
Robinson, Ida (Bishop), 145
Rodeheaver, Homer, 147
Roman Catholic Church, 1, 2, 76–77, 78, 143–
    44, 167. See also Catholicism/Catholics
Romans Road, 24
Rome, 188
Romero, Oscar, 186
Rublev, Anton, 36–37
Ryther, Mother, 2

Sabbath, 1, 115
sacrament, church as, 74–75, 78. See also bap-
    tism; Lord's Supper, the
Saddleback Church (CA), 39
salvation/sōtēria, 119–20, 125–26, 128, 187–88
Salvation Army, the, 85, 154–55
Samaria, 16, 29, 93, 94, 127
Samaritan woman, 13, 26
Sankey, Ira, 147–48
Sarah, 36, 183
Satan, 84
Schroeder, Roger, 109n39
Scotland, 152
Seattle, 2, 55–56, 68, 85
Second Great Awakening, 121
Second Vatican Council. See Vatican II
seekers, 40–41, 43–45, 46–47, 58, 147, 163, 171
    liturgical evangelism, 74, 77, 79, 80–81
Seoul, 39
Sermon on the Mount, 83, 85, 107
servant, church as, 54–55, 63–64, 88, 163–64
service evangelism, 114
Seymour, William, 145
shalom, 119
shalom revival, 153–54, 156
sharing/proclaiming the gospel, 23–25, 45, 59,
    125–26, 187–89. See also message bearing
    action and, 128–29, 131, 186–87
Shaw, Mark, 140–41

Sheen, Fulton (Archbishop), 167
Sherwood Baptist Church (GA), 170
Sider, Ron, 123
Simeon, 70
sin, 126–27, 129–30, 139, 172
Sinai, 96
slavery, 121–22
small group evangelism, 7, 25, 27, 31–48, 50, 63, 74, 80, 81, 87, 150, 152, 179, 181
    hospitality, 33–34, 36–37, 40–41, 43–44, 48
Snapchat, 173–74
Social Gospel, 113, 130
social justice, 122–23, 125–27, 129–30, 179
    evangelism and, 113–15, 122–23, 186–87
    Jesus Christ and, 115–18
    revivals and, 121–22, 153–54
    sin, denouncing, 126–27
social media, 59, 67, 135, 146, 163–64, 167–71, 172–74, 184
    dangers of, 176–77
social networks, 160, 163–64
Solomon (king), 155
Southern Baptist, 5, 99
sovereignty of God, 139–41
spiritual disciplines, 22, 72, 83, 93
spirituality, attractive, 46–47
spiritual pilgrimage, 23
Sri Lanka, 5
Stackhouse, Ian, 106, 107
Stearns, Richard, 131
Stebbins, Tom, 12, 26
Stephen (apostle), 51, 71, 188
Stetzer, Ed, 189
Stewart, James S., 148
Stoddard, Solomon, 139–40, 142, 148
Stone, Barton W., 142
Stone, Bryan P., 168, 168n34, 185
Straton, John Roach, 165
Strong, Josiah, 130n36
Sunday, Billy, 17, 144, 155
Sunday, Helen "Ma," 144–45
Sunday school classes, 59, 63
Sunrise Church (CA), 109
surveys, 38, 98
    neighborhood, 57, 61–62, 132
Swaggart, Jimmy, 186
Sweet, Leonard, 49–50, 160, 168
Sweet, William Warren, 136
synagogues, 34, 70–72, 75–76, 115

tabernacle, 15
Taft, Robert, 76n15
Talbot School of Theology, 99
TED talk, 42
television, 145, 157–58, 159, 166, 167–68, 170, 177, 186
    visitation evangelism, 60n35, 62
temple, 70
testimony, 24
Timothy, 160
transformation, 66, 106–7
transparency, 40–41, 46, 60, 62
transportation, 2, 144, 154, 159, 160, 161, 164–65, 185
Trinity, the, 35–37, 48
Twain, Mark, 135
Twitter, 164, 167, 173, 175, 190

unchurched people, 38, 103, 186–87, 189
Underground Railroad, 122
United Lutheran Church in America, 57
United Methodists. See Methodism/ Methodists
University of Chicago, 136
Utley, Uldine, 145

Vatican II, 76
visitation/episkeptomai, 50–52, 65, 67–68
visitation evangelism, 7, 8, 27, 74, 80, 81, 87, 103, 147, 154, 188
    church and, 53–54, 59–61, 62–64, 65
    Holy Spirit, 65–66
    Jesus Christ and, 52, 53–54, 68
    prayer, 59, 61, 64, 66
Voke app, 42

Walker, Patricia, 104n30, 167
Ware, Kallistos, 36
Washington, DC, 57
Washington, George, 154
Watergate, 18–19
Watson, David Lowes, 38, 114n5
Webber, Robert, 69, 77, 78
websites, 171–72, 175, 183
Wesley, John, 37–38, 40, 83, 133
Wheaton College, 77, 99
Whittemore, Emma, 56, 68
Wilcrest Baptist Church (TX), 3, 104n29

Willow Creek Community Church (IL), 39
Wilson, Walter P., 159–60n8, 176
Winter, Ralph, 94–95
Woman's Christian Temperance Union, 2
Woo, Rodney, 3, 4, 104n29
Woodworth-Etter, Maria, 143–44
World Vision, 131
World War I, 57, 155
World War II, 3, 122

worship, 7, 33, 59, 72–75, 78–79, 88, 117
Wuthnow, Robert, 38–39, 46–47, 50, 58

YMCA, 18
Yoido Full Gospel Church (South Korea), 39–40
YouTube, 167, 173

Zacchaeus, 127–28